Everybody's Guide to Emotional Well-Being

Everybody's Guide to Emotional Well-Being

Helping Yourself
Get Help

J. INGRAM WALKER, M.D.

Published in San Francisco by
HARBOR PUBLISHING

Distributed by G. P. Putnam's Sons

For information contact Harbor Publishing, 1668 Lombard Street, San
Francisco, CA 94123.

Printed in the United States of America.

Credits:

☐ Pages 34–5: Eliciting the Relaxation Response from THE RELAXATION
RESPONSE by Herbert Benson, M.D., with Miriam Z. Klipper. Copyright
© 1975 by William Morrow and Company, Inc. Adapted by permission of
the publisher.

☐ Page 165: From pp. 3–4 "20 Achievers at an Advanced Age" in THE
BOOK OF LISTS by David Wallechinsky, Irving Wallace, and Amy
Wallace. Copyright © 1977 by David Wallechinsky, Irving Wallace, and
Amy Wallace. Abridged and adapted by permission of William Morrow &
Company.

Cover design: Design Office/Bruce Kortebein

Composition and interior design: Printed Page Graphics

Text printer & binder: Fairfield Graphics

ISBN: 0-936602-34-1 paper
        0-936602-35-X cloth

This book is dedicated to Milton L. Miller, M.D.,
who taught me the value of integrated insight.

Acknowledgments

From the many people who gave me encouragement while writing this book, I am especially grateful to H. Keith H. Brodie, M.D., Jesse O. Cavenar, M.D., and William Burgower who, with their constant support and help, have enabled me to pursue my career beyond my greatest expectations. I am most appreciative for the secretarial services of Virginia Clegg, without whose energy and enthusiasm this book would never have been completed. I give special thanks to my patients. Their spunk, endurance, and good humor supplied the heart for most of the examples found in this book. Finally, to my wife, Vickie, and to our children, Wende and Brad, goes my deepest appreciation, for their love has made living and working worthwhile.

J. Ingram Walker, M.D.

Contents

Part III: Getting Help: Psychotherapy and Psychotropic Medication   *207*

Part IV: For Family and Friends— How to Help   *249*

Everybody's Guide to Emotional Well-Being

Part I
Emotional Well-Being
and How to Achieve It

Chapter 1
Why This Book Was Written

We live in a psychiatric age. Over the past decade, hundreds of books—many of them best-sellers—have been written on emotional problems. Books have told us where our erroneous zones are, how to become our own best friends, and everything that we have wanted to know about sex. We know the games people play, and that I'm OK and you're OK. We have learned to pull our own strings and how to win through intimidation. There has even been a book on sports psyching. After we are all tired out from winning, we can revive ourselves with the relaxation response or discover inner energy and overcome stress with Transcendental Meditation. Before bedtime we can settle down for some serious reading on life's passages, Type A behavior and the heart, or death and dying.

And now there is yet another book on psychiatry—this one, *Everybody's Guide to Emotional Well Being.* Why, you may justifiably ask, has another book been written on an already worn-out subject? Why, so to speak, is the tired horse being ridden around the track again? The reason is simple: the proliferation of psychiatric knowledge has led to confusion. Most of the books giving psychiatric advice have been incomplete. There has been no synthesis, no organization, and the scattered knowledge has occasionally been more harmful than helpful.

In helping people of all ages deal with their emotional problems, I have seen a great need for a book that explains simply but in detail the causes and meaning of psychiatric illness and gives the various treatment options available for these disorders. This book is written, then, to give facts about psychiatric illness, not advice. Psychiatric patients—and the families of psychiatric patients and people with emotional problems—have a right to know more about their problems and how to effectively get help for them.

Despite all the books written on psychiatric knowledge, people still hunger for more understanding. I never cease to be amazed when at a party, or on the tennis court, or some obscure place I am introduced to a stranger as a psychiatrist. Almost immediately that stranger looks at me with questioning eyes and, half jokingly, half seriously, says, "I sure need your help." In all likelihood these strangers *don't* need my help but they *could* benefit from a basic understanding of emotional problems. That is what this book is all about.

You may not particularly like statistics, but these from the best-selling textbook by James Coleman, *Abnormal Psychology and Modern Life*, confirm what I've already said. In the United States,

20,000,000	people are neurotics
3,000,000	are psychotic
5,000,000	are psychopathic (antisocial) personalities
12,000,000	are alcoholic
2,000,000	are dependent on heroin, barbiturates, and other dangerous psychoactive drugs
6,500,000	are mentally retarded
250,000	attempt suicide each year
6,000,000	children and teenagers are emotionally disturbed
1,000,000	students withdraw from college each year as a result of emotional problems

And these are all low estimates!

Now that I have given you some facts, let me tell you how you can benefit from this book. The purpose of this book is two-fold: (1) to help you understand the basic principles of psychiatry and (2) to enable you to develop more skills in dealing with everyday problems. More specifically, there are 12 things this book will help you understand:

1. Your basic personality
2. The development of emotional problems
3. Dreams and other phenomena of the unconscious
4. The difference between psychosis and neurosis
5. The cause, course, and treatment of anxiety, depression, and schizophrenia
6. Methods of relaxing and coping with stress
7. Drug and alcohol abuse
8. Sexual problems
9. Emotional problems of children and adolescents
10. Emotional problems of aging
11. The uses and abuses of psychiatric drugs
12. How psychotherapy works

This book will help you better understand emotional problems and become able to help yourself or members of your family acquire the most appropriate treatment available if the need ever arises for psychiatric help. In addition, by understanding emotional development you can learn to become self-fulfilled, rather than bitter, depressed, or indifferent. People who know about their emotional needs find their lives incomparably more stimulating and more satisfying than people who do not.

Chapter 2
What's Normal?
(Will the Real Crazy Person Please Stand?)

People worry about going crazy: they are nervous and depressed; they can't sleep; they overeat; they don't enjoy sex as much as they think they should; they are unhappy. Is this normal behavior? If not, where does normal behavior end and abnormal behavior begin? How does stress cause abnormal behavior? What causes emotional illness? How is abnormal behavior classified? These questions are answered in this chapter.

What Is Normal Behavior?

There are many ways to define normal behavior. For example, to the humanist, individuals who develop their talents to the fullest potential are normal. To the behaviorist, a normal individual is one who deals with problems effectively. To the interpersonal psychiatrist, one who develops satisfactory relationships with others is normal.

Using definitions from statistical norms would place a genius among the abnormal; personal adjustment as a norm ignores the individual's role in society; individuals who adjust to the restraints of society might be considered normal even though their personal discomfort might be overwhelming. Perhaps the psychoanalyst Theodore Lidz best summarized the concept of normality: "There is no proper standard of normality, no proper way of life, but rather different types of workable integrations. Everyone has defects, weaknesses, hidden shames, and guilts, but they are usually offset, if not balanced, by assets."

Most psychiatrists define normal behavior as the ability to adapt to the environment while maintaining the capacity for pleasure. More specifically, psychologist James C. Coleman lists six criteria that are essential to mental health:

1. *Attitudes toward the self.* The individual has a realistic estimation of his or her abilities and deficiencies.
2. *Perception of reality.* The individual is able to distinguish the imagined from the actual.
3. *Stress tolerance.* The individual is capable of using a wide range of thoughts, feelings, and actions to tolerate stress, and if temporarily disturbed, is capable of prompt return to functioning.
4. *Interpersonal competency.* The individual has social and emotional assets that enable intimate relationships to be formed.

NORMAL CHALLENGES THROUGH THE YEARS

Age	Challenge
16–22	Leaving the family and adjusting to peer group values
23–28	Search for personal identity and the ability to develop intimacy
29–34	Settling down: finding order and stability in work and relationships
35–43	One last chance to make it big in one's career
43–50	Increasing attention to old values: nurturing, teaching, and serving others
After 50	Enjoying the simple pleasures of daily life

Source: Levinson, Daniel J.: *Seasons of a Man's Life.* New York; Knopf, 1978.

5. *Autonomy.* The individual has the ability to work effectively and independently.
6. *Self-fulfilling capacity.* The individual has the persistence to develop his or her potential and talents to the fullest.

Strengths in these areas generate flexibility that enables successful functioning over long periods of time and renders the individual resistant to psychiatric symptoms even with the most overpowering environmental stresses.

What Causes Emotional Illness?

In a very strict sense, almost no one is completely normal. For example, everyone has inner conflicts and responds with anxiety or depression to a greater or lesser extent when stress arises. Conflict, which is a normal event in life, fosters emotional growth, but with ill-timed severe stress can foster psychiatric symptoms in even the most well-adjusted individual.

Several environmental factors contribute to the individual's resistance or susceptibility to emotional illness. Genetic defects may predispose the individual to mental retardation, schizophrenia, or manic-depressive illness. Congenital or acquired physical handicaps may make adjustment more difficult; innate differences in sensitivity, temperament, and activity may prompt

TOO MUCH OF A GOOD THING LEADS TO PROBLEMS

Normal Personality Traits	Psychiatric Term for Excess Traits
Warm	Hysterical
Methodical	Compulsive
Sensitive	Paranoid
Stoic	Schizoid
Love of self	Narcissistic
Firm	Rigid
Self-reliant	Avoidant
Assertive	Aggressive
Dependent	Passive

different responses to environmental pressures. Early psychic trauma such as maternal deprivation during the infantile stage of development may predispose the individual to a greater sensitivity to environmental pressures later. Parental rejection, overprotection, or overpermissiveness all lead to more sensitivity to environmental pressures. Early communication failures, sibling rivalry, undesirable parental models, poverty, and low economic status also weaken the response to additional stress.

In the 1960s, a large group of scientists led by Thomas Holmes and Richard Rahe developed the Social Readjustment Rating Scale (see the table), ranking the environmental stresses that may lead to symptom formation. Their scale ranks 43 critical changes in the life of an individual according to the severity of their impact. The death of a spouse—the most severe change of all—has a value of 100 points, while a minor infraction of the law has a ranking of 11 points. In between fall such events as marital separation, 65 points; retirement, 45 points; troubles with a boss, 23 points. When events over a single year total 150–199 points, approximately 25 percent of people develop illness; with 200–299 points, 50 percent develop physical or emotional symptoms; and with over 300 points, 79 percent become symptomatic (that is, show severe disturbance).

THE SOCIAL READJUSTMENT RATING SCALE

Life Event	Life Change Units
1. Death of spouse	100
2. Divorce	73
3. Marital separation	65
4. Jail term	63
5. Death of close family member	63
6. Personal injury or illness	63
7. Marriage	50
8. Being fired at work	47
9. Marital reconciliation	45
10. Retirement	45

11.	Change in health of family member	44
12.	Pregnancy	40
13.	Sex difficulties	39
14.	Addition of new family member	39
15.	Business readjustment	39
16.	Change in financial state	38
17.	Death of close friend	37
18.	Change to different line of work	36
19.	Change in number of arguments with spouse	35
20.	Mortgage over $10,000	31
21.	Foreclosure of mortgage or loan	30
22.	Change in responsibilities at work	29
23.	Son or daughter leaving home	29
24.	Trouble with in-laws	29
25.	Outstanding personal achievement	28
26.	Wife beginning or stopping work	26
27.	Beginning or ending school	26
28.	Change in living conditions	25
29.	Revision of personal habits	24
30.	Trouble with boss	23
31.	Change in work hours or conditions	20
32.	Change in residence	20
33.	Change in schools	20
34.	Change in recreation	19
35.	Change in church activities	19
36.	Change in social activities	18
37.	Mortgage or loan less than $10,000	17
38.	Change in sleeping habits	16
39.	Change in number of family get-togethers	15
40.	Change in eating habits	15
41.	Vacation	13
42.	Christmas	12
43.	Minor violations of the law	11

Source: Adapted from Thomas H. Holmes and Richard H. Rahe, "The social readjustment rating scale," *Journal of Psychosomatic Research, 1967, 11*:213.

How Is Abnormal Behavior Classified?

Just as there is no good concept of abnormality, neither is it easy to classify patients according to distinct clinical entities. Most mentally ill individuals possess a mixture of symptoms. In general, however, mental disorders can be broken down into five major categories:

1. Psychoses
2. Disorders of mood
3. Neuroses
4. Personality disorders
5. Psychosomatic disorders

What Is Psychosis?

Psychotic individuals are out of touch with reality. These people hear and see things we cannot; they withdraw into their own worlds, say strange things, and laugh or cry inappropriately. They may, on occasion, be violent; they are always unnerving to people unfamiliar with their strange way of sitting, walking, and talking.

Basically there are four types of psychoses: schizophrenia, organic brain disease, mania, and, on rare occasions, depression. Schizophrenia, one of our most formidable health problems, is probably a group of diseases—some schirophrenias are caused by an abnormal chemical; other schizophrenic conditions are caused by childhood deprivation; still others result from brain abnormalities. Whatever the cause, schizophrenics all have virtually the same symptom characteristics. Schizophrenics hear voices that no one else hears; they feel they are controlled by outside forces, that their thoughts are broadcast out to others, and that radio, television, and newspapers are giving them special messages.

Individuals with organic brain syndrome have a physical cause for their abnormal behavior—drugs, stroke, poor brain circulation, or other diseases of brain function. These people are more confused than anything else. They can't remember where they are; they don't know the date; their judgment is impaired. If the underlying cause for the maladaptive thinking can be removed, these individuals recover normal brain function. Unfortunately, many causes of organic brain syndrome are untreatable, although the psychiatrist can certainly help improve the patient's symptoms.

Mania is less common than schizophrenia and organic brain syndrome, but it is no less disruptive. Manics talk incessantly, move around in high gear, and seem to be on top of the world; they laugh, talk, greet strangers as if they were long-lost friends, tell jokes, sing songs, and dress outlandishly—two or three hats or ties, perhaps a couple of belts, three or four wristwatches or trinkets. Their behavior soon becomes a nuisance to others, and their reckless driving and foolish spending sprees endanger their health and well-being.

Untreated manics eventually develop a profound, severe depression. Almost a fourth of the population will experience significant depressions sometime during their lifetimes, but very few become psychotically depressed. Individuals who are psychotically depressed are suicidal; they cannot take care of their basic needs; they are disheveled and unkempt; they won't eat, and they can't sleep. Depression is one illness that psychiatrists can treat, and treat well; almost all depressed individuals get better with the proper treatment.

Are All People with a Mood Disorder Psychotic?

No. Most individuals with a mood disorder—depressed individuals or those with a mild form of mania (called *hypomania* by psychiatrists)—remain in touch with reality. Mood dysfunctions are the most common illness encountered by mental health workers, and there are a variety of effective treatment methods.

What Is Neurosis?

The term *neurosis* is old, and was first coined by Freud to signify a conflict—a conflict between impulse and reality. We all have conflicts. Some of us want to make love to our neighbor's wife, but reality holds us back (hopefully). Others would like to sock the boss in the nose, but reality prevents us. Sometimes we get unreasonably angry at our children and then feel guilty. Conflicts may be conscious or unconscious (that is, outside our awareness). The more we are aware of our conflicts, the more maturely we manage them; the less aware we are, the more our conflicts manage us.

Neurotic conflicts may cause us to act in different ways. Some of us with conflicts have anxiety as the major symptom—hence the term *anxiety neurosis.* Others behave in a compulsive manner—hence the term *compulsive neurosis.* Still others become fearful of acts or objects (riding elevators, for example) in an attempt to manage unconscious conflicts—hence the term *phobic neurosis.* Discovering what these conflicts are, what causes them, and adopting more useful ways to handle the conflicts will take away the symptoms.

What Are Personality Disorders?

Somewhere between neuroses and psychoses fall the *personality disorders.* These people aren't out of touch with reality, and although they have conflicts they are generally unbothered by them. The main problem with people with personality disorders (also called *character disorders*) is their behavior. They seem to get into trouble again and again—yet they don't learn from their mistakes. Most (but not all) people with drug and alcohol abuse have personality disorders. The most serious personality disorder is the antisocial type—the habitual criminal. Other individuals are constantly late for work, obstinate, and unreliable (passive-aggressive type). Others are shy, withdrawn, and clinging (dependent type). There are many other personality types, and I am sure you can name them as well as I: just look around at your acquaintances, pick out their major characteristics, and label them.

The suggestion I just made gets us into a subject that is a serious problem for psychiatrists—when are personality patterns merely the mark of an individual, the behavior that makes that individual unique, and when is the personality pattern an illness? I like to answer that question this way: if an individual bothers society with his or her behavior, he or she may benefit from treatment; or, if an individual becomes disturbed by his or her personality traits, he or she can be helped by psychiatry.

What Are the Psychosomatic Disorders?

Psychosomatic disorders are physical illnesses in which emotional problems play a part. Ulcers, asthma, headaches, and many others are real physical illnesses—but emotional stress contributes to their development. These illnesses are helped with a combination of physical treatments and emotional support. More about this interesting set of illnesses later.

Who Treats Emotional Problems?

A variety of professionals treat emotional disturbances. Here is a brief overview:

1. The *psychiatrist*, a medical doctor who specializes in the treatment of mental disturbances, has four years of specialty education after obtaining an M.D. (medical doctor) degree. The psychiatrist has training in biological and medical treatments as well as training in psychotherapy. Two years after graduating from a residency training program, the psychiatrist is eligible to take an examination given by the American Board of Psychiatry and Neurology. If he or she passes, the psychiatrist is board certified. Although there are 26,000 psychiatrists in the United States, only 40 percent are board certified. Many non-board certified psychiatrists are perfectly capable—they just haven't chosen to go through the examination process.

2. The *psychoanalyst* is generally a psychiatrist who has had specialized training in the analytic process. Although most analysts are physicians, individuals with advanced training in

many fields can study in psychoanalytic institutes. In these institutes, trainees learn psychoanalytic theory and methods, and are analyzed themselves by an experienced analyst. There are approximately 2,500 psychoanalysts in the United States.

3. A *clinical psychologist* is not an M.D. and may or may not have a Ph.D. (doctoral) degree in psychology. The American Board of Professional Psychology certifies psychologists who have Ph.D. degrees and have had at least one year of training in a mental hospital or a mental health clinic. Some clinical psychologists, however, practice psychotherapy and administer psychological tests with only a master's degree (M.A.) or less.

4. A *psychiatric social worker* generally takes a two-year course after college for the M.S.W. degree (Master of Social Work). Most psychiatric social workers deal with family situations and help the patient with practical problems at home and in the community. For certification by the American Academy of Social Workers, candidates must work for two years under the supervision of a certified social worker and pass the academy's examination.

5. A *psychiatric nurse* is an R.N. (registered nurse) who has had special training in dealing with emotionally disturbed people.

6. The *paraprofessionals* are individuals without specialized degrees who work in conjunction with a professional.

7. Some *physicians* who are not psychiatrists use psychotherapeutic techniques in their daily practice.

8. The *neurologist* is an M.D. with 2½ years of specialty training in diseases of the nervous system (such as epilepsy and stroke) and six months of training in psychiatry.

Part II
Emotional Problems:
Causes and Symptoms

Chapter 3
Anxiety
(Butterflies and Other Nuisances)

Need it be necessary to define anxiety for anyone who has lived in our society? Present in all of us to some degree at some time, anxiety varies from the anticipatory stimulus of an exciting venture to an immobilizing panic that renders us helpless. In a moderate degree, anxiety constructively increases effort and alertness; in the pathological form, anxiety is the source of most emotional disorders. This chapter discusses pathological anxiety: its causes, symptoms, and treatment.

How Does Anxiety Differ from Fear?

Fear is the unpleasant response to an external threat; anxiety is a painful reaction to an internal conflict. Fear persists only as long as the danger lasts; anxiety lingers to produce physical and emotional symptoms.

What Happens to Your Body Under the Influence of Anxiety?

In his book *The Stress of Life*, Dr. Hans Selye, M.D., explains how the body responds to anxiety. When we become anxious, from either an actual physical threat or a perceived threat, the nerve cells in the part of the brain called the *hypothalamus* become excited. Anxiety causes the hypothalamus to release a hormone called CRH, which in turn signals the pituitary gland to release another hormone called ACTH. ACTH then enters the bloodstream and, on reaching the adrenal glands, causes them to release the hormone adrenalin.

Adrenalin, the "flight or fight" hormone, causes alertness, a rapid heartbeat, rapid breathing, speeds the reaction time, and improves perception. In short, adrenalin makes you either want to fight or to run away.

This "fight or flight" mechanism is beneficial when a definite danger needs to be resisted. However, this response becomes harmful if it persists or it is inappropriately triggered by minor events in everyday situations. If you are anxious about something, your body is put into a constant low-key state of stress, and your adrenal glands are continually producing enough adrenalin to ready your body for an encounter—one that will probably never happen.

Fear fades away when the dangerous situation passes, but anxiety may persist to produce chronic effects on the skeletal, gastrointestinal, and cardiovascular system. Clumsiness, tremor, nervous tics, choking sensations, and breathlessness become chronic symptoms of anxiety. An increase in skeletal muscle tone can produce a generalized fatigue and weakness due to prolonged energy expenditure.

What Causes Anxiety?

Basically anxiety is thought to develop from a combination of factors—stress, childhood conflicts, and faulty learning.

How Does Stress Contribute to Anxiety?

Our response to environmental conditions varies widely depending on cultural, family, and personal experiences. An unanticipated traumatic event such as a near-accident can elicit physiologic effects of anxiety. However, the anticipation of a stressful event is often more anxiety provoking than the event itself; for example, stomach cramps and nausea before school exams, or the rapid pulse and sweating before a job interview. Even the absence of stress is in itself a kind of stress. Experimental volunteers subjected to extreme environmental deprivation develop symptoms of anxiety. Because of our enormous adaptative capacity, most of us adjust to the everyday stress of living; but once problems escalate faster than they can be solved, clinical anxiety results.

How Do Childhood Conflicts Contribute to Anxiety?

According to Freudian analytic theory, unconscious childhood conflicts may produce anxiety. Unfortunately, because these conflicts are outside of our conscious awareness, our efforts to relieve the anxious feelings are inappropriate and ineffective. Several childhood conflicts may persist into adulthood and produce anxiety:

1. The childhood fear of losing love, affection, and support can persist into adulthood, producing anxiety. As adults, we may be getting as much love and attention as necessary, but because we were deprived of love in childhood, we may fear that adult affection will also eventually be withdrawn. This fear may be outside of our awareness so that we become chronically anxious without knowing why.
2. We may harbor unconscious resentment and anger based on past childhood conflicts. We may fear losing control of these aggressive impulses, a fear that, in turn, produces the symptoms of chronic anxiety. Likewise, the fear of losing control of bottled-up sexual impulses can also contribute to anxiety.
3. It is well documented that many individuals fear success. In many individuals, this success fear is related, in part, to childhood conflicts over competition with the parent of the same sex.
4. Fear of transgressing moral and ethical values can produce anxiety.

Here is an important point: the cause of our anxiety is often repressed—we are unaware of the cause. The only symptom of these childhood fears is a vague uncomfortable feeling of anxiety. Most of the time this anxiety can be well controlled with productive work, hobbies, helping others, or recreational pursuits. Symptoms of anxiety result when these activities become incapable of completely repressing the childhood conflicts.

For example, a college freshman developed the fear of going out-of-doors. Although it was necessary for this student to leave the dormitory to attend classes, he could not walk across the campus without rapid heartbeat, sweating, and shortness of breath. A psychiatric interview revealed that when the student was five years old his mother and father were divorced, leaving him alone with his mother. Although the father lived in a nearby town, he never visited his son after the divorce. The boy lost himself in his studies, becoming an outstanding student and receiving praise from his mother because she was certain he was going to "amount to something" (in contrast to his "ne'er-do-well" father). After graduating from high school, it was necessary for the boy to leave home to fulfill his mother's prophecy, but soon after the fall semester began he developed the fear of going out-of-doors. The student reported never having experienced anger. He showed no outward resentment toward his father's continual neglect and talked of him in a bland, detached way. Moreover, he recalled vividly an occasion when, as a small boy, he had gone hunting with a cousin and had killed a squirrel. He was horrified by this act and swore that he would never again harm any living creature. Soon after this incident, the boy decided to pursue a career in veterinary medicine.

It is understandable that divorce of his parents had a powerful effect on the student when he was a little boy and left him with a serious conflict over aggression. His father left at a time when the boy was competing with his father for his mother's attention. Because of the boy's powerful unconscious wishes to be rid of his father, he blamed himself for the departure of his father. As a result, he experienced a fearful respect for his aggressive urges, which he began to keep under strict control. College presented an opportunity for the student to supersede his uneducated father and stirred up the old fear of aggresssion; this feeling was displaced onto the fear of going outside. The fear of going outside not only prevented the student from going to class (and thus superseding his father) but also offered the opportunity for the student to return to his beloved mother. During psychoanalysis, the student recovered a repressed memory of his father severely beating him whenever he crossed the street—the source of the fear of the outside. With therapy, the student became more aware of his competitive feelings toward his father and began to realize that success would cause him no physical harm. He was able to return to college and complete his studies.

Can Faulty Learning Contribute to Anxiety?

Often the perception of a stressful event depends on what the individual has learned to appraise as dangerous or threatening. What one person perceives as stressful, another may experience as stimulating. An inappropriate, unrealistic anxiety response is often a manifestation of learned habits.

Studies of animals demonstrate this process; for example, a rat is placed on a grill. Ten seconds later an electrical current is passed through the area of the grill on which the rat is standing. The rat soon learns to scamper to the opposite end of the grill and escape into a nonelectrified compartment. After a few repetitions of this procedure, the rat's fear becomes conditioned, and it will run to the opposite end as soon as being placed on the grill—even when the current is turned off.

Human beings can also be conditioned to fear certain situations. For example, an individual who has lived through a hotel fire may never want to sleep in a hotel again; an individual who has a particularly harsh and critical teacher may learn to fear all authority figures. Another example of learned anxiety is the stress disorder that is precipitated by combat. Soldiers returning from a war may jump to the ground whenever they hear a loud noise that reminds them of combat sounds.

What Are the Results of Anxiety?

Anxiety can produce a variety of neurotic conditions—phobias, panic attacks, compulsions, depersonalization, and conversion reactions. Many people can accomplish great deeds in spite of (or in some cases, because of) their neurotic conflicts (see the box).

What Are Phobias?

A phobic disorder is the persistent avoidance of an object, activity, or situation because of irrational fears. The individual realizes that the fear is unreasonable but continues to avoid the particular situation because to do otherwise would lead to incapacitating anxiety. Some individuals may fear crowds, others may fear closed or open spaces, bridges, tunnels, and so forth. The following case shows how a fear of going to churches developed.

A 19-year-old student who lived at home while attending a local college developed panic attacks while sitting in church. The student would begin to sweat profusely, breathe rapidly, become nauseated, and fear that he would vomit and embarrass

---

FAMOUS NEUROTICS

Marcel Proust—Proust lived the last few years of his life in a corklined room, which he hoped would prevent dust from provoking an asthma attack.

Oscar Levant—If he encountered a semicolon while reading, Levant would force himself to reread the paragraph. He claimed to have given up reading the *New Yorker* magazine because it contained too many semicolons.

Sigmund Freud—For ten years or so, Freud suffered from a death phobia, fear of traveling by rail, and anxiety so distressing that, at times, he was unable to write or concentrate his thoughts. There is an unmistakable connection between Freud's anxiety and his work. His anxiety compelled him to find the cause of his distress; thus he developed the theories of psychoanalysis.

Henry Houdini—Houdini's daring underwater escapes and ingenious tricks were a reaction to the fear of death, especially death by respiratory disease, which had killed his two brothers.

---

himself. The patient became phobic of church and soon refused to attend services or to leave home unaccompanied. Treatment revealed that the patient came from an extremely religious background; his parents strongly wanted him to attend a seminary after college graduation. The student had no desire to enter the ministry but was reluctant to rebel against his parents' wishes. The fear of churches had its origin in expected punishment for the student's unconscious anger toward his parents for dominating his life. The student's fear was deconditioned using relaxing techniques (as described later). Psychotherapy helped the patient understand that he was free to choose his own career.

Often phobias can be simply treated by deconditioning techniques as the following case exemplifies. A middle-aged suc-

---

A FEW FANTASTIC PHOBIAS
(There are 662 more that aren't in this list)

Acrophobia—fear of heights

Agoraphobia—fear of open places

Ailurophobia—fear of cats

Androphobia—fear of men

Anthrophobia—fear of people

Arachibutyrophobia—fear of peanut butter sticking to the roof of the mouth

Astraphobia—fear of storms, lightning, thunder

Baccilophia—fear of microbes

Ballistophobia—fear of bullets

Ceraunophobia—fear of thunder

Claustrophobia—fear of enclosed places

Decidophobia—fear of making decisions

Ergophobia—fear of work

Gynephobia—fear of women

Hematophobia—fear of blood

Hydrophobia—fear of water

Iatrophobia—fear of doctors

Nosophobia—fear of disease

Nucleomitiphobia—fear of nuclear bombs

Nyctophobia—fear of night

Ochlophobia—fear of crowds

Peccatophobia—fear of sinning

Pyrophobia—fear of fire

Sophophobia—fear of learning

Thanatophobia—fear of death

Topophobia—fear of performing (i.e. stage fright)

Xenophobia—fear of strangers

Zoophobia—fear of animals

cessful businessman was fearful of riding elevators but functioned quite well in all other respects. As a child, the patient had been repeatedly locked in closets by his older brothers. This childhood experience was later displaced onto a fear of elevators. The elevator phobia was successfully treated by using an exposure technique. The therapist accompanied the patient to the hospital elevator and repeatedly rode up and down with him. Initially the patient was terror stricken; but after ten minutes he appeared somewhat relaxed and within 20 minutes experienced no fear. Next, the stop button was pushed, causing the elevator to jerk to a stop between floors. The patient's anxiety level initially soared but within a few minutes he learned to tolerate being "trapped" between floors. Next the patient was allowed to ride alone, and although fearful at first, within 45 minutes he was riding the elevator comfortably. After another hour of "practice" and a repeat session a few days later, the patient's phobia completely disappeared.

What Causes Panic Attacks?

A panic condition is an acute, terrifying apprehension accompanied by rapid heartbeat, nausea, tremulousness, dizziness, weakness, shortness of breath, and occasionally chest pain. These attacks usually occur once a week or more often, and the individual commonly is unable to determine what precipitated the attack.

Many of the physical symptoms associated with a panic attack result from hyperventilation (overbreathing). Any fear-producing situation can cause a person to overbreathe. This increased breathing rate may be so slight that the individual fails to realize that he or she is overbreathing. Nevertheless, if sufficiently prolonged, overbreathing can cause an imbalance of the chemicals in the bloodstream. The overbreathing causes the individual to blow off more carbon dioxide than is desirable. This lowered carbon dioxide level leads to a fall in the blood bicarbonate, producing light-headedness, increased sweating, feelings of pressure in the chest, and palpitations. All these symptoms cause an increase in the rate of breathing and consequently a further increase in the symptoms. The fingers, toes, and the areas around the mouth may begin to tingle, and occasionally the individual faints. Rarely, convulsions may be produced by hyperventilation.

The following case illustrates how emotional conflicts can produce panic attacks and hyperventilation. A 28-year-old married woman came to my office complaining of episodes of fainting. I gave the patient a complete medical work-up including blood studies, urinalysis, chest Xray, thyroid tests, and a glucose tolerance test. These examinations all produced normal results, but she continued to experience fainting episodes. On careful questioning, it became apparent that her frequent fainting was associated with problems of parenting. Often after having an argument with her four-year-old daughter, the patient would become faint; occasionally she would experience this sensation when driving her child to kindergarten. Just before feeling faint, the patient experienced many of the sensations associated with the hyperventilation syndrome. Between attacks the patient felt weak and tired, slept poorly, and had frequent headaches. Psychotherapy sessions revealed the patient's unconscious hostility toward her child. Before her pregnancy the patient had had a satisfying job as an executive secretary to the vice president of a large corporation. The patient had experienced an uncomfortable pregnancy, and delivery was especially difficult. At the time she had thought she might die, and her breathing was difficult. After her child was born, she felt compelled to become a "good mother" and stay at home. Whenever she became angry at her daughter, she had conscious thoughts of "this child is going to be the death of me." The patient was helped to understand that she could return to her satisfying job and remain a good mother. In subsequent visits she was encouraged to express her "unacceptable" feelings toward her daughter. After several months of treatment, the patient's symptoms began to clear and she happily returned to work (and became a better mother).

What Causes Compulsive Behavior?

Compulsive behavior is characterized by persistently performing certain rituals despite the wish to stop. There is a wide range of compulsive behavior. The most common ritual is frequent hand washing. Another symptom is checking and rechecking the doors of the home to make certain they are locked. One of my patients kept opening and closing his cigarette lighter to see if the flame was extinguished; another kept opening and closing the refrigerator to make certain that the light inside had gone out. Behind all these senseless acts was an attempt to relieve anxiety. The patients felt silly performing these acts but were overwhelmed with anxiety when they failed to do so.

Compulsive acts serve to defend against anxiety. Performing a lot of foolish tasks prevents the individual from worrying about what is really bothering him or her—guilt, for example, as the following case illustrates:

A 24-year-old medical student felt compelled to wash his hands before and after visiting each patient. Soon he began washing his hands after each part of the examination was completed. Rather quickly the student's supervisor noticed this strange behavior and referred the student to me for treatment. When I saw the patient, he told me that he felt compelled to carry out certain activities that he knew were bizarre but nevertheless were out of his power to control. Every night he read a different chapter from his Bible, picked out a verse that he felt was important, and memorized it before going to bed. His clothes had to be placed on the dressing table, with his pants stacked neatly on the bottom of the pile, followed by his shirt, and underwear. Three pairs of socks were placed next to his clothes; his shoes had to be placed under the bed with only the toes of the shoes visible. The laces of the shoes had to be crossed over each other three times. Before getting into bed, he had to knock on his chest three times and, on reclining, say the Lord's Prayer three times. Failure to do any of these things caused overwhelming anxiety. The student explained that the activities in threes stood for Father, Son, and Holy Ghost. Brought up in a strict environment by a tyrannical father and ambitious mother, this student felt driven to medical school by his mother's wishes for him to do well and his determination to out-do his father. The student viewed his successful entrance into medical school as a hostile act toward his unsuccessful father. Thus, most of his rituals and religious preoccupations were attempts to relieve unconscious guilt over superseding his father. With treatment, the student gradually improved and was able to reenter medical school and complete his degree.

How Does Anxiety Produce Fatigue?

Individuals with anxiety live in a state of worry, apprehension, and uneasiness. These individuals are overconscientious and have difficulty making decisions. Once a choice is made, they tend to ruminate over whether the choice is right or wrong. Constant worry produces chronic fatigue and the inability to concentrate. The following case is an example:

A jumpy, apprehensive, and rather timid 27-year-old elementary school teacher entered my office complaining of chronic fatigue and weakness. During the interview the patient revealed somewhat reluctantly that she had been dating a choir leader at a local church for which she sang. The choir master insisted on premarital sexual relations to make certain of their sexual compatibility before their marriage. Although this idea was against her religious training, she found him sexually attractive, loved him very much, and did not want to lose him. She was unable to make up her mind. First, the patient considered herself unattractive and felt that the choir leader was only trying to seduce her. Second, she feared losing the man she loved. Third, her desire for sexual relations engendered guilt feelings. Fourth, she feared that if she were to have sexual relations she would be punished with pregnancy. She became anxious, irritable, and could not sleep well at night. The patient received supportive psychotherapy aimed at helping her work on a reasonable solution. Subsequently, the choir leader was driven out of town after it was rumored that the pastor's wife became pregnant by him. Psychotherapy helped the patient deal with these unfortunate events, and she gradually began to adjust. She remained shy and somewhat high-strung, but no longer experienced episodes of acute anxiety. Several years later she married a local farmer and has been relatively happy since.

What Is a Stress Reaction?

A stress reaction is chronic anxiety that occurs following a car accident or other traumatic events such as fires, airplane crashes, floods, earthquakes, rape, assault, or combat. Generally the symptoms remit within six months after the onset of the trauma, although occasionally symptoms may last for decades.

The following case is an example of a stress reaction secondary to an automobile accident. A 19-year-old woman was driving home, after having had an argument with her boyfriend, when the brakes of her car went out on a slippery curve. The car overturned several times, and somehow her arm was severed just below the shoulder joint. The patient was immediately flown to a nearby medical center where her arm was reattached. Several days following the accident the patient began to complain of painful flashbacks, at which time she would vividly remember the accident. She feared going to sleep because of recurrent nightmares of the event. Occasionally she would have brief periods of unreality during which she felt her arm would detach from her body and wave goodbye to her. I was asked to see the patient to help her deal with her emotional conflicts surrounding the accident. I told the patient that it was important for her to talk about the accident as much as possible so that she could put it behind her. I encouraged her to start talking about the accident during the day so she would stop dreaming about it at night. Because the patient was somewhat of a local celebrity, I encouraged her to talk to the press and television people about her accident. She also began to collect newspaper reports of the event. The patient also talked with her boyfriend about the events preceding the accident. As she began to discuss the accident openly she began to adjust to this overwhelming trauma. One year following the patient's accident, she had regained approximately 50 percent use of her left arm and was planning to marry her boyfriend. She was no longer bothered about the car accident in any way.

What Is the Vietnam Stress Syndrome?

Burt, drafted one month after high school graduation, considered basic training a joke. Throughout boot camp he laughed and joshed with his friends; on the plane ride to Vietnam, they sang bawdy barroom songs. As the plane landed on the solitary strip at Con Thien, they were suddenly fired on by the enemy. A few seconds later, a buddy standing next to him was blown to bits. "Suddenly," Burt said later, "it wasn't a joke any more—these guys were serious." Burt spent most of his time in the jungles of Vietnam fighting desperately for unknown villages and hills, only to have the bureaucracy give up the hard-won territory. A few weeks later, Burt and his buddies would be back fighting for the same territory again. Burt witnessed tortures and atrocities. On returning to the United States, he was spat on and cursed as a "baby killer."

Eleven years later, Burt continues to dream about the war. Whenever a car backfires or a door slams, Burt falls to the ground. Helicopters flying overhead make him momentarily feel he is back in Vietnam. In addition, Burt is angry and upset with the federal government; he has trouble trusting anyone, and his frequent difficulties with employers causes him to drift from job to job. He is married, but unhappily. He occasionally gets drunk and beats his wife; at other times he cries like a baby in her arms.

Burt is one of an estimated 500,000–700,000 Vietnam veterans who suffer from posttraumatic stress disorder secondary to the Vietnam War. Symptoms include

1. Traumatic dreams of the war
2. Flashbacks—feeling as if the war were recurring
3. Startle reactions
4. Difficulty trusting others
5. Emotional numbness—feeling "half-dead"
6. Difficulty in relationships with other people.
7. Survival guilt—guilt about surviving when others died

The treatment for this condition involves getting the veteran to join a group therapy session with other Vietnam veterans. Group therapy allows the veteran to talk about and reexperience the war in the presence of others who understand his difficulties. As with all therapies, group therapy of this sort is painful, but worthwhile. It often takes from one to three years of treatment for the veteran to begin to feel better about himself and others. Burt, for example, has been in group therapy for two years. He is doing much better. He no longer beats his wife and has maintained the same job for eight months. He continues to occasionally dream about the war whenever he is stressed, and he feels guilt over having survived the war when some of his best friends died in Vietnam. It will probably take Burt another year or two to put the war behind him so that he can live a more satisfying life.

Unfortunately, many Vietnam veterans with Burt's symptoms have yet to seek treatment. Part of the reason for this is their anger at the federal government and their mistrust for any bureaucratic program. To partially alleviate this situation, the federal government has established 130 "storefront" centers that are located in urban areas throughout the United States. The Vietnam veteran can go to one of these centers "with no strings attached." The centers are operated by other Vietnam veterans who have special training in treating emotional problems of the war. Once the veteran begins to trust the "storefront center" counselors, he more easily accepts referral to the Veterans Administration hospitals for more intensive group therapy if it is needed.

Although the Vietnam War was unique in many ways, all war is hell: Many, many (the exact number no one knows) World War II and Korean War veterans have the same symptoms that Burt has. These unfortunate individuals have "burned out," leading lives of no joy and no productivity.

Many people ask me why some individuals can tolerate war better than others. I can't answer that one completely, and, as far as I know, no one else has all the answers either. Perhaps some veterans reacted adversely to the war because of a poor childhood, while some experienced more stress than others. Maybe so much stress occurred over such a brief period of time that the individual "cracked." Some people are simply emotionally stronger than others. Whatever the cause for the stress reaction of war, the syndrome can be effectively treated if the veteran is willing to seek and stay with group therapy until the conflicts have been resolved.

What Is Multiple Personality?

Multiple personality is the occurrence of several distinct, fully integrated personalities in the same individual. Such people assume the role of one individual for hours, days, and even months, and then suddenly flip into another personality. *Three Faces of Eve* by Drs. C. H. Thigpen and H. M. Cleckley, and *Sybil* by F. R. Schreiber, are two celebrated reports. Multiple personality, extremely rare, is not to be confused with schizophrenia (see Chapter 5). More common but still exceedingly rare, psychogenic fugue is the assumption of a new identity and the inability to recall one's prior identity. Both these disorders result from overwhelming anxiety. The anxiety is so severe that the individual "blanks out" or assumes another personality.

An example of psychogenic fugue is the following. A 34-year-old married contractor became overwhelmed with unpaid bills. One day he simply disappeared. One and one-half years later he was recognized by a friend who was passing through another state. The contractor had assumed a new identity as a pastor for a fundamentalist church and had remarried. As he tells it, he remembers driving out of his old home town; the next thing he remembers is waking up by the side of the road, his head bloodied and all identification missing. The contractor wandered to the nearest town where he eventually got a job as a bag-boy in a grocery store. A few weeks later the contractor "received the call" and began preaching the gospel. Whether this is an example of psychogenic fugue or malingering, neither I, nor any of the other psychiatrists who examined the contractor-pastor, could tell. The patient did return to his home town and pay his bills. Just prior to his bigamy trial, the contractor-pastor disappeared again. Another attack of psychogenic fugue? Who knows.

What Causes Symptoms of Depersonalization?

Depersonalization involves the temporary feeling of self-estrangement or unreality. The individual feels that he or she is in a dreamlike state; actions seem mechanical; there may be a sense of seeming to view oneself from a distance. Such episodes can be precipitated by anxiety, fatigue, or toxic illness.

The following case represents an example of depersonalization. A 23-year-old female graduate student in a university school of fine arts came to the student health center with a complaint of overwhelming anxiety and unreality. Often when sketching she would feel as though her mind had floated upward and that she could view her body from above. This feeling was so disturbing that she would be forced to stop work. After a few minutes the sensation would pass, but would occasionally recur after she returned to her sketching. As the diagnostic interview continued, the patient revealed that her parents wanted her to pursue a career in engineering and that she had become acutely anxious after having entered the school of fine arts against her parent's wishes. Psychotherapy centered around the patient's conflict with her parents concerning her career choice. As her conflict cleared, so did the feelings of depersonalization.

What Are Conversion Reactions?

Conversion disorder derives its name from the "conversion" of anxiety into a physical symptom. For example, after becoming enraged with his employer, a man suddenly may suffer "paralysis" of his arm to prevent him from striking his boss. This paralysis results from the unconscious anxiety that the individual's anger had precipitated. Several decades ago, conversion disorders were extremely common. Recently, however, conversion symptoms have been extremely rare for some reason—probably the increasing sophistication of the general population. When it does occur, the conversion symptom often develops during a period of extreme stress. Unsuccessful love affairs, an unhappy marriage, fear of pregnancy, and sexual difficulties are frequent precipitants of conversion symptoms in women, while threats to self-esteem or problems at work may result in conversion reaction in men. War trauma or the recent loss of a loved one may contribute to the development of conversion symptoms.

Most theories on the cause of conversion disorders originate with Freudian theory: a conflict between an unconscious wish and fear of the wish produces anxiety; the anxiety, in turn, is converted into a physical symptom. The symptom expresses the repressed wish while at the same time offering relief from the emotional conflict. In addition, the conversion symptom provides an escape from an intolerable social situation or an excuse for failure.

Patients with conversion disorders are best treated by a psychiatrist. The goal of therapy is to remove the symptom and to help the patient achieve a more constructive method for dealing with anxiety in the future. Hypnosis is the treatment of choice for removing the symptom. Analytic psychotherapy can help prevent recurrences.

The following example represents a successful treatment case. An 18-year-old woman developed blindness a few days following an episode in which her boyfriend, overcome with passion, had ripped off his pants, exposing his erect penis. The patient had spent most of the spring and summer evenings parked down a dark country lane, kissing and hugging with her boyfriend. Each time he pleaded for sexual intercourse, she would sharply rebuke him, but they continued to park because she enjoyed his tender caresses, and he savored the anticipated sexual conquest. On one warm summer night, exasperated by what he perceived to be seductive behavior, the boyfriend forcefully attempted sexual intercourse. The woman jumped from the car and ran home. Several days later she could not see. An ophthalmologist examined the patient and found no physical cause for her blindness. She was referred to a psychiatrist for treatment. Hypnotherapy helped rid the patient of some of her acute anxiety and her vision returned. Psychotherapy centered on helping the patient accept her womanhood by working through her conflicts concerning adult sexual activity and her legitimate fears of forcible intercourse.

What Is the Best Treatment for Anxiety?

There are a variety of effective treatments for anxiety; the best treatment depends on the particular situation. I discuss some of the treatments here and other treatments in Chapter 15.

What Are Some Methods to Aid in Relaxation?

Relaxation techniques are especially helpful in learning to deal with anxiety. As the mind becomes anxious, the body begins to tense; this body tension produces more anxiety, setting up a vicious cycle. Relaxation techniques help break up this vicious cycle. Although a number of techniques successfully produce relaxation, perhaps the most popular has been Transcendental Meditation (TM). Individuals taught meditation by a trained TM instructor are given a secret phrase, called a *mantra*. While sitting in a comfortable position, the meditator then repeats this phrase mentally over and over again. Practitioners meditate for 20 minutes, twice daily. A Harvard cardiologist, Herbert Benson, found that meditation appears to be effective in reducing oxygen consumption, respiratory rate, heart rate, and blood pressure. In addition, the blood lactate (associated with anxiety and skeletal muscle metabolism) is decreased; metabolic rate is lowered; and drug use, alcohol consumption, and cigarette smoking diminishes. When a meditator is connected to an electroencephalogram (which measures brainwaves), the meditator is found to have an increase in alpha waves, indicating that this altered state of consciousness differs from sleep.

Benson tested the TM meditators and found that the use of a specific, secret mantra taught by TM instructors is unnecessary. Any phrase works just as well. The following set of instructions recommended by Benson (1975, pages 114–15) represent a modified form of meditation called the *relaxation response*.

1. Sit quietly in a comfortable position.
2. Close your eyes.
3. Deeply relax all your muscles, beginning at your feet and progressing up to your face. Keep them relaxed.

4. Breathe through your nose. Become aware of your breathing. Breathe easily and naturally. As you breathe out, say the word *one* silently to yourself.

5. Continue for 10 to 20 minutes. You may open your eyes to check the time but do not use an alarm. When you finish, sit quietly for several minutes, at first with your eyes closed, later with them open.

6. Do not worry about whether you are successful in achieving a deep level of relaxation. Maintain a passive attitude and permit relaxation to occur at its own pace. When distracting thoughts occur, try to ignore them by not dwelling upon them, and return to repeating *one*.

With practice, you should be able to achieve the relaxation response with little effort. Practice the technique once or twice daily, but not within two hours of a meal, because the digestive process seems to interfere with the elicitation of anticipated changes. If you practice this procedure of generalized relaxation, you will begin to gradually feel more and more comfortable. If you are especially tense and don't seem to be responding to TM or the relaxation response, it might be beneficial to receive a few sessions from a hypnotherapist or a behavioral therapist who specializes in relaxation techniques. Or you can purchase relaxation tape recordings.

After you have mastered the relaxation response, practice a 10-second relaxation exercise throughout the day to help break up the spiraling tension that accumulates during stressful periods. During the 10-second exercise, you merely take a deep breath and slowly exhale while telling yourself to relax, imagine the tension draining out of your body and remember the pleasant way that you felt with the Relaxation Response. Perform this 10-second exercise whenever you begin to feel yourself tensing up.

What Is Systematic Desensitization?

Systematic desensitization simply means exposing someone to a fear-producing situation in a step-by-step manner. The businessman who was afraid of elevators (mentioned earlier in this chapter) got rid of his elevator fear by gradually being exposed to riding an elevator. He was desensitized to his elevator fear in a systematic way. Systematic desensitization works well for phobias and other unrealistic anxieties, but you will probably need a professional (usually a behavioral therapist) to help guide you through a hierarchy of your fears. Other behavioral techniques are also good for reducing anxiety (see Chapter 15).

What Is Goal-Directed Psychotherapy?

Individuals with anxiety disorders and emotional difficulties related to environmental stresses often respond to brief psychotherapy sessions with the goal of helping them deal with the current life situation that's troubling them. In goal-directed psychotherapy, the individual, with the help of a therapist, tries to answer the following questions: (1) What am I troubled about? and (2) What can I do to alter the situation to make this situation more tolerable?

The following case is an example of how I use a combination of relaxation therapy and goal-directed therapy to help individuals overcome conflicts that are producing anxiety. A 28-year-old housewife complained of irritability, palpitations, and vague, unpleasant apprehension. On the initial visit, the patient and I set a goal of therapy consisting of helping her learn more effective ways of dealing with anxiety and to explore the environmental source of her apprehension. Ten 20-minute, once-weekly sessions were scheduled. The first three sessions were spent training in the relaxation response. The patient was given a cassette tape recording of the first session to take home. The next two sessions were spent in reinforcing the relaxation response. The patient was encouraged to practice the relaxation response twice daily at home as well as to perform 10-second relaxation exercises when tension built up during the day. The fourth through ninth sessions were spent in exploring environmental factors contributing to her stress. It became evident that the patient's main conflict was her great expectation of herself as a mother. The patient felt as if she had failed whenever she became irritated with her two preschool children. In addition she had few interests outside of the home and was essentially a slave to her own demands. She felt guilty whenever she considered leaving her children with a babysitter because her mother had always sacrificed for her and she felt that she must do likewise for her children. The patient was encouraged to get out of the house, and she began to take tennis lessons and became more active in the community affairs. Her husband was pleased with her new-found enthusiasm and was more than willing to help her change her lifestyle patterns. The last session was spent in going over with the patient all that she had learned. She was helped to understand that if her old patterns of behavior returned in the future they could be dealt with effectively once she became alert to the factors that precipitated them. Of course, not all cases are this easy, but this example gives you an idea of what can be done in a relatively short period of time if you are highly motivated to change and have a cooperative family.

Who Needs Professional Help?

If you continue to be anxious and tense after having tried the relaxation techniques listed in this book, then you should see your family physician. He or she might want to help you with additional relaxation techniques or might help you explore the causes of your anxiety. If you are undergoing a particularly stressful situation, your physician may decide to prescribe some minor tranquilizers for a week or two. These medications will be discussed in great detail in Chapter 14, but let me make one warning now: *never take any minor tranquilizer for longer than two weeks.* Such medications dull the senses and may lead to depression. They gradually take away your enthusiasm for everyday activities and may, after a long period of time, become addicting. In some individuals, the minor tranquilizers, including Valium, lead to an increase in irritability and anger.

If after receiving help from your family practitioner, you are continuing to have emotional difficulties, you should seriously consider seeing a psychiatrist. There are a variety of psychotherapeutic techniques used for the treatment of anxiety symptoms. The accompanying box lists the techniques that are specific for each type of problem. These treatment techniques will be more fully explained in Chapter 15.

PSYCHOTHERAPEUTIC TECHNIQUES USED TO TREAT ANXIETY

Symptoms	Treatment
Phobic symptoms	Behavioral therapy (systematic desensitization)
Anxiety related to difficulty in getting along with other people	Group therapy
Generalized anxiety	Psychoanalysis
Conversion reaction	Hypnotherapy and analytic therapy
Brief situational disturbance producing anxiety	Minor tranquilizers for no longer than two weeks
Panic disorder	Psychotherapy to help uncover the reason for the anxiety attacks (analytic therapy)
Compulsions	Behavioral modifications
Posttraumatic stress disorder	Talking about the stress over and over with a family physician or a psychiatrist until the symptoms gradually disappear
Depersonalization disorder	Analytic therapy

Chapter 4
Depression
(Singing the Blues and How to Stop)

Almost everyone experiences occasional feelings of mild depression—there are days when we all ask the question "What's the use?" A slowed gait, gloomy expression, and a slumped posture tells the world "I'm miserable." These low periods attack even the most exuberant optimist at times, but they rarely persist.

Then there are the periods of deep despair brought about by a death of a loved one, the loss of a job or a serious illness. Such despair can be so black at times that treatment becomes necessary. But in most cases time and care from loved ones relieve the suffering and normal functioning gradually returns.

In millions of other people, however, depression occurs for no definite reason and it may linger for months or even years. At any given time, 7 percent of the population shows evidence of clinically significant depressive symptoms. During the course of a lifetime, over one-fourth of the population (that's right—one out of four) will have a severe depressive episode.

This chapter tells how to distinguish depression that needs medical treatment versus that kind of treatment that can be expected to lift almost spontaneously. The types of depression, the various causes of depression, and ways of getting help are also discussed.

What Are the Types of Depression?

Basically, there are three types of depression. The first type, often the mildest, comes on as a reaction to a stressful event or a significant loss.

This type of depression will gradually clear in a few months' time with proper help from loved ones and friends. Occasionally, however, the stressful event can be so overwhelming that the depressed individual loses weight, has difficulty sleeping, a poor appetite, decreased sexual interest, and loses interest for

FAMOUS DEPRESSED PEOPLE

Hamlet—Depression prevented the melancholy Dane from avenging his father's death. Hamlet said: "How weary, stale, flat, and unprofitable seem to me all the uses of this world."

Abraham Lincoln—Endured recurrent episodes of depression during the years he practiced law and later as President of the United States. When a young man he refused to carry a pocket knife for fear he would kill himself with it.

Sylvia Plath—American writer who described her depression in the novel, *The Bell Jar*. She committed suicide at the age of 31.

Edwin E. "Buzz" Aldrin, Jr.—The second man to walk on the moon became depressed from the stress of post-flight publicity.

Senator Thomas P. Eagleton—In 1972 withdrew as Democratic candidate for Vice-President after it was revealed that he had been hospitalized three times for depression and received shock therapy twice. A majority of individuals surveyed in a national poll thought that he was qualified for the job despite his history of illness.

Edgar Allen Poe—The brooding author rarely smiled; he was depressed and intoxicated most of his short life.

almost everything. The individual is tired, draggy, easily fatigued. Physical complaints—headache, diarrhea, upset stomach, and muscular aches and pains—are common. When these symptoms occur and persist for over six weeks or so, the individual needs medical treatment.

For example, a 34-year-old man, Jim, came to my office after experiencing a series of setbacks. Several months before his visit, funding for a research project he was working on had been cut back and he was terminated from his job. Soon after that event, his wife had a second miscarriage in as many years. To compound matters, Jim's father died suddenly after suffering a massive heart attack.

FAMOUS MANIC DEPRESSIVES

King Saul of Israel—I Samuel records his plight. Uncontrollable outbursts of irritability and suspiciousness alternated with a depressed state. While manic he tried to kill David and later his own son, Jonathan. On another occasion he stripped off all his clothes and lay down naked all that day and night. When in a depressed state he committed suicide.

Ernest Hemingway—Manic phases of activity—fishing, hunting, writing, fighting, loving—alternated with depressions. When manic he believed he was immortal, which may partially explain his frequent accidents and automobile collisions. Committed suicide in 1961.

George III of England—The "mad monarch" asked rapid fire questions while waiting for answers, bolted his food, rode his horse to death, and had episodes of sleep depriving energy.

Theodore Roosevelt—Irrepressible—all action and energy—he could work for days with little sleep: was constantly occupied with talking, telephoning, and writing. During his governorship and presidency wrote 150,000 letters and wrote an estimated 18 million words in his lifetime.

Winston Churchill—Brilliant, impulsive, and domineering, Britain's Prime Minister had high periods when he talked nonstop and said whatever came to mind, alternating with bouts of deep depression that he called his "Black Dog."

Robert Schumann—The peak years of his musical output occurred during his manic phase; while depressed he created nothing. He tried to drown himself in the Rhine—spent the last two years of his life in a mental hospital.

Jim gave the appearance of being totally washed out—no energy, no enthusiasm, no hope. He sat slumped in the chair, his eyes downcast and his hands folded in his lap. Jim's speech was slow and halting and, unlike people with a normal mood, he did not change his body position throughout the entire interview.

Jim reported that he first began having difficulty after he lost his job. He found himself waking early in the morning, anxious and tense and unable to return to sleep. After his wife's miscarriage, Jim's despondency increased. He would sit around the house, numb, thinking of nothing, doing nothing. His weight began to fall off, and his sexual interest diminished entirely. With his father's death, hopelessness and helplessness set in. He began to have crying spells and suicidal thoughts. His family finally persuaded him to seek help.

Because of the severity of Jim's depression, I decided to admit him to the hospital for a brief period of time. While he was there, I started him on a tricyclic antidepressant medication, and he began to have daily supportive psychotherapy sessions consisting mainly of my listening, empathizing, and encouraging him. After a few weeks Jim was able to see hope for the future, and he began to look for a new job on discharge three weeks after the initiation of hospitalization.

Jim continued with weekly supportive psychotherapy sessions and was maintained on the antidepressant medication for six months. Jim's appetite and sexual energy returned, and he was sleeping soundly at night. He was able to find another job that paid slightly less than his former one, but suited his talents more. A couple of years after his acute depression, Jim called to tell me that his wife had given birth to a seven-pound, four-ounce healthy baby boy. He also said that his climb up the promotion ladder at work was progressing well.

The second type of depression is much more common and even more puzzling than the depression that is related to a specific stress. This type of depression comes on almost spontaneously. There appears to be no particular cause for the depression, but the downcast mood is devastating and can lead to suicide without the proper treatment. Individuals with this spontaneous type of depression will have all the signs and symptoms that the first type experienced. The difference between the two depends on the precipitating event: Individuals with the first type of depression have a definite stress that results in their illness; those with the second type have no discernible cause for their depression. Because there is no environmental cause for the second type, researchers believe that there is some biological cause (a chemical imbalance in the brain) that produces the depression.

For example, Elizabeth—like Jim—also looked depressed when she came to see me. Her eyes had that same downcast gaze, her hands did not move from her lap, and the normal posture shifts were absent. She cried easily as she reported the same symptoms of depression, namely, waking early in the morning, decreased appetite, decreased energy, feelings of hopelessness and helplessness, and diminished sexual energy. Elizabeth's history, however, differed from Jim's: there was no precipitating event. She had two healthy children, her husband had an executive position for a textile company, and she had an active social calendar—but for some reason she was depressed. Elizabeth reported that she had experienced periodic episodes of depression since her college days. These episodes would come on rather suddenly and last for several months, only to clear up spontaneously. She had never seen a psychiatrist or any other physician for her problems, but, being a rather stoic individual, she preferred to weather these depressive episodes on her own, pretending to her family and friends that she was doing well. She had come to see me this time only because she couldn't seem to shake this depression—it had lasted for over six months and the symptoms seemed to her to be getting worse.

Because Elizabeth had the biological signs of depression (sleep disturbance, weight loss, decreased energy, and diminished sex drive) I started her on the same antidepressant that I used in Jim's case. After a few weeks of drug therapy, her depressive symptoms began to lift. I thoroughly explored with Elizabeth the possibility of psychosocial factors contributing to her illness. I could find none. She had an excellent childhood and seemed to be close to both her mother and father. During times when she was not depressed, Elizabeth was loving and energetic, and she appeared to be free from competitive or sexual conflicts. Interestingly, Elizabeth had a strong family history of depression. She had a brother, an aunt, and a grandmother who also had episodic melancholy.

Because Elizabeth appeared to be biologically predisposed to depression, I decided to continue the tricyclic antidepressant medication at therapeutic levels for eight months and then gradually decrease them to a low-dose maintenance level. I have followed her progress closely now for five years, and she has done well without a recurrence of depressive episodes on 25 mg of Elavil at bedtime. Whenever I attempt to discontinue this medication, her biological symptoms again return. (Please keep in mind that the tricyclic antidepressants, of which Elavil is one, differ markedly from the benzodiazepines—Valium, for example. These differences are discussed in greater detail in Chapter 14. Let me say here that in my opinion the benzodiazepines should *never* be used in maintenance therapy, whereas in some cases the tricyclic antidepressants are necessary for long-term use.)

The third type of depression is associated with episodes of mania. Individuals with this type of depression have mood swings: a depressive episode alternates with periods of elated mood, at which time the individual is so euphoric that he or she spends money indiscriminately, talks incessantly, and stays "on the go," perhaps not sleeping for several nights, calling friends at any hour, day or night, and generally being a nuisance. Between these periods of depression and mania, the individual may be normal for several months and even years. Sometimes an individual may have one manic attack and then have a normal period of mood for a decade or so before becoming depressed or manic again.

For example, most of the time Melvin had a delightful personality—a winning manner, a bright smile, and a high level of ambition and energy. When he entered a room, people immediately lit up from his bright aura. Unfortunately, Melvin's energy level occasionally got out of hand. At times he became so elated that he couldn't work effectively and was braggish and impulsive. On one occasion he became angry when his boss would not buy him a new company car. He stalked out of the office, drove hastily to a car dealership, and purchased a $25,000, bright red Cadillac. He then went to the country club and lavishly bought drinks for everyone. He began making telephone calls to his old girlfriends and arranged to meet two of them for dinner that night at the same restaurant. He never kept the date. His elated mood quickly turned to anger when the bartender made some remarks, and a brawl broke out. The police took Melvin to the hospital instead of jail only because they knew his history of mental illness.

Until 1974 Melvin had a long-time history of these manic episodes alternating with periods of normal mood and acute episodes of depression. The depressive episodes would be characterized by the same symptoms that Jim and Elizabeth showed. Since 1974, the year the Federal Drug Administration approved lithium carbonate for the use in treating manic-depressive illness, Melvin has been well stabilized on this medication. He continues to have an engaging personality but no longer has the severe mood swings that he suffered previously. Lithium will be discussed in greater detail later on in this chapter, as well as in Chapter 14.

What Are the Symptoms of Depression?

There are many symptoms of depression. Almost all depressed patients are unable to enjoy their work and hobbies. Most depressed patients have a slow gait and diminished body movements. They lack spontaneity, their eyes are downcast, and they just plain look depressed. Most depressed patients ruminate over perceived past failures. They feel guilty and blame themselves needlessly. Indecisiveness, decreased concentration, and inattentiveness are also common.

Is Anxiety a Symptom of Depression?

Depressed patients frequently complain of being anxious, tense, uptight, and nervous. These individuals wring their hands, pace the floor, and look worried and anxious. Sometimes these complaints may prompt the physician to prescribe a minor tranquilizer (again, usually Valium), and the patient gets worse instead of better.

Jane, for example, was a depressed woman who for years had been treated with Valium. When I first saw Jane, she gave the appearance of being acutely anxious. Indeed, her major complaint was "I'm nervous all the time." Her hands shook and her lip quivered; she was jumpy and irritable. She said she needed a presciption for Valium or she would "go crazy." I listened to her complaints carefully. It became evident that Jane had a severe depression; anxiety was only a secondary symptom. Compounding her problem was her Valium addiction. To shorten a long story and not go into detail about the difficulties psychiatrists sometimes have, let me say that I was eventually able to get Jane to take the appropriate medication; namely, a tricyclic antidepressant. She was gradually withdrawn from Valium and began to feel much better. Because many psychological factors were contributing to her depression—her mother died when Jane was two, among other things—I referred Jane to a psychoanalyst for intensive psychotherapy. She is progressing well without medications.

Who Needs Treatment for Depression?

You would benefit from professional treatment if you have what are commonly known as the biological signs of depression— sleep disturbance (usually with waking up several times in the middle of the night and waking up early in the morning with trouble going back to sleep), a change in appetite with weight loss (rarely, there may be a massive weight gain), diminished sexual interest, and decreased energy. Of course, those individuals who have experienced a recent, significant loss will often have these biological signs. The key is the length of time that these biological signs last. The cutoff time between those individuals who need treatment and those who don't is generally six weeks. Those individuals who have the biological signs of depression that last for longer than six weeks deserve treatment.

One of the biggest troubles that doctors have in managing depressed patients is convincing them that they are depressed. If you are depressed, you may not realize it and instead may complain of physical symptoms—low back pain, diarrhea, headache, shortness of breath, and so forth. Of course these physical symptoms need to be investigated with a thorough physical and laboratory examination, but if no cause for the physical complaints can be found, don't be surprised if your doctor tells you he or she thinks you are depressed.

Who Commits Suicide?

Every 20 minutes someone in the United States commits suicide. There are approximately 25,000 successful suicides annually; probably twice that number are misclassified and unreported. Suicide ranks as the tenth leading cause of death in the United States, as the second leading cause of death in the 15 to 20-year-old age group, and the first cause among physicians under age 40.

Although deaths from suicide approximate 50,000 each year, some surveys report transient suicidal thoughts in about 15 percent of the general population (33 million people). If you have a family member who is depressed, it is helpful for you to know which type of individual has a serious potential for suicide and which might just have a transient suicidal thought. The following criteria may serve as a guide to assess suicidal potential in a person who has thought of suicide:

1. The suicide rate for single individuals is two times higher than that of married individuals.
2. Men successfully commit suicide three times more often than women, while women attempt suicide two or three times more often than men.
3. Suicide risk increases with age.
4. Protestants have a higher suicide rate than Jews or Catholics.
5. Suicide rate is highest in the lower socioeconomic classes.
6. Suicide rates are higher among white than among nonwhites.

7. Suicide rates are higher in patients who have the biological signs of depression; namely, decreased appetite, weight loss, decreased sex drive, and sleep disturbance.
8. Patients who express feelings of hopelessness are especially vulnerable to suicide.
9. Alcohol and drug abuse increase the potential of suicide.
10. The presence of auditory hallucinations telling a person to commit suicide increases suicidal risks.
11. Homosexual orientation increases the risk of suicide.
12. Individuals with chronic illness or intractable pain run an increased risk of suicide.
13. A family history of suicide increases the risk of suicide.
14. An individual who has begun to give away personal property is an increased risk.
15. A history of a previous attempt is found in 50 to 80 percent of those who ultimately commit suicide.
16. People who have no plans for the future are vulnerable to suicide.
17. Living alone increases risk.
18. A recent loss is associated with increased risk.
19. Recent surgery or childbirth increases risk.
20. Financial difficulty increases risk.

Although many factors help determine which disturbed individuals will ultimately commit suicide, a depressed person should be considered suicidally dangerous until proven otherwise. If a family member is suicidal, he or she should be hospitalized, because it is almost impossible to stay with an individual all the time. If you leave that individual alone for just a few minutes, he or she is likely to commit the act.

For example, a depressed man had been talking about killing himself. His wife, who perceived hospitalization as a stigma, preferred to watch over him at home. She was determined to stay with him night and day until he gave up his suicidal ruminations. After a few days, the patient appeared to be responding to his wife's attention. He seemed more alert and cheerful and reported that he was starving for vanilla ice cream. His wife, elated with his progress, quickly jumped into the car and drove down to the corner convenience store. When she returned five minutes later, she found her husband dead from a self-inflicted gunshot wound to the head.

At times it is almost impossible to prevent someone from committing suicide. One young man, a bachelor, called to tell his mother and father that he was going to the beach for a two-week vacation. He then had his newspaper and mail delivery temporarily discontinued. He drove his car out into the country, parked it down an abandoned road, and walked back to his home. He locked all the doors and windows, went into the bathroom, nailed it shut, took all the drugs he could find in the medicine cabinet, climbed into the bathtub, and slashed his wrists. His suicide was not discovered until three weeks later.

Who Becomes Depressed?

Approximately twice as many females as males will have a depressive disorder in the course of their lifetimes. Generally speaking, patients with depressive disorders are somewhat higher in social class, education, and occupational level than are patients with schizophrenia. Although there is an increased incidence of mild depression in separated, divorced, or widowed individuals, the hospital rates for depression are about the same in married individuals as in single persons. Although depressions may occur at any age, including childhood, peak incidences occur at middle age and late middle age.

Is Depression Inherited?

Twin studies seem to indicate that the predisposition for depression is inherited. If an identical twin becomes depressed, 40 percent of the time the other twin will also be depressed. If an unidentical twin becomes depressed, 11 percent of the time the other twin will also become depressed. Both of these figures are higher than the depressive rate for the normal population. Studies involving relatives of depressed patients also indicate that the predisposition for depression is inherited. In one study, just over 10 percent of 408 relatives of depressed patients were found to also be depressed; the rate for depression in the normal population is about 7 percent.

Is Depression Caused by a Chemical?

There are definite indications that at least some depressions are caused by a chemical imbalance in the brain. Depressed individuals seem to be deficient in chemicals (called *neurotransmitters*) that facilitate the spread of impulses across central nervous system connections. Researchers have established that neurotransmitters regulate movement of nerve impulses in the area of the brain that controls emotion. A decrease in the activity of the transmitters seems to be related to depression, while an increase in activity is related to mania.

Do Environmental Factors Contribute to Depression?

Loss through separation, divorce, or death, or loss of a job or prestige can produce depression. Failure, whether perceived or real, may result in a diminution of an individual's self-confidence, contributing to depression. Depression-prone individuals are extrasensitive to failure. These individuals often base their feelings of self-worth on the opinions of others, while at the same time they feel driven to excel. When their achievements do not reach expectations of excellence, depression sets in. Individuals who talk of pressures on the job generally mean the pressures they are putting on themselves.

For example, a high school basketball coach became clinically depressed when his team failed to win the state championship for an unprecedented third consecutive year. He felt that the loss of the championship game proved that he was an inferior coach and forever precluded his coaching in college, a goal that he had coveted to "show that I'm man enough to make it in the big time."

Occasionally an individual becomes depressed after a promotion or apparent success. This paradoxical depression can occur for two reasons: (1) the individual may feel guilty about success, equating successful assertion with hostile aggression, or (2) the individual may believe that he or she is inadequate to cope with the increased responsibility of success. For example, soon after being promoted to the largest church in the district, a 41-year-old Methodist pastor became depressed. He felt that his small-town background did not equip him to deal with the pressures of a city congregation. His depression led to a failure to capitalize on his promotion, and he was transferred back to a smaller church where he felt more comfortable.

Do Childhood Experiences Contribute to Depression?

Some psychiatrists believe that a tendency to depression can be related to childhood experiences. Some depression-prone individuals have experienced real or perceived parental loss of love during early childhood, resulting in frustration or anger. Fearing his or her own anger, the child learns to turn the anger against him- or herself into self-criticism and depression. The child then attempts to win approval through achievement, undertaking the development of strength and security against feelings of helplessness and dependency. The depression-prone individual learns to isolate and deny his or her real feelings through achievement. But with perceived failure, or the loss of loved ones or valued possessions, depression becomes likely.

For example, Ralph, a 33-year-old dentist, was success oriented. When he was a child, his father would drive him incessantly to achieve. At Little League baseball games, when Ralph struck out his father would not speak to him. When he hit a home run, his father would beam and brag all around town about his son's athletic achievements. His father insisted on Ralph being the best in everything, and Ralph, because he was talented, was able to perform well in athletics and academics. Ralph became conflicted. He both hated his father and, at the same time, longed for his father's approval. He decided to win his father's affection by becoming supergood. Ralph blossomed into a high school athlete whom recruiters courted. He played first string for the state university, graduated from college with honors, and, through hard work, finished dental school in three years. Following graduation, he quickly established a lucrative practice, married a beautiful woman, and began devoting most of his time to improving his golf game. He soon became good enough to enter local and regional tournaments, and he became more and more obsessed with improving his game. Ralph's self-esteem was based entirely on achievement. Whenever he lost a golf match, he would agonize over it for days. He was highly successful but felt miserable: his success was not enough, somehow. It was difficult even for me, as a psychiatrist, trained to understand human nature, to conceive of how Ralph would consider himself a failure. Of course, deep down inside, Ralph was still a little boy trying to hit that home run for his father and always fearing that he would strike out. Although a winner, Ralph always considered himself to be a loser. And in a way he was, because he could never gain what he desired most—unconditional love from his father.

Can Our Thoughts Make Us Depressed?

Even before Norman Vincent Peale wrote *The Power of Positive Thinking*, commonsense knowledge told us that the way we think determines how we feel. More recently the noted psychiatrist, Aaron Beck, has scientifically documented that depressed mood is in large part determined by the way people think. According to Beck, an individual becomes depressed because he or she makes negative generalizations about these traits, such as "I'm no good because I'm weak" or "I'm nothing because I'm unattractive." Beck believes these sweeping negative generalizations about oneself, the world, and the future produce depression. Depressed individuals tend to magnify negative experiences, disqualify prior positive experiences, and selectively recall negative material at the expense of positive memories.

Beck has also found that depressed patients use the directive "should" inappropriately, such as "I should study four hours a night no matter what." "All or nothing" directives are also common, such as "If I am not successful, life has no meaning." As a result of negative thinking, the individual begins to feel badly, and is soon locked into a vicious cycle of distorted thinking, depressed mood, and maladaptive behavior.

For example, I saw a middle-aged man, Frank, who was depressed. No wonder—during the interview, he kept saying "should" over and over again: "I should be a better father; I should go to the church tomorrow and help with the picnic; I should send my wife more flowers; I should work harder so that I can be promoted sooner."

I took a directive approach with Frank. I told Frank that I wanted him to cut out the "shoulds." I told him to get a rubber band and wear it around his wrist. Whenever he said, "should," he was to pop himself with the rubber band. He laughed at my ridiculous request, but he agreed to try it.

I next told Frank that whenever he felt obligated to do something for someone else, I expected him to do something that he enjoyed doing for himself instead. I also had him replace every negative thought with a positive thought and encouraged him to have fun, kick up his heels, and to act weird and wonderful.

We laughed and joked a lot during the therapy sessions. I would gently and humorously chide him about his "should" and "ought to." I told Frank over and over again that mental health, in my definition, was the ability to work productively, love

ACCENTUATING THE POSITIVE

Negative Statement	Positive Statement
I hate fog because it's so depressing.	I like fog because of the way it silhouettes the trees.
I hate rain because it keeps me from playing tennis.	I love a rainy night—I think I'll write a song about it.
Lemons are sour.	I'll make lemonade.
My boss is rigid.	Working for my boss will teach me self discipline.
My neighbor's new car makes me sick with envy.	My neighbor is an inspiration; I will get a second job so I can buy a faster car than my neighbor's.
I hate it when my mother-in-law visits; all she talks about is her bridge game.	I'll get my mother-in-law to teach me how to play bridge when she visits.

others, and enjoy recreational pursuits. I told him that he had flunked two out of three of those criteria, and so far he had received an F in mental health. Whenever he would come out with a "should" or "ought to," I would say to him, "Well, I see you are continuing to flunk mental health." Rather quickly Frank began to loosen up. Actually, all he had ever wanted was permission from some authority figure to enjoy life more. When I began to tell him it was OK to have fun, he began to make rapid progress.

Can Depression Be Treated?

Depression is probably one of the easiest of all illnesses to treat. Unfortunately, only 20 to 25 percent of depressed patients ever receive treatment. This figure is astounding. Think of the thousands of people who spend a lifetime of misery when almost all of them could be helped with treatment. Although depression is just about as common as the common cold, there are better treatments for depression than for the sniffly nose.

Only 5 percent of depressed patients are treated by psychiatrists; the remainder are treated by primary-care physicians. Most depressed patients do not need the expert management of a psychiatrist; primary-care physicians can prescribe the correct medications and treat the disorder just as well. The various treatment methods are discussed in the following sections.

What Are Tricyclic Antidepressants?

If you have decreased appetite, weight loss, diminished sex drive, decreased energy, and poor sleep, you will probably benefit from the tricyclic antidepressant medications. These symptoms of depression point to a biochemical imbalance in the brain. Although this biochemical imbalance cannot be tested for in a regular chemical lab, scientific research has shown that the symptoms are due to a deficiency of certain chemicals that help transfer impulses from one brain cell to another. Tricyclic antidepressants are not addicting. They are not tranquilizers, sleeping pills, or narcotics. They merely restore the chemical balance in the brain cells and help you feel better.

If you take this type of medication, you will have a few initial side effects from the drug. These side effects are not particularly harmful. In a way, it's good to have them initially because it indicates that the medicine is getting into the bloodstream and will soon begin working. Generally the first effect of a tricyclic antidepressant is the return of better sleep patterns. A dry mouth, possibly some blurred vision, and perhaps a little difficulty in urination may also occur. These side effects generally clear up in a few days as your body begins to adjust to the medication. Your physician will begin you on a low dose of the tricyclic and gradually increase the dose, to minimize the side effects. (Within a few months there will be a new generation of antidepressants that will revolutionize drug therapy of depression. These new drugs—just as effective as the tricyclics— promise to be better because they have fewer side effects).

As the tricyclic medication begins to go to work, you will continue to sleep better. Within two to three weeks, your appetite and energy level should pick up. Generally you should be maintained on the medication for six months (although you will feel almost completely well within a few weeks) to completely restore all of the brain biochemistry.

What Are Monoamine Oxidase Inhibitors?

The monoamine oxidase inhibitors (MAOIs) are compounds that interfere with the metabolism of the brain cell neurotransmitters. These compounds seem to be especially effective if you are depressed and also show signs of anxiety. However, the MAOIs can cause serious side effects if you fail to maintain rather rigid dietary restrictions. Therefore these drugs, although they are extremely effective for depression, are generally used only if you fail to respond to the tricyclic drugs. Because the MAOIs have antianxiety and antiphobic properties, these drugs may be used as a first-line treatment if you have a depression associated with phobic and panic attacks.

The most dangerous side effect from MAOIs results from high blood pressure when the medication is taken in combination with certain food and drugs. Cheese, beer, or any protein that has undergone putrefaction can release norepinephrine (a neurotransmitter) from storage sites. Norepinephrine may grow to alarming levels when a patient is on MAOIs and fails to follow the proper diet. Severe high blood pressure can result when norepinephrine becomes elevated. The MAOIs are discussed in more detail in Chapter 14.

Are Other Medications Useful in the Treatment of Depression?

Some individuals become so depressed that they become out of touch with reality. These individuals may have delusions (false beliefs) that, for example, their body is being eaten by worms. Occasionally, depressed patients will hear voices when no one is around.

An example of how a psychotic depression can develop is the case of the mother of a college gymnast. One day at workouts, the gymnast slipped on the parallel bars and suffered a cervical fracture that rendered him quadraplegic. The gymnast gradually accepted the reality of his permanent disability and was able to complete his college education. The student's mother, however, never accepted the permanence of his injury. Instead, she spent three years seeking the opinions of the country's leading neurosurgeons and neurologists. Each negative opinion only increased her search for a cure. Gradually the mother began to believe that the medical community was against her son. She became withdrawn and noncommunicative. She would sit alone in her room rocking back and forth in her chair. She lost weight and could not sleep. On being questioned, she said that voices in her head told her that worms were eating her spine and that she would become quadraplegic also. The mother was so out of touch with reality that she would not benefit from tricyclic antidepressants or MAO inhibitors. Instead, she responded well to antipsychotic medications. These medications are discussed in detail in Chapter 14.

The stimulants, such as amphetamine, dextroamphetamine, and methylphenidate (Ritalin), are ineffective in the treatment of depression.

Is Shock Treatment Helpful in Treating Depression?

Shock therapy (electroconvulsive therapy, or ECT) is definitely effective in the treatment of depression. Unfortunately, ECT has received a great deal of bad press. For example, Ken Kesey's book and the film made from it, *One Flew Over the Cuckoo's Nest* showed ECT being used as a punishment rather than a treatment. ECT is safe, effective, and usually does not cause permanent memory loss. Most psychiatrists reserve ECT for those patients who fail to respond to adequate dosages of the appropriate medications, or for those who are sufficiently dangerous to themselves to merit treatment that is more rapid than medication. (ECT works in a few days, while it often takes medications two or three weeks to begin working.) Chapter 14 provides further material on ECT.

How Does Psychotherapy Work?

A therapist can help you talk about bottled-up resentments and regrets that contribute to the depressed mood. Therapists who are analytically oriented can help you look for childhood origins of depression. Those who believe that negative thoughts contribute to depression can help you eliminate negative thinking. A therapist can also help you plan and carry out potentially enjoyable activities. All these psychotherapeutic maneuvers can be complemented with antidepressant medications. Psychotherapy is discussed further in Chapter 15.

Can Depression Be Prevented?

Now that depression can be successfully treated, the next goal for medicine is to work out preventive techniques. Depression can be prevented to a certain extent by getting the individual to a physician as soon as possible. Relapses can be fended off through drugs and intensified psychotherapy. But even more important is the task of defeating depression before it has a chance to take hold. New discoveries about genetic factors may some day help identify possible depressives before their symptoms become manifest. Public education too, can help individuals recognize depressing environments and enable them to deal more intelligently with environmental stresses.

How Does Mania Differ from Depression?

Mania is the exact opposite of depression. Manic individuals are hyperactive, talk excessively, and have an elevated mood. Blessed with unbounded enthusiasm, the mania-prone individual pursues tasks with gusto and gaiety. Imperceptibly, these energetic characteristics may escalate to pathological proportions: A warm and friendly manner turns into an elevated irritable mood; engaging conversation converts to senseless talk. The manic patient may telephone acquaintances regardless of the time of day, or inappropriately share intimate personal secrets with complete strangers. Buying sprees, foolish business ventures, and reckless driving add to the personality disruption.

During an acute manic attack, the individual dresses outlandishly: the individual may be wearing two or three watches, several hats, necklaces, or belts. Occasionally the manic may be delusional—the individual may believe that he or she is a special emissary from God or a secret agent from the Federal Bureau of Investigation. Sometimes, the manic condition may escalate into a delirious state characterized by incoherent speech, purposeless activity, and confusion.

I have already given an example of Melvin, a salesman who had episodes of mania alternating with depression. Mr. Jameson represents an example of a manic who seemed never to have severe depressive episodes—but when he became manic he was truly wild. Mr. Jameson was a tobacco farmer who did extremely well when he took his lithium carbonate regularly. Unfortunately, during the harvesting season, Mr. Jameson would sometimes forget to take his medication, or he would falsely believe that the medicine was slowing him down. On one such summer during harvest season he stopped his medicine completely for three weeks. He began to get more and more hyperactive and disorganized. He finally decided that he needed to start taking his medicines, but when he could not find his pills, he got into his truck, intending to drive to the clinic. Unfortunately, the truck wouldn't start, so he began walking. The clinic was some 30 miles from his home, so to help him in his long journey he began singing religious songs. As he walked, he became more and more enthusiastic in his singing. As the day got hotter, he began to gradually disrobe. When the police picked him up, he was walking along the side of the highway singing hosannas, clad only in his work boots. He responded well to hospitalization and medication adjustment. Thereafter his wife made certain that he took his medications regularly. He no longer entertains the sheriff's department with his singing, but he is a much better tobacco farmer.

How Common Is Mania?

Researchers have found that about 0.5 percent of the population will have a manic episode sometime over the course of their lifetimes. The disorder is equally as common in men as in women.

What Happens to a Person Who Has a Manic Attack?

Typically, manic attacks begin around age 30. Symptoms of a manic attack begin suddenly and escalate rapidly over a period of a few days. Manic attacks generally alternate with depressive episodes, with periods of normal mood in between. There may be several years between attacks, or attacks may recur as often as three or four times a year. Modern treatment with lithium has both shortened the length of a single attack and decreased the rate of occurrence.

Is Mania Inherited?

Manic illnees is 10 to 25 times higher in relatives of manic patients than in the general population. Some family studies suggest that mania may be connected with an autosomal dominant gene. There is some evidence that a few cases may be linked to an abnormality of the sex chromosomes.

Is Mania Caused by a Biochemical Abnormality?

There is increasing evidence that mania is secondary to the increase in neurotransmitters. Just as depression is caused by a deficiency of neurotransmitters, mania is caused by an increase in these chemicals. Some forms of mania may be related to an imbalance of sodium and potassium and other electrolytes in the body.

Can Mania Be Treated?

One of the great success stories in mental health treatment is the use of lithium for the treatment of mania. Lithium is discussed in greater detail in Chapter 14, but let me mention an amazing financial statistic here. The National Institute of Mental Health (NIMH) estimates that the use of lithium has saved our country over $4 billion by helping formerly hopeless manic patients return to useful work.

Who Needs to See a Psychiatrist?

Most depressions can be effectively treated by your physician. The following traits deserve a referral to a psychiatrist or other mental health care specialist:

1. Suicidal urges
2. Depression or mania that has caused irrational thinking
3. Failure to respond to drug therapy
4. A history of manic episodes

Remember, almost all people with depression or mania will get better if they seek the proper care.

Chapter 5
Schizophrenia
(Opening the Doors
to the Back Wards)

If a member of your family has been diagnosed as a schizo-phrenic, when you first hear the pronouncement a shudder of fear probably went down your spine. Schizophrenia is horrible, you think. It's like cancer, or worse. Images of disheveled recluses huddled in the back wards of dusty, dungeonlike state hospitals come to mind. Schizophrenia isn't like that. The available treat-ments and the outcome of schizophrenia have improved remark-ably in the past few decades. The purpose of this chapter is to dispel the myths and misconceptions about schizophrenia and to give you an idea of the symptoms, causes, and treatments. An understanding about schizophrenia can reassure you that the illness is not as horrible as you first imagined.

How Many People Have Schizophrenia?

About 1 percent of the population will have a schizophrenic episode during the course of a lifetime. Approximately 150,000 new schizophrenic episodes occur in the United States every year; worldwide, there are 2 million new cases of schizophrenia every year. What's more, one-fourth of all hospital beds and one-half of all mental hospital beds in the United States are occupied by schizophrenics. The cost of schizophrenia in the United States (mostly due to a loss of productivity) is estimated to be from $11 to $19 billion annually, with only 25 percent of schizophrenics being able to return to full-time employment.

What Are the Symptoms of Schizophrenia?

Schizophrenia results from a disturbance in thought. Schizophrenics think people can read their minds and that powerful forces are controlling them. They may be paranoid or hear voices talking inside their heads. Because of this overwhelming thought disturbance, schizophrenics do poorly at work or in school and gradually withdraw into their own world. Furthermore, most schizophrenics separate their emotions from their intellectual processes. For example, a schizophrenic might be thinking about upsetting ideas while giving the appearance of indifference (called *flat affect* by psychiatrists).

SCHIZOPHRENICS IN LITERATURE

Ophelia—After her father is killed by Hamlet, the man she loves, she regresses to bizarre and inappropriate behavior. As Claudius reported, "Poor Ophelia, divided from herself and her fair judgment without the which we are pictures of near beasts."

Ivan Dmitritch—The student in Anton Chekhov's story "Ward Number Six" undergoes a paranoid schizophrenic collapse: he believes he is a victim of a complicated plot, unseen voices speak to him, and he communicates with divine authority.

Nicole Warren—The heroine in F. Scott Fitzgerald's *Tender is the Night*, who develops acute schizophrenic symptoms following an incestuous relationship with her father.

Don Quixote—Deluded idealist whose imagination turned windmills into giants, solitary inns into castles, and flocks of sheep into armies.

During an acute schizophrenic episode, orientation and intellectual functions remain intact. Although schizophrenics are oriented, without confusion, and occasionally highly intelligent, their abstractions and deductions are strange and illogical. In addition, as a result of their characteristic thought disorder, schizophrenics have a disturbance in communication—their speech may be illogical and at times incomprehensible. For example, an acutely psychotic schizophrenic when first meeting me said,

When you see that wall, you know about life. What's on the other side? Only the wall knows. What's on the other side of me? The other side? Ah, yes, that is the question. Whether it is better to tear down walls or suffer them.

FAMOUS SCHIZOPHRENICS

Virginia Woolf—Novelist who had intermittent psychotic episodes throughout her life. During periods of illness she would talk with imaginary birds in Greek. She believed that the leaves of trees were controlling her thoughts and feelings. She heard sounds in the universe which signalled the birth of a new religion. When not floridly psychotic she was reclusive and depressed. Some authorities think she had manic-depressive illness; others opt for schizophrenia.

Vaslav Nijinsky—Russian ballet dancer who was a patient of Eugene Bleuler—the psychiatrist who coined the term schizophrenia. Najinsky wrote in his *Diary:* "I am God. . . . I love God, and therefore I smile upon myself."

Friedrich Nietzsche—The great 19th Century German philosopher said that in crying out against the madness of God, he had gone mad himself.

Zelda Fitzgerald—Wife of the writer, F. Scott Fitzgerald, Zelda was ill most of her adult life despite receiving the best psychiatric care available. She died in a 1948 Highland Hospital fire.

Vincent Van Gogh—Hot tempered painter who was not recognized as a great artist until long after his death. Sensitive and withdrawn, he believed that people were trying to poison him; on one occasion attacked his friend Gauguin with a razor; later cut off his own ear and presented it to a prostitute; died of a self-inflicted gun-shot wound.

Translated, this statement meant that the patient was unsure of whether he wanted to talk to me about his problems.

Often new words (neologisms) created by schizophrenics express conflicts in a condensed form. A schizophrenic repeatedly used the expression "shacklebotbash." The patient explained that alcohol was the center of his problem ("bot" for bottle) and caused him either to be locked on a psychiatric ward ("shackle") or to get into body-bruising fights ("bash").

Because schizophrenics tend to omit words from a sentence, repeat phrases, invent new words, and misuse words, their prose is often lyrical but cryptic. For example, this ditty was written by an adolescent male schizophrenic on returning from a weekend visit to his parents' summer beach cottage:

> By the sea, we met while walking by the sea. Oft' I've wondered—why?—by the sea. Answers not easily come by while walking by the rolling, roaring, rousing sea. Meeting, mating, meeking by the wandering, wavering, wastering sea.

Schizophrenics are often preoccupied with religion and symbolism. For example, a schizophrenic wrote,

> "Bacchus [ancient Roman god of wine] Lord of the rings (or Wrings), has made my bones turn away from Mother Mary and the Mother of Mothers as well. For God has created Bacchus as He created Succubus and Incubus—The Holy Trinity— so that no man sins. God save the Queen."

Are There Different Types of Schizophrenics?

There are five types of schizophrenics. The hebephrenic type—characterized by silly, inappropriate behavior, neglect of personal habits, and odd grimacing—reflects a regressed, childlike orientation. For example, a quiet honor student began to show bizarre behavior on entering college. He would interrupt classes by his inappropriate laughter and gesturing. His roommate noticed him standing before the mirror for hours posturing and grimacing. On hospital admission, the patient was incoherent and excited. The next day, he stared vacantly at the floor, at times breaking into a silly giggle. Over the next few weeks, the patient began to masturbate publicly, occasionally ate his own feces, and refused to bathe or change clothes. Large doses of antipsychotics eventually controlled the patient's bizarre behavior, but he remained hospitalized for many years.

A relatively rare condition, catatonia, is characterized by a mute, motionless patient who may assume statuelike postures for days or weeks as a way of escaping the demands of the real world. An illustration in Silvano Arieti's classical book *Interpretations of Schizophrenia* shows a nude catatonic patient crouched on his haunches, his arms squeezed between his knees and chest. The caption states that the patient allows an attendant to dress him and accompany him for a daily walk. But on returning to the ward, he resumes the uncomfortable position, which he has maintained for several years except for his brief morning stroll.

The most common of the schizophrenias, paranoid schizophrenia, is typified by powerful delusions of persecution often associated with auditory hallucinations. For example, a 26-year-old college graduate became convinced that people thought he was a homosexual, and he felt that the club members where he worked as a tennis instructor were mocking him. He began going to church regularly and began praying and reading the Bible continuously at night after work in an attempt, as he stated, "to find a way to get people to like me." Soon he started preaching to the club members, and his religious convictions isolated him even more from the community. In an attempt to gain spiritual purity, he decided to blind himself by dipping his head into a bucket of Lysol. He entered the emergency room several hours after the attempt and, with absolutely no emotion, vacantly told his story: "I wanted to blind myself so I could be more like Jesus. I was sad when I failed because I wanted to be friendly." After leaving the hospital against medical advice, the patient shot himself in the hand when he heard what he perceived to be a commandment from Jesus. Although no longer dangerous to himself, the patient remains delusional despite massive doses of antipsychotic medication. He occasionally works as a janitor, but has no friends.

The undifferentiated subtype includes that vast wasteland of the schizophrenias in which no symptom complex predominates. Those patients who fail to meet the diagnostic criteria for the other schizophrenic subtypes would be included here. For example, a sullen and shiftless 48-year-old unmarried man spent most of his days wandering the streets. Frequently, he would stand on the street corner yelling, "My name is Smitty and I'm looking for trouble." His attorney, whose office was on the fourteenth floor of a downtown office building, reported that on a clear, windless day, he could hear the patient shouting on the streets below. Occasionally the patient would enter the bank where he received money from a family trust fund and would shout obscenities. The clerks and tellers, accustomed to his behavior, never looked up from their work. The patient would report hearing voices calling him "bad names" and occasionally would put a sign in front of his house that stated, "This house is free of sin." The patient was tolerated by the community as a harmless crank and was regarded as somewhat of a local landmark.

Residual schizophrenia includes those patients who have a history of a schizophrenic episode, but whose clinical picture fails to show prominent psychotic symptoms in the present. However, signs of schizophrenia persist, such as emotional blunting, social withdrawal, and a mild communication disorder. For example, a 32-year-old unmarried woman had had an acute catatonic episode when she was 24 years old. At that time she entered the hospital, babbling incoherently and imitating the actions and words of the psychiatrist. On the third hospital day, she assumed the posture of someone being crucified and had to be tube-fed until she responded to high doses of antipsychotics. The patient has been free of prominent psychotic symptoms for almost eight years, although she seldom leaves her home except to shop for groceries with her mother; she never smiles and only occasionally speaks. Her behavior is regarded as "strange" by her neighbors.

What Causes Schizophrenia?

Several factors—genetic, biochemical, family problems, and personality conflicts—contribute to the development of schizophrenia. Because of the multiple causes and the wide variety of symptoms, most psychiatrists believe that what we now consider to be schizophrenias may later turn out to be one, two, or maybe even more separate disorders, each with a different cause. In this section, I discuss several of the possible causes of schizophrenia.

Is Schizophrenia Inherited?

The risk for developing schizophrenia during the course of a lifetime in the general population is 1 percent. Parents of schizophrenics have a risk of 5 percent, siblings of schizophrenics, 10 percent, children with one schizophrenic parent, 10–15 percent, and children with two schizophrenic parents, 30–40 percent. Even more compelling evidence for a genetic factor has come from the comparison of adopted individuals with their biological and foster parents. In 1966, L. L. Heston found that almost a fourth of individuals born to schizophrenic mothers but reared away from them became schizophrenic, while none of the individuals born to nonschizophrenic mothers and adopted away became schizophrenic. In subsequent studies, several other research teams have confirmed a genetic predisposition for schizophrenia.

Although research indicates a genetically transmitted predisposition to schizophrenia, those studies fail to eliminate a syndrome of multiple causes of—or several diseases with different modes of—genetic transmission. So far, studies suggest that environmental as well as genetic factors play a role in the development of schizophrenia. Individuals with a mild degree of predisposition might develop schizophrenia under extremely stressful situations, while others with a high degree of predisposition may become schizophrenic with little or no unusual stress.

Is There a Chemical That Causes Schizophrenia?

Because of the compelling evidence that the predisposition for schizophrenia is inherited, for many years numerous researchers have tried to isolate a chemical that might be responsible for the inheritance of the core symptoms of schizophrenia. Over the years, research teams have isolated what they thought to be the definitive causative agent in the bloodstream, only to have their findings disproved by more detailed study. Research continues, but the elusive chemical—if there is one—has not been found.

However, one biochemical theory of schizophrenia is worth mentioning. Research by a number of scientists has shown that the brain consists of millions of nerve cells. In between each nerve cell is a tiny gap known as a *synapse*. Electrical impulses travel from one nerve cell to another by jumping across this gap with the aid of the chemical mediators known as neurotransmitters. There are at least a half dozen chemical mediators in the human brain. Using a series of remarkable experiments, several scientists have proposed that one of these chemical mediators, dopamine, may be responsible for schizophrenia. Too high a level of dopamine in the brain allows a bombardment of nerve impulses, which (as the theory goes) produces schizophrenic symptoms. Antipsychotic medication is believed to work by blocking excessive dopamine release. This blockage, in turn, diminishes the number of nerve discharges and the amount of schizophrenic symptoms.

If dopamine is a contributing factor in schizophrenia, what causes an excess of the compound in the brain? Is it genetically determined? Probably—in some cases. In other cases, psychological factors may cause an increase in dopamine. So far, the dopamine hypothesis is just that—a theory that is yet to be definitely proven.

Do Family Problems Cause Schizophrenia?

Whatever the biological predisposition to schizophrenia, the intervening variables of life experiences are instrumental in producing the final clinical picture of the illness. Mothers, fathers, and families of schizophrenics have, by one investigator or another, been blamed for the cause of the illness. The development of schizophrenia, however, is more complicated than a simple cause and effect process.

The schizophrenogenic mother, described as cold, rejecting, and impervious to the needs of others, has been a favorite target for investigators since Freida Fromm-Reichman first coined the phrase in 1948 (she was the psychoanalyst in the book *Never Promise Me a Rose Garden*). According to Fromm-Reichman, the schizophrenogenic mother, lacking emotional warmth yet overprotective and smothering, appears to foster immaturity and pervasive feelings of inadequacy in her children. Although these mothers have received a great deal of attention, the foremost authority of schizophrenia, Silvano Arieti, contends that mothers of schizophrenics fit the image of the schizophrenogenic mother in only 25 percent of cases.

Likewise, the father of a schizophrenic has been described as passive, ineffectual, and aloof by some investigators. Other psychiatrists have emphasized the father's insecurity and his constant need for admiration. The majority of the fathers of schizophrenics, however, fail to meet these criteria.

More common in schizophrenic families is what the anthropologist Gregory Bateson calls the "double-bind" phenomenon—a double message for which there is no correct choice. For example, a mother may tell her child, "Go out and play with your friends." At the same time, her tone and body language convey that the mother would prefer for the child to stay with her. In this situation, if the child fails to play with his or her friends, the mother will be angry; if he or she does play with friends, she will be disappointed. There is no solution: each choice is wrong, yet because the child depends on the mother for emotional sustenance, the conflict is inescapable. Bateson feels that schizophrenics are exposed to numerous double-bind situations in childhood and that psychosis eventually develops to deal with this faulty communication.

Many paths lead to schizophrenia. Some children born with seemingly innate irritability could engender the wrath of the most loving of mothers, impairing communication to such an extent as to set the course toward an inevitable psychosis. Other naturally calm children turn schizoid if exposed to a cruel, harsh mother. Still others are born to chaotic families from which the only escape is schizophrenia. Finally, some, genetically impaired, have the passage to schizophrenia fixed even before birth.

Is Schizophrenia Curable?

Although approximately 5 percent of patients recover completely after an acute schizophrenic episode, the majority go on to develop some form of a chronic condition. A little over half of schizophrenics will have a lifetime course of repeated remissions and flare-ups, 30 percent will be able to return to fairly good functioning in society, and 10 percent will develop a progressive chronic condition requiring long-term hospitalization.

With drug therapy (the antipsychotic medication works by blocking the excess dopamine in the brain cells), eight out of ten schizophrenics can become symptom-free in a few months, but over half of these individuals will have one or more relapses sometime during their lifetimes. Those who remain on medication and visit a psychiatrist regularly have a much greater chance of remaining symptom free than those patients who fail to take their medication and irregularly visit their physicians.

For example, a 21-year-old college student entered the clinic babbling incoherently. His wide-eyed stare, gross hand tremor, and excessive perspiration told, without words, of the fear he was experiencing. Occasionally the patient would look quickly to the right or left as if he had heard a voice, and then cry out pathetically. After being admitted to the ward and started on antipsychotics, the patient's acute panic abated, but he talked loosely:

> They are after me to make me a female. I was in chemistry lab and someone put estrogen in my beaker. The estrogen was a powerful estrogen from the moon that caused my thoughts to come in waves, to flow back and forth like the tide. It caused me to think

thoughts and to do things that I cannot tell. I don't know. Thoughts came out of my head and were broadcast out over a loudspeaker that was in my brain. I think it was the moon goddess. But why don't girls like me? I flow like the tide, in and out.

After a three-month hospitalization, the patient's thought pattern returned to normal. He remembered the panic and the fear that he had and was perplexed about what had caused him, as he put it, "to be so crazy." He denied using drugs or alcohol, which could have produced an acute psychotic break. He did talk of being shy, of never having dated, and of feeling pressured at school to make good grades.

I continued to see the patient on a weekly basis after hospital discharge. He remained on medication because without it he quickly became paranoid. With encouragement, he began dating and by cutting back on his course hours, he was able to graduate from college within a six-year period.

The patient continues to be shy and awkward, especially around the opposite sex. When pressured on his job as an industrial chemist, he becomes paranoid. With medications and twice-monthly counseling sessions, however, the patient has remained out of the hospital. He lives alone, but works regularly, occasionally goes to the local college football games, and enjoys hiking in the mountains. He leads a far more satisfying life than many of us who are not schizophrenic.

What about Psychotherapy?

A trusting relationship with a psychotherapist can help the schizophrenic function in the real world again. Unfortunately, with each step toward improvement the schizophrenic tends to retreat into fantasy, so that the patient, the physician and the patient's family are constantly dealing with frustration and disappointment. A sign of progress comes when the schizophrenic experiences an intense depression as he or she realizes the severity of the condition. After the patient works through the depressive phase, he or she must learn to cope with family and environment. Even after optimal social functioning is achieved, under stress the individual tends to decompensate into a psychotic episode, and hospitalization may be neceseary for a brief time. Need for rehospitalization should be approached in as positive a manner as possible, with the physician and family emphasizing the gains that can be made and looking forward to attempting to avert hospitalization in the future.

Chapter 6
Psychosomatic Illness
(Broken Hearts and Tired Blood)

The term *psychosomatic reaction* is used here to designate those illnesses in which emotional factors contribute to the existence of a physical disease. Because emotional factors influence all body processes, broadly conceptualized every disease is psychosomatic. Indeed, in two major epidemiological surveys, significant psychological components were found in greater than 60 percent of patients with physical complaints.

How Does Stress Produce Physical Illness?

The theme underlying all psychosomatic theories involves stress. In 1926 while still a medical student, 19-year-old Hans Selye began investigating what it meant to be sick—the nonspecific effects of illness and the connecting links between diseases. Selye had noticed that individuals show characteristic fatigue and general discomfort following either a physical or a emotional event. Exploring these similarities, Selye subjected rats to traumatic injury, extreme changes in temperature, bacterial infection, and prolonged immobilization. After persistent stress, autopsies of the dead animals revealed enlarged adrenal glands, bleeding ulcers, and atrophied lymph and thymus glands.

Selye suggested that there is a general adaptation syndrome involving three stages: the alarm reaction, the stage of resistance, and the stage of exhaustion. The first stage involves the fight or flight reaction of the autonomic nervous system, as described in Chapter 3. In the second part of the reaction, the hypothalamus continues to stimulate the pituitary to produce hormonal and neural changes throughout the body until the stressful situation has passed. Continued stress leads to the stage of exhaustion. If the individual cannot get enough rest to restore the body's equilibrium, deterioration and finally death occurs. With these experiments, Selye demonstrated the negative effects caused by emotional tension such as frustration or suppressed rage.

As mentioned in Chapter 2, Holmes and Rahe have found an almost linear relationship between stressful changes in life events and the frequency of illness. The more life change units (LCU) the individual experiences, the greater the chance for developing an illness (see the table in Chapter 2). Although the type of illness cannot be predicted by the LCU score, life changes can help distinguish individuals vulnerable to illness.

In addition, stresses of everyday living that cannot be easily quantitated—a traffic jam, a disparaging remark from an employer, a family argument—can produce biochemical reactions such as increased pulse, elevated blood pressure, decreased immune response, and increased respiration. Failure to deal with these emotional changes usually leads to chronic illness.

The concept of stress fails to answer why some individuals develop psychosomatic disorders rather than another type of illness—or why a few develop no illness at all. Most of us cope with stress by ventilating our anger and frustration through crying, laughing, shouting, screaming, or simply talking about our feelings. But patients prone to psychosomatic illness may be incapable of expressing feelings appropriately. Stressful conflicts are bottled up, surfacing in the form of psychosomatic illness.

How Does Personality Contribute to Illness?

Many attempts have been made to explain why the damaging effects of chronic arousal become concentrated in a specific organ system. In a massive volume, *Emotions and Bodily Changes*, Flanders Dunbar attempted to connect particular personality profiles with specific organic illnesses. For example, she proposed that hypertensive patients showed a lifelong pattern of anxiety, perfectionism, and difficulty with authority figures. More recent research has refuted most of her proposals as oversimplifications. However, Friedman and Rosenman explored the same issues in their popular book *Type A Behavior and Your Heart*. They concluded that Type A behavior—characterized by excessive competitive drive, aggressiveness, impatience, and a

---

TYPE A AND TYPE B PERSONALITY TRAITS

Type A	*Type B*
1. Excessive competitive drive	1. Lack of sense of urgency
2. Ambitiousness and achievement oriented	2. No need to display achievements
3. Chronic sense of urgency	3. Lack of free-floating hostility
4. Inclination to multiple commitments	4. The ability to play for fun and relaxation rather than competition.
5. Concern for meeting deadlines	5. Ability to relax without guilt
6. Impatience	6. Ability to work without agitation
7. Inability to relax without feeling guilty	
8. Drive to accomplish tasks quickly	
9. Preoccupation with quantity rather than quality	
10. Behavior is unrelated to anxiety, fear or worry	

Source: Adapted from M. Friedman and R. Rosenman, *Type A Behavior and Your Heart* (New York: Knopf, 1974).

---

sense of urgency—lead to coronary heart disease three times more often than Type B behavior, which is characterized by an easy-going attitude (see the boxed lists of traits). Yet even this finding is inconclusive: most Type A personalities escape heart attacks while some Type B personalities suffer coronaries.

To a certain extent, psychosomatic illness can be a learned response. Respiratory patterns approximating asthmatic breathing can be induced by experimentally reinforcing certain breathing behavior. Thus, psychosomatic illness may develop through accidental conditioning. As the psychologist Paul Long states, "A child may learn the visceral responses of chronic indigestion by being allowed to stay home from school when he has an upset stomach."

ARE YOU TYPE A?

The more "yes" answers you give to the following questions, the more likely you are to have Type A tendencies:

1. Do you utter the last few words of your sentences far more rapidly than the opening words? (This characteristic implies impatience.)
2. Do you move, walk and eat rapidly?
3. Do you become impatient with slow highway drivers?
4. Do you try to do two things at once?
5. Do you try to dominate conversations?
6. Do you feel guilty when you try to relax?
7. Do you fail to observe the beautiful things around you?
8. Are you preoccupied with material possessions?
9. Are you constantly trying to crowd more and more tasks and activities into your work schedule?
10. Do you feel competitive with people who you feel are like you?
11. Do you frequently clench your fist or grind your teeth?
12. Do you believe that your success depends on your ability to get things done faster than others?
13. Do you find yourself evaluating activities in terms of "numbers?"

Source: Adapted from M. Friedman and R. Rosenman, *Type A Behavior and Your Heart* (New York: Knopf, 1974).

The development of illness might also depend on the individual's susceptibility to a disease of a certain type. In 1950, H. G. Wolf suggested that individuals can be classified as "heart reactors," "stomach reactors," and so on, depending on the particular types of physical condition that stress characteristically produces in them. A stressful situation may produce hypertension in one individual, peptic ulcers in another, and some other illness in a third, depending on the constitutional predisposition of the individual.

Franz Alexander designated seven psychosomatic disorders: asthma, peptic ulcer, ulcerative colitis, hypertension, thyrotoxicosis, neurodermatitis, and rheumatoid arthritis. He proposed that these illnesses resulted from a particular kind of emotional conflict. Thus, for example, frustrated dependency may lead to peptic ulcer. Or chronically inhibited rage may produce hypertension. Subsequent research has failed to show that a specific emotional conflict always leads to a certain psychosomatic illness. Instead, research suggests that severe stress, regardless of type, predisposes, precipitates, reinforces, or aggravates almost all illnesses.

The development of a psychosomatic illness is a complex process. In an individual who fails to adjust to stress, chronic tension develops, which produces tissue damage. Unresolved psychological conflicts, the inability to appropriately express emotions, constitutional predisposing factors, and reinforcement through conditioning all contribute, in a lesser or greater degree, to the development of psychosomatic illness (see figure). These illnesses are discussed in the following sections.

How Psychosomatic Illness Arises

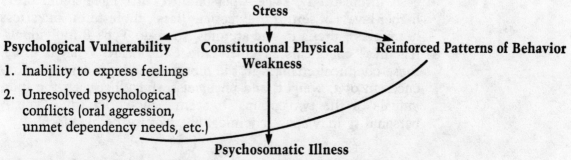

Stress

Psychological Vulnerability   Constitutional Physical   Reinforced Patterns of Behavior
                                        Weakness

1. Inability to express feelings

2. Unresolved psychological
   conflicts (oral aggression,
   unmet dependency needs, etc.)

Psychosomatic Illness

Coronary Artery Disease

The leading cause of death in the United States, cardiovascular disease, afflicts an estimated 28 million Americans. Each year 1 million Americans experience a myocardial infarction (heart attack). About one-half of these survive. Of those who survive 20 percent—about 100,000 people annually—are disabled.

What Factors Contribute to Heart Disease?

Research over the past few years has classified the role of both psychological and physiological phenomena in contributing to coronary heart disease. Obesity, smoking, increased blood triglyceride, congenital malformations, a sedentary lifestyle, a family history of heart disease, and certain diseases such as hypertension and diabetes are clearly identified as major risk factors in coronary artery disease.

In addition, the stress caused by sudden environmental changes also contribute to coronary disease. Stress researchers Richard Rahe and Ernest Lindy, in gathering life change information on 39 individuals who died suddenly from coronary disease, found a threefold increase in stressful life events during the six months immediately preceding their deaths. Similarly, there was a 40 percent higher than expected death rate from coronary disease in a sample of 4,000 widowers during the first six months of bereavement.

As mentioned earlier, Friedman and Rosenman have described a behavior pattern—Type A—that contributes to the development of cardiovascular disease. In contrast, Type B personalities have a significantly lower rate for cardiovascular disease. Interestingly, Type A personalities also have significantly higher levels of serum triglycerides (fats), cholesterol, and stress hormones (adrenalin and steroids) than do Type B individuals. All these chemicals adversely affect the heart. What is more, these chemical changes in the blood are independent of differences in diet, weight, and physical activity between the individuals of the two groups. It seems, then, that the Type A personality may cause chemical changes in the blood.

Are You a Type A Personality?

George, a successful physician and a friend of mine, recently scheduled an appointment for professional consultation. I had not seen George for some time, and when he entered my office, I hardly recognized him. He looked haggard and worn. He was much thinner and more jittery than when I'd last seen him. Circles under his eyes indicated lack of sleep.

As I began to talk with George, he spilled out the following story. His principal complaints were depression, difficulty concentrating, tension and anxiety of four to five months' duration, chronic fatigue, the inability to enjoy life, and a 10-pound weight loss in the past several months.

He was unable to date the onset of his illness, but knew that it had been building up for at least six months. He could not remember when he last had a vacation.

George went on to tell me about his daily routine. He saw 30 to 40 patients a day in his busy general practice, never sitting longer than necessary with a patient, preferring instead to rush from examining room to examining room (he has four), barking orders to his nurses and assistants.

During the lunch hour, George would hurriedly engulf a sandwich as he returned business calls. At the end of the day, he took pride in counting the number of patients he had seen and the telephone calls he had made. While driving swiftly home from his office, he would dictate letters and charts on his battery-operated Dictaphone.

On arriving home, he changed into jogging clothes, and— with stopwatch in hand—tried to break his sprinting time of the day before. Competitively devoted to tennis during the summer months, he would go into a rage when he lost, yet feel vaguely dissatisfied when he won. He spent the winter months in the weight room trying to lift more than those half his age could lift. Thoughts of acquiring more money and the finest material possessions interfered with his ability to relate warmly to his wife and children.

George has a Type A personality. He is not alone. Friedman and Rosenman concluded that Type A personality characterized by excessive competitive drive, preoccupation with material possessions, and a sense of urgency is endemic to middle-class, upwardly mobile people.

Type A individuals base their self-esteem on their possessions and achievements. This pattern develops early in life when children are praised for what they have done, rather than for what they have tried. In adolescence, people begin to search for ways to maintain self-esteem. They soon become motivated to receive praise and acceptance rather than to do something because of the intrinsic joy of the task. Schools (by rewarding good grades) and employers (by giving raises and promotions) massively reinforce the Type A behavior pattern.

How Can Type A Behavior Be Changed?

Giving up the tyrannical habits of Type A and replacing them with a more relaxed attitude can help prevent heart attacks. Changing ingrained personality traits requires persistence and dedication. Probably the biggest obstacle you will face in giving up Type A behavior is your belief in the old way of doing things. You may feel that your time urgency and competitive drive have been the reasons for your success. But people who have changed their behavior tell me they soon found their "hurry" sickness and hostile competitive drive to be a handicap rather than an asset.

Ralph is a periodontist who began restructuring his life after reading *Type A Behavior and Your Heart*. He became aware of what he was doing to himself one day when he was frenetically trying to get home in rush hour traffic. After having run a red light, he suddenly began to question his lifestyle. Why was he rushing? Why was he trying to get home so fast? He began to realize that his frenetic pace caused him to become more and more irritable. Usually, when he arrived home, he was so upset he would snap at his wife and children and rush to the golf course.

This time, as Ralph drove the rest of the way home at a leisurely pace, he began thinking about his work schedule. He later told me,

For the first time in my life, I realized how much trouble I had been getting into by constantly rushing. The cases that I had the most trouble with almost invariably were due to my desire to get the case done quickly. Those procedures that I did too quickly usually ended up costing me more time in the long run because of the effort that it took to correct my mistakes. I began to understand that my Type A behavior was a handicap rather than an asset.

So Ralph canceled his daily golf game (he realized he really didn't want to play anyway) and sat down to chat with his family. In essence, he made a confession and told them he realized his hurried pace was causing problems. He asked for their help in changing his lifestyle.

Ralph began leaving his office a little bit later at the end of the day to avoid the rush hour traffic. After supper he would meet with the family, at which time each would talk about what they had done during the day. His family decided they should start reading stories aloud to each other, and Ralph rediscovered the joys of *Treasure Island*, *The Black Stallion*, and *Tom Sawyer*. Just the other day, Ralph told me,

I began to realize how the time urgency and my overachieving attitude were driving me away from my family and friends. A lot of my rushing around was an attempt to prevent myself from realizing how lonesome I felt, and I was feeling lonesome because of my rushing. Now that I'm spending more time with my family, I don't rush as much, and I'm getting just as much done at work as before.

For others, such hyperactivity can represent an attempt to gain a lasting state of security. As one patient, who was always trying to do several things at one time, told me recently,

For the first time in my life, I realistically appraised my abilities and my inadequacies. I had to admit to myself that I was not a whiz kid. Since coming to grips with that realization, I have been less harried and less merciless on myself. I've also learned how to improve the quality of my work by budgeting my time better.

It required great persistence for my patients to rid themselves of their tyrannizing habits. They didn't change their habits overnight. On the contrary, they had to work diligently (and continue to work) to restructure their attitudes. How did they do it?

In the first place, both of them took a look at the way they were leading their lives and decided that they were dissatisfied. Next, they examined their personal strengths and weaknesses. In making a meaningful self-appraisal, my friends determined, as best they could, exactly how intelligent and creative they were. Admitting to themselves that they were "above average" reduced their need to constantly challenge others. After assessing their individual attitudes, they began to take a hard look at some of their friends. Soon they began to open themselves to new friendships that would expand their interests.

You don't have to wait until you have a heart attack, get divorced, or alienate your children before you begin changing your personality. Type A behavior can be due to a hostile competitive drive, a sense of urgency, and the desire for material possessions. To rid yourself of Type A behavior, cultivate the opposite attitudes—affection and love, relaxation, and a humanistic philosophy.

In *Type A Behavior and Your Heart*, Friedman and Rosenman devised drills to combat the three basic characteristics of Type A behavior: (1) "hurry" sickness, (2) hostility, and (3) preoccupation with material possessions. Read, study, and work on these drills daily. Those of you who feel you need extra help should study the book in detail.

Friedman and Rosenman list 18 drills against "hurry" sickness. In condensed form, 6 of those drills follow.

1. Try to figure out why you are always rushing.
2. Remind yourself that life is always full of unfinished business.
3. Ask yourself, "Will this task matter five years from now?"
4. Ask yourself, "Do I really have anything to say that others want to hear or should hear right now?"

5. Remind yourself that if you don't protect your allotment of time, no one else will.
6. Before completion, interrupt tasks that induce stress and tension.

The best drill against hostility is to remind yourself that you *are* hostile. This awareness will help you keep from exploding at minor irritations. In addition, strive to diminish your sensitivity to the provocations of others, while at the same time taking the opportunity to give thanks to those who give you help. Don't inflict your ideals on others (people who are harsh on others are extra harsh and demanding on themselves). Finally, even though it may appear contrived and hypocritical, smile. (To change inward feelings, first change external appearances.)

Friedman and Rosenman list nine exercises under one heading, "a drill toward things worth being." Four of those exercises are condensed as follows:

1. Remind yourself that once a reasonable economic security is established, improving your intellect and personality is more important than acquiring material possessions.
2. Seek time to be alone.
3. Cultivate spiritually rewarding friendships.
4. Allocate time for reading classic literature.

Now let's get back to my friend George. After a long talk, I finally persuaded George to take a two-week vacation with his family. He returned much improved. We then sat down together to plan out a less taxing work schedule.

George read the book *Type A Behavior and Your Heart* and agreed that he had many characteristics of Type A personality. He began to see just how he was wrecking his personal life.

As George later told me, "I began to realize that I never lost a patient's business because I did a job too well or too slowly. But I have lost some in hurrying; I did a job poorly. Every time I got in trouble with a patient, I was going too fast and working at a frenzied pace."

After mulling over his lifestyle, George decided to change some things about himself. It hasn't been easy. As George said,

> Around other Type A individuals, I have to constantly remind myself not to become obsessed with the same things they are concerned about. Each social event I attend, I consciously remind myself that I suffer from a personality conflict that makes me want to acquire more and more things and outdo my friends. By reminding myself that I have this problem, I have been able to decrease my hostility and greediness and have opened myself to more rewarding friendships. Instead of trying to increase my bank account and get by the stupid deadlines I used to set for myself, I spend quality time with my family and friends. Limiting my workload has caused me to make a little less money, but I feel more relaxed and carefree and am enjoying the pleasures that the money I make brings.

George is gradually cultivating a peace of mind that enables him to take better care of his patients, while at the same time he is preventing personal emotional problems. He's happier, and his appearance these days shows it.

If you have Type A personality, you can change, too. By slowly ridding yourself of the hurry and hostility that dominates your personality, you can find your life far more satisfying and more rewarding.

Is Type B Behavior Nonproductive?

After giving a talk on how to change Type A behavior, I was questioned by a grandmotherly woman from the audience. She said, "Dr. Walker, I don't seem to have any of those traits you were talking about. I can sit around for hours reading and listening to music if I want to, and it doesn't bother me. My husband says I go kind of slow but I get things done. Is there something wrong with me?" I reassured this pleasant lady that Type B behavior, rather than being "wrong," was to be cultivated. I congratulated her on her ability to go slow, "enjoy the music," and get things done at the same time. I told her of an idol of mine who was Type B through and through, but had a highly rewarding and successful life.

This man, Connett, is a 51-year-old physician who has a thriving practice in general medicine. He continues to see many of the same patients that he started with almost 30 years ago, and he now cares for the children and some of the grandchildren of some of those original patients. Although he is extremely busy, Connett never seems to hurry. Connett always seems to have time to chat with his patients, whom he considers his friends, and is most satisfied in doing a thorough job. He never hesitates to refer a patient when he feels someone else can help that patient better; he accepts that he is not the smartest doctor around. Returning home following a busy day in the office, Connett invariably takes a pleasant walk around the neighborhood with his wife. On Wednesday afternoons, he plays golf for fun and relaxation, slicing notoriously, putting poorly, and laughing loudly about his always pathetic score. Connett is a connoisseur of fine books, a believer in a God who controls the order of the universe, and seems unconcerned by the petty annoyances of life. Little bothered by the quest for possessions, he is invigoratingly healthy and fit, and destined to live a long and happy life.

How Else Can Heart Disease Be Prevented?

Eliminating the other major risk factors for coronary artery disease is perhaps just as important as giving up the habits of Type A behavior. Hypertension, cigarette smoking, and a diet high in saturated fats, cholesterol, and calories have been identified as major risk factors for coronary disease. So avoid smoking and overeating. In addition, have an annual physical examination. And if your blood pressure or serum cholesterol are elevated, cooperate with your doctor's treatment recommendations.

What Happens After a Heart Attack?

Probably no illness is more devastating than a heart attack. Physiological and psychological factors combine to overwhelm the victim with legitimate questions: "Will I live?" "Will I work again?" "Will I ever be the same?" "Can I enjoy sex again?"

Although the sequence and intensity of the responses may vary, heart attack victims typically demonstrate specific behavior patterns. Individuals may delay three to four hours before seeking medical care—blaming their problem on gastrointestinal upset or respiratory difficulties. After this brief period of denial, anxiety gradually grows, peaking on the second day. By the third or fourth hospital day, as the person's physiologic condition stabilizes, a growing awareness of the lasting significance of the illness precipitates a depression and a marked dependency on the medical staff. Demanding and irritable behavior marks the intermittent anger that the individual often feels. During the second week of convalescence, resolution and acceptance gradually allows the individual to cooperate more realistically in the treatment program. Unfortunately, psychological adjustment often fails to progress as smoothly as just outlined, and emotional problems may contribute to poor recovery.

For example, Clay, a 47-year-old powerline worker, suffered a mild cardiac infarction, and was advised that he would be unable to return to strenuous "high-line" work. Once an aggressive, independent individual, Clay became a cardiac cripple. He was totally preoccupied with fear of chest pain and demanded constant attention from his wife. Clay's physician gradually helped him view his illness more realistically. The physician told Clay that although he was no longer able to do strenuous work, he was not useless. The physician encouraged Clay to take a job as powerline supervisor, emphasizing to the patient the importance of the job as an advisor to others. Furthermore, Clay was instructed that normal sexual activity need not be restricted. Finally, Clay was informed of the benefits of exercise. As his self-concept improved, Clay began to become less dependent on his wife and finally returned to work as a foreman.

How Can Psychological Problems After a Heart Attack Be Overcome?

Following a heart attack an individual may recover physically, but have emotional problems that prevent the return to a normal lifestyle. Some of these problems include phobias, work or sexual inhibitions, fear of being alone, and physical complaints centering on the heart. Often these problems can be overcome with reassurance and a specific program of steadily increasing activities.

For example, on the second day after his heart attack, Buck, a 53-year-old furniture worker, became anxious, began to sweat profusely, and had feelings of impending doom. Buck's anxiety attack was precipitated by a brief visit from his wife, who told him not to worry about his family because they would live with her parents until he was able to work again. This fiercely independent man viewed his heart attack as a crippling blow. He had always provided for his family without help from anyone, and now they were going to have to move out of their rented home and live with his in-laws. He felt weak, damaged, and angry. He resented the prospect of being financially unable to provide for his family's needs and having to rely on his relatives. Yet, at the same time, he was afraid that if he returned to work he would have another heart attack and die. Buck was encouraged to talk about his fears and anger. He was gradually led to understand that temporarily depending on others did not prevent him from being a man. When Buck accepted his physician's assurance that he would be able to return to work again with proper rehabilitation, his anxiety diminished.

Most heart attack victims complain of weakness during convalescence. This weakness is a natural consequence of prolonged bed rest. Yet, because they are weak, convalescents may be afraid to get out of bed, which only increases the feeling of weakness. Thus fear begins to snowball. Physicians often help these people understand the debilitating effects of simple bed rest by telling them about the interesting study performed by Paul Saltin and his associates. Three healthy sedentary students and two trained athletes were placed on three weeks of bed rest. The sedentary individuals took an average of 11 days to regain their pre-bed rest maximal strength; the athletes took an average of 35 days. In addition to educating patients about the debilitating effects of bed rest, physicians often offer treadmill testing just before hospital discharge to help reassure patients that they are capable of doing much more than they would have otherwise imagined. Patients can be taught to monitor their own pulse rates and can be given specific exercise programs to follow that will allow a gradual increase of the heart rate with progressive activity. Families should be discouraged from treating the patient as a cardiac cripple.

The strain on the heart during sexual intercourse is equivalent to climbing a flight of stairs. Therefore, patients can generally be expected to return to sexual activity approximately six weeks after a coronary attack. Those individuals who have excessive anxiety about resuming sexual intercourse are encouraged to begin with mutual body massage, progressing to mutual massage of the genital areas. Coitus follows, with the post-coronary patient assuming the supine position. Finally, the usual patterns of intercourse can be resumed.

Hypertension (High Blood Pressure)

Hypertension, defined as blood pressure above 160 mm Hg systolic (the first figure of a blood pressure reading) or 95 mm Hg diastolic (the second figure), plagues one in every five Americans. Of the three major risk factors for cardiovascular disease—hypertension, cigarette smoking, and high cholesterol levels—hypertension is the most easily controlled. Hypertension is directly responsible for 60,000 deaths in America annually. In a 20-year research project involving over 4,000 people, patients with hypertension had twice as many deaths. They also showed a threefold increase in coronary heart disease, and seven times the number of cerebral vascular accidents than those without hypertension. Unfortunately, only one-third of the 23 million Americans with hypertension comply with their medical treatment.

What Emotional Factors Contribute to Hypertension?

In 1939 Franz Alexander proposed that hypertensive patients possess chronically inhibited aggressive impulses in which the individual covers hostility with outward serenity and affability.

More recent studies have failed to establish a specific personality profile for hypertensive patients. Yet evidence continues to accumulate implicating emotional stress as a major influence on the development of hypertension: overcrowding, disruptive social conditions, job stress, and poverty have been incriminated. The plight of American blacks—with an incidence of hypertension twice that of American whites—supports the hypothesis that sociocultural factors influence the course of hypertensive disease. Black Americans experience more poverty and more overcrowding, move more frequently, and have higher rates of divorce than their white compatriots.

What Can Be Done About Hypertension?

Medication can control blood pressure in 80 to 85 percent of hypertensives who comply with treatment. Unfortunately, failure to adhere to antihypertensive medication treatment results in U.S. death and disability costs of $3 of 5 billion annually. The pollster Lou Harris, in his 1973 survey on public knowledge of high blood pressure, found that only one-third of hypertensives and one-fourth of the general population knew that hypertension means high blood pressure. In addition, only half of the general population knew that hypertension could cause other illnesses or that hypertension was a serious disease. The first method in increasing compliance with medical treatment, then, is medical education. You, the reader of this book, will know that you should get a blood pressure reading regularly (at least once a year). In addition, you will know that taking medication will prevent hypertensives from developing serious illness. You can also pass along your knowledge to family and friends.

Many people ask me, "How can I get my husband (or wife) to take his (or her) medicines?" Simple: provide positive reinforcement for compliance, including encouragement, praise, and the demonstration of concern, approval, and interest. Try to get your spouse to take the medication at the same time of the day. And ask the physician to provide the drug in once-a-day dosage, if possible (the more times a drug must be taken, the greater the likelihood of missing a dose).

What About Biofeedback?

Biofeedback is a method using electrical instrumentation to provide an individual with knowledge of internal body processes. It has been used in the treatment of hypertension as well as to treat irregular heartbeat, low back pain, tension and migraine headache, and various other medical conditions. Biofeedback works like this: an individual goes into a soundproof room and reclines in a comfortable chair. Electrodes are connected to the forehead, the hands, and the area over the heart. Information about the heart rate, brain waves, and muscle tone are then fed into a small machine, which converts this information into a light signal displayed on a bar graph. The more tense an individual is, the higher the light signal appears on the graph; the less tense, the lower the position of the light. With aid from an instructor, the individual learns to lower the position of the light beam, and hence to relax. The more relaxed an individual, the more normal the blood pressure will become.

For example, a 43-year-old rather obsessive schoolteacher had suffered from severe migraine headaches since she was in college. I tried to help this teacher by instructing her in relaxation techniques as described in Chapter 3. But she just couldn't seem to get the hang of it. She would try so hard to relax that she would actually become more tense. Finally, I referred her to a psychologist for biofeedback training. After the patient was "wired up" and reclined in a comfortable chair in a soundproof room, she became obsessed with lowering the position of the

BRAIN WAVES: IS THERE ANYTHING GOING ON UP THERE?

An electroencephalogram (EEG) correlates the amount of electrical activity in the brain with a person's arousal level.

	Brain Wave Activity	*Arousal Level*
Beta rhythm	13–30 cycles per second	mentally active
Alpha rhythm	8–13 cycles per second	meditative concentration
Theta rhythm	4–7 cycles per second	drowsiness
Delta rhythm	0.5–3 cycles per second	deep sleep

light on the display graph. The patient worked so hard at trying to get the light to move downward that she actually went into a mild trance. Her muscles relaxed, and the tension seemed to drain out of her body. The more relaxed she became, the lower the light descended on the bar graph. Suddenly she realized that the light was descending and she became excited and tense— the light went back up. After a few sessions, however, she was able to use this biofeedback mechanism to teach herself to relax. She learned from the feedback of her own body processes. Once she learned what it meant to relax, she was able to use these techniques to help control her headaches.

Gastrointestinal Disorders

The gastrointestinal system, an important focus in early childhood development, provides the site for a variety of emotional reactions. The satisfaction gained through feeding, the tension engendered by hunger, and the pleasure derived from the early sucking process all influence the development of trust and security in the young child. Bowel training offers an opportunity for gaining approval and autonomy. Because central issues of need and independence are closely connected with the intestinal tract, it is understandable that psychosomatic problems of the gastrointestinal system are extensive. In this section, peptic ulcer diseases, obesity, and anorexia nervosa are discussed.

How Do Personality and Stress Determine Ulcer Formation?

Franz Alexander suggested that ulcer-prone individuals have an unconscious but strong infantile wish for love. This desire to be cared for, associated with the need to be fed, results in gastric hyperactivity. Because the wish to be cared for conflicts with the mature drive for independence, some ulcer-prone individuals seem to compensate for their dependent needs by becoming superindependent (or *counterdependent*). Others openly demonstrate their wishes for passive, clinging behavior. Under stress, these so-called oral characters develop ulcers.

Another researcher, I. A. Mirsky, found that emotions correlated with the level of the digestive enzyme pepsinogen. In comparing serum pepsinogen levels with psychological data in healthy men, Mirsky found that those who went on to develop duodenal ulcers had high pepsinogen levels and in addition had an unconscious longing for love. When these predisposed individuals were subjected to stress, ulcers developed.

As in all psychosomatic diseases, a single specific causative agent for peptic ulcer disease remains undiscovered. The disease continues to be attributed to a combination of factors including inherited, emotional, environmental, and physiological elements.

How Can Ulcers Be Prevented?

The possibility of emotional loss, job stress, and separation from loved ones can contribute to ulcer formation. Therefore, people who are prone to ulcer development can often prevent further attacks by preparing for stressful events in advance. By getting professional help during the time that the life stresses are building up, the person who has had ulcer problems in the past can prevent a return of the ulcer symptoms. Supportive therapy, often more effective than long-term psychotherapy, is best administered by an understanding family physician.

For example, a tax accountant always seemed to have an ulcer flare-up around the income tax deadline. During this time, the accountant would frantically work in an attempt to keep up with his clients' demands. He would take aspirin for his almost constant headaches and would slug down three or four drinks at night to help him go to sleep. (By the way, aspirin plus alcohol almost always equals ulcers.) After the accountant was admitted to the intensive care unit for a third consecutive year with a bleeding ulcer, he finally listened to his physician. The accountant cut back on the number of clients that he served. And he threw away his bottles of aspirin and alcohol. The next year, with a lot of encouragement from his physician to keep calm and slow down, the patient remained out of the hospital.

What Can Be Done for Obesity?

Between 30 and 40 million Americans are at least 20 percent overweight, and another 15 million are at least 30 percent overweight. Obesity increases morbidity and mortality and drains the pocketbook of those afflicted. Each year, $70–80 million are spent on appetite suppressant drugs, the diet industry reaps $10 billion yearly off the obese (from book sales, diet clinics, consultations, fad diets, and other means), and the cost of excess food ranges from $350 to 700 million for every 10 million obese Americans. Constitutional, emotional, social, and environmental factors all contribute to the development and maintenance of obesity. No medical or self-help treatment method has been shown to provide lasting benefit to those individuals suffering from this illness; multimodal behavior therapy is the most effective treatment.

A successful program of weight control involves four components: sensible nutrition, diet, exercise, and behavior modification. Because fat contains twice as many calories as protein or carbohydrate, the obese individual should learn that good nutrition begins with eliminating foods high in natural fats and oils. Foods should be cooked without oil and poached or steamed rather than fried or sauteed. Vegetables low in calories and high in vitamins help satisfy hunger pains by supplying bulk to the diet. Fresh foods are better than processed foods (processed foods contain three times as many calories). Because counting calories reinforces the notion of dieting as a temporary deprivation, individuals need to cut down on caloric intake gradually by making minor modifications in the diet—eliminating a pat of butter every day, stopping the habit of a midnight snack, foregoing the before-dinner cocktail, and so forth. In addition to a walking or jogging program, individuals can be encouraged to climb stairs rather than use the elevator; when possible, stand up rather than sit (standing uses more calories); and combine activity with fun (golf, tennis, swimming). The individual should use the following behavior modification tips:

1. Shop for foods from a prepared list (makes it easier to resist buying junk foods).

2. Keep as little food as possible around the house.
3. Keep high-calorie foods stored in opaque containers (so the food cannot be seen, thus reducing temptation).
4. Always eat in the same place (cuts down on snacks).
5. Use a small plate (makes skimpy portions look like more).
6. Chew each bite well and swallow before taking another bite.

Training in self-reinforcement and continued support from persuasive family members are necessary to help the individuals maintain weight loss.

What Is Anorexia Nervosa?

Anorexia nervosa is a relatively rare disorder (5 to 75 people per 100,000 are afflicted). It is characterized by voluntary resistance to eating, resulting in a weight loss of 20 percent or more of the usual body weight. According to the foremost authority on anorexia nervosa, Hilda Bruch, the most frequently found characteristic of anorexics are (1) a disturbance of body image (patients think they look fat despite their emaciation), (2) an inability to correctly perceive hunger stimuli, and (3) denial of fatigue with a subjective feeling of not being tired.

Bruch believes that anorexia nervosa represents a desperate struggle for a self-respecting identity. According to Bruch, anorexics attempt, by refusing food, to become respected members of their families, capable of mature, independent relations. In other words, anorexics feel controlled by their parents; they rebel by not eating. The nutritional disorganization has two phases—an absence of desire for food and uncontrollable impulses to gorge one's self, often followed by self-induced vomiting. Patients exercise vigorously to keep their weight down.

For example, an emaciated 88-pound college student was admitted to the hospital in an acute state of malnutrition. Although the patient looked like an escapee from a concentration camp, she insisted that she was overweight. She refused to eat more than three or four bites of food at mealtime and would spend most of the day exercising in an attempt to "get off another pound or two." A series of rewards and punishments was set up to encourage the student's eating habits. She was confined to her room until she gained five pounds. After gaining five pounds, she was allowed to sit in the psychiatric day unit, but was not allowed off the ward until she had gained another five pounds. If she were caught doing calisthenics, she had to return to her room and stay for 24 hours. In addition, the patient received intensive psychotherapy to help discover the origins of her false body perception, and her family was involved in the treatment program. Essentially, this young lady had a fear of growing up. She unconsciously wanted to remain "Daddy's little girl," and feared the responsibilities of sexual maturity. After a long period of hospitalization and several years of psychotherapy, the patient is well adjusted and engaged to be married.

Although several treatment modalities have proved successful, behavior therapy combined with family therapy shows the most consistent effectiveness and should be carried out in the hospital under the supervision of trained personnel. Despite treatment, mortality rates for this severe illness may be as high as 15 percent.

Musculoskeletal Disorders

How Do Emotional Factors Influence Rheumatoid Arthritis?

Most arthritic patients have psychological problems, but whether the emotional difficulties result from the illness or contribute to the development of the illness cannot as yet be determined. Many arthritic patients perceive their parents as being stern disciplinarians; Alexander suggests that parental restrictions have prevented the arthritis-prone child from directly expressing hostility. Alexander found a marked tendency toward outdoor activity in arthritis-prone individuals—which, he suggested, helps discharge aggressive feelings. When physical activity becomes inadequate to handle the abundant hostility, the resulting increase in muscle tone produces or exacerbates arthritis. The theory, although interesting, has not been substantiated in every case.

As with all psychosomatic illnesses, rheumatoid arthritis patients respond best to a supportive relationship with an understanding physician. Because a change in life circumstances can cause a flare-up of symptoms, the arthritic individual should talk with the physician about emotional problems. Physician and patient should meet at regular intervals to discuss ways the patient can better deal with this traumatic illness. Change in life circumstances should always be explored. At times, hospitalization may be necessary as a temporary haven from stressful life situations that are causing a flare-up of symptoms. Because many arthritic patients are depressed, a person who has arthritis should be alert for signs of depression; namely, sleep disturbance, decreased appetite, weight loss, decreased sex drive, and decreased energy (see the chapter on depression). An antidepressant medication can relieve these symptoms and may, at times, also help with the arthritic symptoms.

After a trusting relationship develops between the arthritic patient and the physician, the patient may voluntarily begin to express feelings of frustration or talk of deprivation and maltreatment in childhood. Because arthritic patients often have difficulty in dealing with anger, usually only after a long relationship with the physician will the patient feel free to talk about that hostility that he or she has for family and friends. Although psychiatric consultation is rarely necessary, some arthritic patients may want to see a psychiatrist if they wish to further understand their emotional problems.

Can Other Musculoskeletal Diseases Be Psychosomatic?

Systemic lupus erythematosus (SLE), psoriatic arthritis, ankylosing spondylitis, and other diseases of the muscles and connective tissue may be made more severe by stressful life events. A trusting relationship with the patient should be cultivated by the physician, as described in the section on rheumatoid arthritis.

Respiratory Disorders

Do Emotions Affect Asthma?

Anxiety, emotional events, and allergic reactions precipitate asthmatic attacks. In addition, precipitating circumstances appear to be conditional responses. One patient experienced an asthmatic attack whenever she was exposed to roses; interestingly, she also had an attack when shown a papier-mache rose. The asthmatic attack has been attributed to the suppressed cry for the mother. And fear of separation has been proposed as the asthmatic's chief emotional conflict.

Hypnosis, biofeedback, interruption of stressful interactions in the family, and antidepressants have been found as useful adjuncts in medical treatment of asthma. Long-term psychoanalytic psychotherapy has helped some asthmatics resolve dependency problems.

Do Emotions Affect Skin Disease?

The venerable psychiatrist Lawrence C. Kolb reports that significant psychological factors are found in over 75 percent of patients with skin diseases of all types. Current research, however, has failed to establish a specific personality profile in any skin disease. Rather, a variety of psychosocial stresses as well as inherited and physiological factors precipitate and aggravate skin disorders. Psychological treatment depends on the specific case. Those patients who have difficulty expressing anger often respond to once-weekly, time-limited (10 weeks) psychotherapy centered on current areas of conflict in which the physician helps the patient learn to become appropriately assertive. In those patients with anxiety, relaxation techniques help. And behavior modification can alter the bad habit of scratching.

What Is Hypochondriasis?

Hypochondriasis is an unrealistic interpretation of physical signs or sensations, resulting in a preoccupation with the fear of having disease.

For example, a 42-year-old woman, Rose, came to the medical clinic with a six-year history of abdominal pain that she was convinced was cancer. For most of her life, Rose had been dominated by her tyrannical father who never gave her the love and attention she craved. When Rose was 36 years of age, her father died of cancer of the colon. Soon after, she developed abdominal pain. Her complaints gradually escalated as her identification with and unconscious hostility toward her father increased. Rose began coming to the clinic almost daily with complaints of bloody stools (on examination the feces were found to be free of blood) and the belief that she had cancer. She felt that none of the clinic physicians listened to her, just as her tyrannical father had not. Psychotherapy helped decrease some of her complaints, although she never entirely gave up the belief that she had cancer.

A more common variant of hypochondriasis is known as *somatization disorder.* Patients with somatization disorders have a lifelong preoccupation with physical illnesses. These patients frequently report that they are anxious and depressed and have a history of suicidal gestures; they may be under the care of several physicians at one time. Drug abuse is a potential hazard. Unstable marriages and irregular work histories are common. Somatization disorders have been reported in 1 percent of women but are rarely diagnosed in men. The following case study is an example of somatization disorder.

A 27-year-old woman urgently poured out a litany of complaints in a pleading but hostile voice. The patient reported frequent episodes of nausea and vomiting, and lifted her blouse to reveal a roadmap of surgical scars. When asked about previous medication, she produced a brown sack containing no less than 22 prescriptions from five different physicians. Most of the medications were narcotics, analgesics, minor tranquilizers, sedative-hypnotics, and laxatives. Headaches, musculoskeletal problems, and painful menstruation had dominated her life. The patient had never experienced sexual pleasure. A physical examination and routine laboratory test revealed no serious medical problem. The patient stormed out of the clinic when the physician failed to admit her to the hospital.

Such individuals are extremely difficult to treat. If you have a loved one whom you suspect of having somatization disorder, the best you can do is attempt to have that individual see one physician and stick with him or her. The physician should perform all the necessary laboratory tests to rule out organic disease and then make regularly scheduled appointments with the individual. Once the patient begins to trust the physician, the physical complaints will diminish. Somatization is a serious, lifelong illness and requires the constant attention of an understanding, nonjudgmental physician.

The physician's goal is to establish regular appointment times with the patient. Encouraging the patient to keep the appointment no matter how well the patient is feeling implies that the physician cares for the patient. This maneuver diminishes complaints and establishes a relationship based on trust rather than illness. The patient initially may be seen for 20 to 30 minutes weekly, but as a trusting relationship develops the duration of the patient's visit can be diminished to 10 to 15 minutes twice monthly.

An increase in the patient's physical complaints generally indicates environmental stresses. Unnecessary diagnostic work-ups, medication, and physician shopping can be prevented if the family helps the patient stick with one physician.

Conclusion

Norman Cousins, the editor of *Saturday Review*, wrote an intriguing article in the most prestigious of all medical journals, the *New England Journal of Medicine*, concerning his bout with ankylosing spondylitis (a rheumatoidlike disorder). When Cousins failed to benefit from regular medical treatment, he asked his physician to release him from the hospital. (He thought the hospital too noisy and too impersonal.) Cousins then checked into a hotel room where he read inspirational and humorous literature, watched film clips from the television show *Candid Camera*, and took massive doses of vitamin C. Although flat on his back with pain when the experiment began, Cousins was soon able to walk and within a few months was able to return to full-time work. Cousins attributes his recovery to the cultivation of positive emotions such as optimism, laughter, and love.

I make this note not to discourage hospitalization, because the benefits of hospitalization far outweigh the hazards; nor to advocate the use of vitamin C, because that debate is still undecided; but rather to encourage the use of positive emotions as a part of the treatment of all types of illness. If hate, fear, doubt, depression, and despair can produce physical illness, then love, hope, faith, laughter, and confidence must have therapeutic value. Often engaging the natural resources of body and mind becomes the best one can do to oppose psychosomatic and other serious illnesses.

Chapter 7
Alcohol Abuse
(One for the Road and Other
Ways to Die Young)

Of the estimated 100 million Americans who consume alcoholic beverages, one out of ten (approximately 9 to 10 million) becomes a problem drinker. Almost 20 percent of all hospital care expenses result from alcohol abuse. Untreated alcoholism decreases life expectancy by 10 to 12 years and leads to an increased incidence of liver and heart disease. Alcohol is implicated in 50 percent of federal traffic accidents, 50 percent of homicides, 30 percent of rapes, 80 percent of robberies, 33 percent of suicides, and 62 percent of child abuse cases. In view of the number of alcoholics and the incapacitating, and sometimes fatal, outcome of the disease, alcoholism should be considered the number one major health problem in America.

What Causes Alcoholism?

The eminent psychiatrist George Vaillant says, "The development of alcoholism is as multidetermined and as unpredictable as whether an individual will develop tuberculosis, become a violin player, or move to a large city." Vaillant has listed six factors that have been thought to influence alcohol abuse:

1. Availability. When alcohol is cheap and readily available, consumption goes up.
2. Onset of action. High-proof drinks such as vodka and whiskey lead to alcohol dependency more quickly than less potent drinks such as beer and wines.
3. Physical dependence. The discomfort of withdrawal symptoms reinforces continued drinking.
4. Genetic background. At least some genetic studies indicate that the predisposition for alcoholism may be related to the sex chromosome. Genetic transmission, in part, explains why there is a three to five times higher rate of alcoholism in males than in females.
5. Culture. Higher rates of alcoholism are found in countries that accept drunkenness (Irish and Anglo-Saxon) than those that prohibit drunkenness (Italians and Jews).
6. Childhood environment. Some studies indicate that childhood unhappiness may lead to an increased rate of alcoholism during adulthood.

ALCOHOLICS WHO PROBABLY DRANK THEMSELVES TO DEATH

Dylan Thomas—The shy insecure poet escaped from self-doubt through drinking: Preoccupied with death, his prediction of death before 40 came true: he died at age 39.

F. Scott Fitzgerald—Worked hard, played hard, and drank hard in an effort to find happiness, which he believed was just around the corner. Died at age 44, believing himself to be a failure. His notebooks and letters published in 1945 were entitled *The Crack-up*.

Jack London—Claimed to have begun drinking at age 5. The author of *Call of the Wild* and 49 other volumes, novels, short stories, and essays, drank heavily throughout his life until his death of drug and alcohol overdose at age 40.

Edgar Allen Poe—Died of delirium tremens at age 40.

W. C. Fields—Legendary comedian and alcoholic, Fields drank 2–4 martinis for breakfast each morning and continued drinking throughout the day. Boozing finally caught up with him: he spent his last years in a sanitorium.

What Are the Symptoms of Alcohol Addiction?

The American Psychiatric Association has outlined criteria for a diagnosis of alcohol abuse:

1. Continuous use of alcohol for at least one month
2. Social complications of alcohol abuse reflected in at least one of the following:
   a. Difficulty with family or friends over alcohol abuse
   b. Legal difficulty because of alcohol
   c. Violence demonstrated while intoxicated

3. Either of the following:
   a. Compelling desire to use alcohol
   b. Drinking binges lasting for two or more days

Alcoholics have an uncanny ability to cover up their problems. Furthermore, alcohol abuse may go undetected because the vast majority of alcoholics continue to work, often in responsible jobs, and they tend to have a fairly normal family life. If you expect a family member or friend might be an alcoholic, ask these questions (remembered by the acronym CAGE):

1. Have you ever felt the need to: *C*ut down on your drinking?
2. Have you ever felt: *A*nnoyed by criticism of your drinking?
3. Have you ever had: *G*uilty feelings about your drinking?
4. Do you ever take a morning: *E*ye-opener?

FAMOUS WOMEN ALCOHOLICS

Edna St. Vincent Millay—American lyric poet
Dorothy Parker—American humorist
Vivien Leigh—Film's Scarlet O'Hara
Judy Garland—Actress and performer
Janis Joplin—Singer
Laurette Taylor—Actress

An affirmative response to any of the four questions is incomplete but suggestive evidence of alcoholism. Those individuals who respond positively to more than one of the questions should be confronted with the existence of a drinking problem (also see the box on hazards of drinking).

For example, consider Warren's case. At some level, all his friends realized that Warren had a problem, but they ignored it or denied it, turned their heads, and let it continue until it was too late. Warren could have been a stand-up comedian in Las Vegas; instead, he was an insurance salesman in a middle-sized Texas town, who delighted his clients with his jokes, rapier-like wit, and cheerfulness. Behind this happy-go-lucky facade was an anxious, childlike individual who had never developed a mature self-respect. His father, also an alcoholic, had died when Warren was a young child. Soon after, his mother took the first train out of Texas, bound for her home in Ohio, leaving Warren to be cared for by his father's relatives. As a child, Warren was shy and withdrawn but made good enough grades to get into the state university.

DRINKERS WHO QUIT

Eugene O'Neill—A heavy drinker, the Nobel Prize winning playwright, abruptly quit at the age of 37 after psychotherapy helped him deal with his underlying sexual conflicts.

Robert Young—The father who knows best and the doctor who does best (Marcus Welby, M.D.), Young was a heavy drinker for 30 years until he joined Alcoholics Anonymous.

Dick Van Dyke—The television comedian was done in by his old friend, Jack Daniels. Van Dyke had the last laugh when he finally said "Hit the road, Jack," and now helps other alcoholics say goodbye to booze.

Wilbur Mills—Former congressman from Arkansas who acknowledged his problem at the National Council on Alcoholism in Washington, D.C. May, 1976.

Don Newcombe—Baseball's most valuable player in 1956 gave up drinking when his second wife threatened to leave him.

Betty Ford—Gave up alcohol and Valium when her husband was 38th president of the United States.

It was in college that he first began to drink. He noticed that drinking loosened him up and allowed him to talk and joke with others without his usual anxiety. Warren did not drink enough in college to be classified as an alcoholic. He drank heavily at parties, but avoided daytime drinking and functioned well in school. Just before entering the military after graduation from college, Warren married a woman from his home town.

Warren had difficulties with the regimented military life. He was bored with his job as a communications officer, did not delegate authority well, and feared criticism from his superiors. To relieve his tension, he began to drink daily. After work he would go to the officer's club for what proved to be a gradual increase in drinking habits. At first he would have one or two highballs; this amount gradually increased to five or six drinks nightly with even heavier drinking over the weekends. Warren's jokes and freewheeling spirit while drinking continued to make him the life of every party. He still did not drink while at work and, although his wife thought he drank too much at times, she didn't say anything to him about his drinking because he seemed to be functioning well.

HEALTH HAZARDS ASSOCIATED WITH ALCOHOL CONSUMPTION

1. Esophageal and gastric ulcers
2. Pancreatitis
3. Liver disease
4. Nutritional deficiency
5. Dementia
6. Periperal neuropathy characterized by muscle weakness, pain, and diminished sensitivity to touch
7. Impotence
8. Suicide (one-fourth to one-third of suicides involve alcohol)
9. Heart disease
10. Chronic myopathy, characterized by muscle cramps and weakness
11. Birth defects among children of alcoholic women
12. Automobile and other accidents
13. Assault, rape, and family abuse (as a precipitating factor)

On discharge from the military, Warren joined his cousin's insurance business. As the years passed, Warren assumed more and more responsibility in the business, and as his responsibility increased so did his drinking. His heavy nighttime drinking gradually progressed to an early morning eye-opener; he began to have stomach pains and was frequently sick on Monday mornings.

Warren was a friend of mine. I enjoyed clowning around with him at parties and could laugh loudly for hours at his jokes. I became alarmed when I noticed that he drank three to four times as much as the rest of us at parties. And over the weekends he seemed to always have a beer in his hand. One day I asked him if he ever considered cutting down on his drinking. He gave the standard reply: "Oh yeah, I can cut it back any time I want to." The next time I brought up this subject was several months later, when he entered the hospital with a bleeding

WHAT ARE THE EFFECTS OF ALCOHOL?

Amount of Beverage	Effects	Alcohol Concentration (in serum percent)	Time of Alcohol to Leave Body (hours)
1 cocktail or 1 bottle of beer or 5½ oz. of wine	Slight tension release	0.03	2
2 cocktails or 3 bottles of beer or 11 oz. of wine	Feeling of warmth and mental relaxation	0.06	4
3 cocktails or 5 bottles of beer or 16½ oz. of wine	Exaggerated behavior: Talkative or morose	0.09	6
4 cocktails or 7 bottles of beer or 22 oz. of wine	Unsteadiness in standing or walking	0.12	8
5 cocktails or 27 oz. of wine	Gross intoxication	0.15	10

Source: Coleman, J. Abnormal Psychology and Modern Life. Dallas: Scott, Foresman & Co., 1976.

ulcer. At that time he admitted that he felt vaguely uncomfortable about his drinking, but was somewhat annoyed when I suggested Alcoholics Anonymous (AA). He said that I was the first one that ever suggested that he needed help with his drinking. He said, "All of our friends drink just as much as I do." Warren wouldn't listen to me, and except for his wife no one else seemed overly concerned. A few months after Warren's hospitalization, I left town to enter my psychiatric residency. Some years later I learned from a mutual friend that Warren had died when the car he was driving ran off a bridge; he had been drinking heavily that night.

What impressed me most about Warren's drinking problem was my friend's denial of the abuse. If I hadn't been a doctor, I would have probably ignored it also. After all, to most of us an alcoholic is a skid row bum, not an active, productive citizen who attends church regularly and is a member of the Rotary Club. Then too, if we get enough nerve to challenge a friend with a drinking problem, he or she becomes irritated and ignores us. It is a tough spot for a friend to be in.

Although skid row alcoholic bums are the most visible sign of alcohol abuse, they represent only 3 to 5 percent of alcoholics in the United States. About 5 percent of the country's work force are alcoholics, and another 5 percent are serious abusers of alcohol.

How Common Is Alcoholism in Women?

Because women, especially housewives, can more easily hide their drinking problem, it is difficult to estimate the exact ratio of male to female alcoholics. Until recently, most authorities would say that there were five male alcoholics for every female alcoholic. But with more women seeking treatment for alcoholism, this ratio is diminishing.

Beautiful, active in civic affairs, and a devoted mother, Beth was the last person anyone would expect to have a drinking problem. Beth's husband was a successful executive who traveled a great deal. Tyrannical and old-fashioned, he would not allow Beth to work or develop her talents to the fullest because

"It wouldn't look right at the office." To ease her loneliness and frustration, Beth began to take a nip or two during the day. Her drinking quickly escalated, but her husband, lost in his world of Wall Street mania, failed to notice. Beth began to develop headaches, dizziness, tremors, and shakiness. Alcohol seemed to help these symptoms, so she began to drink in the mornings also.

Beth was admitted to the hospital after her husband, returning home from a business trip, found her passed out on the kitchen floor. On hospital admission, Beth reported a heavy drinking problem that had gone on continuously for almost five years. In addition, she was suicidally depressed. Her husband was appalled—his wife's drinking problem would ruin his business career. He stormed out of the hospital, not waiting to talk to the psychiatrist. In brief, Beth received treatment for her depression, entered into a rehabilitation program, divorced her husband, and moved to another town where she is the administrative secretary of the local chamber of commerce. Her social status has slipped down a couple of notches, but her self-esteem has flourished. She is an active, productive, self-confident individual. Her ex-husband remains a bigot.

How Do I Get a Loved One to Admit That He or She Has a Drinking Problem?

Often, because of the alcoholic's denial of a drinking problem and inability to conceive of life without alcohol, many confrontations from family and friends will be necessary before the individual can begin to agree that he or she has a drinking problem. The alcoholic's family must have the courage to deal with the alcoholic's denial head on—expressing warmth and concern for the loved one and the conviction that professional help is necessary. Most alcoholics postpone a decision to abstain from alcohol until a major crisis forces the issue. If the family chips away at the individual's denial, he or she will be better prepared to seek treatment when a crisis develops.

Emphasizing to the individual the concept that alcohol is a disease helps facilitate acceptance of treatment. The family member might say, "Alcoholism is an illness that can happen to anyone—and just as with other illnesses, you can be helped."

If the individual continues to deny that a drinking problem exists, the family member can ask the loved one to keep a drinking diary and then allow the facts to prove the point. At times the individual may admit to having a drinking problem, but blame the drinking on the stress that he or she is under. For example, the individual might say that the conditions at work are so exasperating that drink offers the only escape. The family member can empathize with this position while at the same time insisting that the alcoholic seek treatment.

Some people say they can't be alcoholic because they only drink beer. That's ridiculous. A 12-oz. can of beer, a 3½-oz. glass of table wine, and 1 oz. of 40-proof liquor all have approximately the same amount of pure ethyl alcohol. Beer drinkers can, most definitely, be alcoholic.

What Are the DTs?

Delirium tremens (the DTs) is a group of symptoms produced by withdrawal from alcohol. DTs usually occur 24 hours following the cessation of heavy drinking and is marked by sweating, rapid heartbeat, acute anxiety, rapid breathing, and confusion. The individual may not know where he is and often has hallucinations. Seeing snakes and having the sensation of having bugs crawling over the body are common hallucinations during alcohol withdrawal. Occasionally an individual may have a grand mal epileptic seizure when withdrawing from alcohol.

One night when I was on duty at a state hospital, I was called to the admitting ward to witness a scene that I will never forget, although I have hence seen it repeated, with variations, many times since that initial exposure to the demons of alcohol withdrawal. A terrified young man was wallowing in his own vomit on the admitting room floor. He was sweating profusely; his breathing was rapid but shallow. Frequently he would let out a piercing scream followed by a cacophony of hoarse cries. He kept repeating, "Please get those spiders, please get them, they are all over my body, take them off, please." He had no idea where he was or what he was doing. With sedation, he began to gradually calm down; proper medical treatment prevented seizures and death. In this respect he was fortunate. The mortality rate for severe delirium tremens often reaches 5 to 15 percent.

How Can DTs Be Treated?

Patients with mild delirium tremens can be managed at home under the care of a physician or a paraprofessional. It is best, however, for a withdrawing alcoholic to be treated at a detoxification center or hospital. In addition to sedation, the alcoholic needs to eat well and to have the proper fluid intake. During withdrawal, the patient will be given vitamin preparations to prevent brain damage. Those individuals who fail to get the proper vitamins during alcohol withdrawal may develop chronic memory loss and confusion.

For example, Bessie, an undernourished and intoxicated 48-year-old woman, came to a church rescue mission complaining of confusion, double vision, and falling spells. During alcohol withdrawal, which included bed rest and a high-calorie diet, Bessie reported visual hallucinations, and her state of consciousness fluctuated from mild confusion to extreme agitation. Bessie's agitation and hallucinations gradually remitted but she remained confused. She cheerfully told detailed but inaccurate stories and would skillfully hide her impaired memory with jocularity and humor. Bessie failed to get the proper vitamin supplements when she was withdrawing from alcohol. Long-term alcohol abuse and mild malnutrition had produced a chronic memory loss.

Is There Hope for the Alcoholic?

The only definitive treatment for alcohol addiction is the hard and narrow path of total abstinence. Abstinence can best be achieved in one of two ways—Alcoholics Anonymous or Antabuse therapy, or, most effectively, the combination of both.

What Is Alcoholics Anonymous?

Alcoholics Anonymous, founded in 1935 by two alcoholics, Bill W. and Dr. Bob, both of whom became abstinent through a "fundamental spiritual change," has grown to over 10,000 groups and more than a million members. AA emphasizes both group and individual treatment approaches. Meetings are devoted to testimonials and discussions of the problems of drink. Through mutual help and reassurance, the alcoholic gains a new sense of confidence and more successful coping abilities.

Alcoholics Anonymous is successful if an individual continues to attend meetings regularly. Of those attending one AA meeting, just less than half continue to attend meetings for three months, but the alcoholic who has regular attendance for 90 days has a 50 percent chance of remaining sober for at least one year.

An extensive survey conducted by the General Service Office of Alcoholics Anonymous found that approximately 40 percent of those in attendance at a typical AA meeting have been sober for less than one year, another 40 percent have been sober for one to five years, and the remaining 20 percent have been sober for more than five years. To put the figures another way: a member of AA for less than a year has a 40 percent chance of going through the next year without a drink, a member with one to five years of sobriety has an 80 percent likelihood of going through the next year without a drink, and a member with more than five years sobriety has a 90 percent chance of going through the next year without drinking.

What Is Antabuse?

Antabuse is a useful adjunct to AA for individuals who drink impulsively. Antabuse (disulfiram) blocks an intermediary step in alcohol metabolism, leading to the accumulation of a byproduct of alcohol (acetaldehyde) in the body. Extreme discomfort, nausea, vomiting, headaches, and dizziness occurs in an individual who drinks only a small amount of alcohol within a two-week period of taking Antabuse. Those individuals with heart disease or an allergy to the drug, or those who have drunk alcohol within the past 24 hours, should not take Antabuse.

Chapter 8
Drug Abuse
(Out in Space and Other Trips)

Drug abuse, whether developing insidiously, as in individuals with chronic anxiety, or as an off-shoot of a youth cult, or even as a reaction to poverty or social injustice, has become a major problem of our society. Marijuana abuse may occur in 14 to 16 percent of the population, 4 to 7 percent of the population abuse amphetamines, and 4 to 7 percent abuse the sedative-hypnotics.

How Common Is Sedative Abuse?

The sedative-hypnotics (see the boxed list of street names) include the barbiturates, most sleeping pills, and the minor tranquilizers such as Valium and Librium. These drugs are the most commonly prescribed drugs in the United States. Last year over 18 million prescriptions were written for the barbiturate drugs; 82 million prescriptions were written for the minor tranquilizers; and another 18 million prescriptions were written for the nonbarbiturate sleeping pills such as Quaaludes.

Valium, the most frequently prescribed of all drugs, accounted for over 60 million prescriptions. In the United States, approximately 100 million prescriptions per year have been written for Valium or other tranquilizers, at a cost approaching 500 million dollars. In any year, 15 percent of American adults are treated with antianxiety drugs, and 6 percent of the population use these medications for more than a month at a time.

What Are the Results of Sedative Abuse?

There is no doubt that the barbiturates and the barbiturate-like sedatives are extremely dangerous. They rapidly produce tolerance—an individual must take increasing amounts of these medications to continue to get the sedative effect of the drug. Eventually the therapeutic dose will equal the lethal dose. The development of tolerance explains the well-publicized deaths of the celebrities who have been taking barbiturates and other sedatives. Individuals who depend on these drugs for sedation continue to take more and more medication to get relief from anxiety and tension until the dosage level becomes so high that the medication kills them.

Withdrawal from barbiturates can produce confusion and seizures. People who are using increasing amounts of these drugs definitely require a physician's care to get them off their medication.

STREET NAMES OF SOME COMMONLY ABUSED SEDATIVE-HYPNOTICS

Trade Name	*Street Name*
Amytal	Blue Heaven, Blue Velvet
Nembutal	Yellowjackets, Yellows, Nembies
Seconal	Reds, Red Devils, Red Birds, Seggy
Tuinal	Reds and Blues, Double Trouble, Rainbows, Tooies
Optimil, Parest, Quaalude, Somnafac Sopor	Sopors

DRUG TERMS

Acapulco Gold
Marijuana

Acid
A strong psychodelic

African Black
Rare, high-quality marijuana

Amphetamines
Compound used as a stimulant to the central nervous system; also known as Beans, Bennies, Black Beauties, Black Mollies, Copilots, Crank, Crossroads, Crystal, Dexies, Double Cross, Meth, Minibennies, Pep Pills, Speed, Rosas, Roses, Thrusters, Truck Drivers, Uppers, Wake-Ups, Whites

Angel Dust
A synthetic hallucinogen; PCP; Phencyclidine

Bad Trip
A psychodelic experience that causes paranoia because of loss of ego and unorganized thought

Bag

1. An ounce of marijuana
2. Approximately 10–30 mg. of heroin
3. Man with the dope

Baggy
A plastic bag commonly used to package ounces of marijuana

Barbiturates
Depressant; often prescribed to induce sedation and sleep; also known as Barbs, Blockbuster, Bluebirds, Blue Devils, Blues, Christmas Trees, Downers, Green Dragons, Mexican Reds, Nebbies, Nimbies, Pajaro Rojo, Pink Ladies, Pinks, Rainbows, Red and Blues, Redbirds, Red Devils, Reds, Sleeping Pills, Stumblers, Yellow Jackets, Yellows

Belladonna
A strong legal psychodelic; can be obtained in a drug store in the form of Asmador; fatal if overdosed

Bennies
Benzedrine, the trademark used for one kind of amphetamine

Big Brother
Trademark of Zig-Zag cigarette papers

Black Mollies
Strong amphetamines

Blue Velvet
A mixture of opium and another drug

Boo
Marijuana

Bong
Kind of a water pipe for smoking marijuana

Bowl
A pipe

Burn Artist
One who is good at stealing

Brick
Usually 2.2 pounds of hashish compressed into a small block for easy shipping

Brownies
Chocolate cake that can be easily spiked with marijuana

Burned
Getting robbed on a drug and sales transaction or receiving the wrong substance during a transaction

Busted
Getting arrested by the police or federal authorities

Buttons
Peyote, a very strong hallucinogen

Buzz
Any feeling produced by a drug or other intoxicant

Cactus
Peyote, a strong hallucinogen

Clean
1. Not possessing drugs
2. Manicured marijuana
3. No longer using addictive narcotics

Cocaine
Blow, C. Coca, Coke, Flake, Girl, Heaven Dust, Lady, Mujer, Nose Candy, Paradise, Perico, Polvo Blanco, Rock Snow, White

Coke
Cocaine, a strong stimulant

Cokey
("Coked-out") Chronic cocaine user

Cold Turkey
Kicking a drug habit with no medication to ease the withdrawal symptoms

Cooker
Any small container that can be used to boil and mix a drug in order to purify and liquefy it, thus enabling the drug to be drawn into a syringe

Crank
Methadrine, a strong stimulant

Cranked Up
On methadrine

Crash
1. Going to sleep
2. Coming down after being high on drugs

Crystal
Methadrine in its purest form

Cured
The completed act of adding another drug to a main drug in order to increase its potency

Decks
Heroin sold in paper envelopes

De Gata
Mexican for heroin

Dex
Dexadrine, a mild stimulant

DMT
A synthetic hallucinogen that is smoked; the effects are similar to LSD

Done Up
Intoxicated

Dope
Any drug used to get intoxicated

Do Up
Injecting a drug into the body; the needle can be inserted in the big toe, back of knee, hip, pudendum or arms

Downers
Barbiturates; depressants

Finger Stall
A rubber cover for a finger used to store dope so that one may

swallow in case of arrest or carry it in the rectum

Fit
A hypodermic needle

Glue Head
One who inhales airplane glue to get intoxicated

Grass
Marijuana

Hash Cannon
A pipe that is open at three places: one inhales through one opening, places the hashish in another and covers the third opening, the third opening can be opened while smoking in order to regulate the mixture of smoke and air entering the lungs

Hashish
Concentrated resin of marijuana; usually two or three puffs will intoxicate a person; Goma de Mota, Hash, Solos

Hash Oil
Thick, dark liquid extract of marijuana plant; usually dropped on cigarette and smoked

Hassle
A minor harassment

Hawaiian Black
Marijuana

Head Shop
A store where one may buy things especially designed for young drug users or sympathizers

Heroin
A strongly physiologically addictive narcotic that is made from, but more potent than morphine; also known as Big H, Caballo, Chiva, Crap, Estuffa, H, Heroina, Hombre, Horse, Junk, Medicine, Mexican Mud, Polvo, Scag, Smack, Stuff, Thing

High
The state of mind under the influence of drugs

Hit
1. Taking a puff of a marijuana cigarette
2. Being injected with a drug
3. To kill someone

Holding
Having illegal drugs on one's person

Jay
Marijuana; Short for joint

Joint
1. A marijuana cigarette
2. The penitentiary

Joints
Doobies

Joy Popping
Injecting under the skin, but not into a vein, also called skin popping

Kiester Stash
Hiding drugs in one's anus

Lid
Generally about 1 oz. of marijuana; the most commonly sold quantity

LSD
The strongest hallucinogen known to man; Acid, Blotter Acid, California Sunshine, Haze, Microdots, Paper Acid, Purple Haze, Sunshine, Wedges, Window Panes

Main Liner
One who injects heroin into his main veins

Marijuana
A tobacco-like substance produced by drying the leaves and flowering tops of the cannabis plant and smoked to produce an intoxicating effect; also known as Acapulco Gold, African Black, Cannabis, Colombian, Ganga, Grass, Griffa, Hawaiian Black, Hemp, Herb, J, Jay, Joint, Mary Jane, Meshican, Moroccan Black, Mota, Mutah, Panama Red, Pot, Reefer, Sativa, Sinsemilla, Smoke, Stick, Tea, Week, Yerba

Mary Jane
Marijuana

Mellow
An expression for contentment

Mellow Yellow
Saffron, a spice that can produce intoxication when smoked; can be obtained in any grocery store

Mescaline
An extract of peyote that also acts as a strong hallucinogen

Meshican
Marijuana

Methaqualone
A synthetic sedative; also known as Quaalude, Quads, Quas, Soapers, Sopes, Sopor, 714's, Ludes

Meth
Methadrine

Mike's
Micrograms, a measurement used in many drugs

Morphine
Principal constituent of opium; used for relief of pain, also known as Cube, First Line, Goma, Morf, Morfina, Morpho, Morphy Mud

Moroccan Black
High quality marijuana from Africa

Mota
Marijuana (Mexican)

Mushrooms
70's name for hallucinogens coming from psilocybin

Narc
A narcotics agent

O.D.

1. An overdose of any drug

2. Too much of anything

Ounce
The most common portion of marijuana sold; usually sold for $35–$125, depending on location of purchase, and usually yielding 15 to 40 cigarettes

Panama Red
Marijuana

Peyote
Hallucinogen derived from peyote cactus; also known as Buttons, Cactus, Mesc, Mescal, Mescal Buttons

Phencyclidine
Hallucinogen; also known as Angel Dust, Crystal, Cyclone, Hog, PCP, Peace, Pill, Rocket Fuel, Supergrass, Tic Tac

Papers
Cigarette papers used to roll marijuana

Pop
Orally taking a drug

Pot
Marijuana

Power Hit (Super Charge or Shotgun)
Forcing smoke out of a marijuana cigarette in one's mouth and blowing the smoke into another person's mouth as he inhales

Psilocybin
A mushroom that acts as a strong hallucinogen

Psychodelic
Being intoxicated on psychodelic

Red Birds
Seconal, a strong depressant

Reefer
Marijuana

Rig (Fit)
Paraphernalia needed to inject drugs into the body

Rip Off
To steal

Roach
The remains of a smoked marijuana cigarette

Roach Clip or Holder
An instrument to hold the end of a marijuana cigarette in order to fully take advantage of the last, most potent puffs

Shoot or Shoot Up
Using a hypodermic needle to inject a drug into the body

Sinsemilla
Popular marijuana from northern coast of California

Smacker
A habitual heroin user

Snort
Inhaling a drug to speed the drug's action

Speed
Methadrine, a very strong stimulant; extremely dangerous and addictive

Speed Ball
Heroin and cocaine injected into different veins simultaneously

Stash
A hiding place for any illegal drugs

Steam Roller
A toilet paper insert with an opening on the side big enough for a marijuana cigarette to fit into the hole snugly; putting one's hand over opened end and inhaling from the other end; the smoke is cool before reaching the lungs

Stoned
The state of the mind under the influence of drugs

STP
A very strong hallucinogen

Strung Out
The poor physical condition of a person who uses intoxicating drugs for a long period of time

Tab
Any drug in tablet form

Tea
Marijuana

THC or T
Chemical unique to marijuana, believed responsible for most of its psychoactive effects

Toke
Drag on marijuana cigarette
Tracks
Scars on the body caused from
needle marks
Trip
Mentally feeling high, either self-
induced or from drugs
Turn On
Using drugs to get intoxicated

Uppers, Ups
The stimulants, such as
amphetamines
Water Pipe (Bong)
A smoking pipe that uses water to
cool the inhaled smoke
Weed
Marijuana
Wired
When one is stimulated or
extremely high by amphetamines

Source: Macdonald, Linda. Drug Terms. In *University Medical* (13C1): 12–13, 1981.

The minor tranquilizers (Valium and Librium) are not nearly as dangerous as the barbiturates and the nonbarbiturate sedatives. Valium and Librium do, however, produce physical dependence when taken for a long period of time (over several months) in high doses. What's more, Valium and Librium cause irritability and depression when taken for longer than a month or two. To avoid complications, these drugs should not be taken for longer than one to two weeks.

There are thousands of Valium addicts in the United States; I will mention one case here and another in Chapter 14. Jack, a 39-year-old truck driver, entered my office demanding a prescription refill for Valium. The youngest of ten children, this rugged individual was forced to drop out of school at the age of 14 years to help support his disabled father. His mother, constantly busy with household chores, was unable to give him the attention and affection he deserved. Married at the age of 16 years, Jack worked hard all of his life until the day he strained his back helping to load a truck. At that time, physical findings were negative but Jack was given a prescription for Valium as a "muscle relaxer." Since his injury, Jack had remained on continuous doses of 40 mg of Valium for five years. Jack, who had not worked since his injury, was receiving workman's compensation of a considerable sum, with the promise of more if his labor union won the lawsuit that was pending for him. He had no intention of getting well, but wanted to ensure that he could continue with his Valium treatment. When I began to gently probe for more information, he stormed out of my office. The Valium, in combination with his deprived childhood, had combined to take away Jack's initiative and responsibility. A once vigorous, productive citizen had been converted into a hostile and bitter drone.

Are Amphetamines Harmful?

An estimated 8 to 10 billion amphetamine pills—enough for 35 doses for every man, woman, and child—are manufactured in the United States each year. They are initially taken to maintain alertness, overcome fatigue, decrease appetite, or create a euphoric state of mind. But the amphetamines, just as the barbiturates, produce tolerance, so that increasingly larger doses are necessary to produce the desired effects. Amphetamine abusers demonstrate poor impulse control, poor reasoning, and hyperactivity. Chronic abuse results in tension, irritability, headaches, nausea, and sleepiness. High doses of amphetamines can produce paranoid symptoms that are indistinguishable from schizophrenia.

For example, the campus police brought Franklin, a 19-year-old college student, to the emergency room of the university hospital. Franklin had been found walking nude through the quad gazing fondly at the moon and singing melodiously, "Come to me, moon goddess." On examination, Franklin's speech was illogical and often incoherent. He believed that he was receiving special messages from the moon goddess, Phoebe, and that together they were going to begin a superrace, the Phoebeians. The patient had all of the characteristics of a full-blown schizophrenic episode. Unlike a schizophrenic, however, his symptoms remitted within a two-week period. He gave a history of heavy amphetamine abuse since entering college one year previously. Initially, the patient had used amphetamines to stay alert while cramming for examinations. A tolerance for the drug quickly developed, and he proceeded to use escalating doses until his psychotic episode began.

What Problems Does Cocaine Produce?

Otherwise known as coke, C, snow, toot, blow, flake, leaf, freeze, happy dust, Peruvian lady, nose candy, or white girl, cocaine is a vegetable alkaloid derived from the leaves of the coca plant found on eastern slopes of the Andes Mountains in Peru. Despite—or because of—the price (cost: $2,200 per ounce) coke is the drug of choice for perhaps millions of status-seeking, upwardly mobile individuals (see box). Unchecked by law enforcement, cocaine is causing significant social and economic shifts in our country.

A snort of cocaine in each nostril can produce an exhilarating half-hour of drive, sparkle, and energy. Its devotees innocently claim that coke produces no hangovers, no physical addiction, no lung cancer, and no burned-out cells in the brain. Nevertheless, cocaine has its dark and destructive side: the euphoric lift that comes with a few brief snorts is followed by depression and irritability. Chronic use can produce hallucinations, paranoia, and physical collapse. A single overdose can cause severe headaches, nausea, and convulsions. "Snorting" has its problems also: sniffing the white powder ensures absorption of the drug into the bloodstream through the mucous mem-

---

SOME FAMOUS PEOPLE WHO USED COCAINE AND REGRETTED IT

1. Linda Blair—star of *The Exorcist*
2. Louise Lasser—TV's Mary Hartmann
3. Michael Tilson Thomas—symphony conductor
4. Keith Richard—Rolling Stone guitarist
5. Flip Wilson—TV personality
6. Ferguson Jenkins—Texas Rangers baseball pitcher
7. Thomas "Hollywood" Henderson—former Dallas Cowboys linebacker
8. Julia Phillips—Academy Award-winning actress
9. Richard Pryor—actor and comedian
10. Mackenzie Phillips—actress

Source: Adapted from *Time Magazine*, July 6, 1981, pp. 62–63.

---

branes, but it also constricts the blood vessels in these membranes, drying up the nose. With repeated cocaine use, ulcers form and the nasal septum can be perforated. "Shooting"— injecting a solution of cocaine directly into the bloodstream— can be especially perilous. The sudden high dose can produce frenetic activity. There is also a greater risk of a fatal overdose, and hepatitis can develop from using dirty syringes.

Although cocaine is physically nonaddictive, without strong withdrawal symptoms, it can damage the liver, produce malnutrition, and increase the risk of heart attacks. Many authorities believe cocaine is the most psychologically addicting drug available—coming down from a high produces a severe letdown that can only be remedied by more cocaine. Bigger and bigger doses often follow and soon the fad becomes a total obsession.

For example, Douglas was referred to the campus mental health services by his advisor after he had nearly come to blows with one of his professors. Douglas admitted to increasing episodes of irritability, difficulty sleeping at night, decreased appetite, and lack of enthusiasm for his studies. He reported that he had begun using cocaine at fraternity parties during his freshman year. He enjoyed the sense of exhilaration and freedom that cocaine induced. At first he used cocaine only at fraternity parties, but soon he began to snort the drug in the library when he became bored with his studies. He soon began to feel that cocaine helped improve his capacity for study, although his grades dropped precipitously and his interpersonal relationships deteriorated. Long-term psychotherapy helped clear up his secondary depression as well as aided him in giving up the drug that was wrecking his life.

What Is PCP?

Phencyclidine (PCP), commonly known as angel dust, hog, rocket fuel, or surfer, is an extremely dangerous hallucinogen. The drug was originally introduced as a surgical anesthetic, but researchers soon found that many of the individuals that were given the medication became psychotic and extremely agitated. Because

PCP produces a stuporous condition with hallucinations, it soon became prominent on the black market. PCP is unfortunately extremely easy to produce. Anyone with a high school chemistry set and a few pennies can produce large quantities of PCP worth thousands of dollars on the black market.

According to a survey conducted by the National Institute of Drug Abuse, almost 6 percent of 12- to 17-year-olds have used PCP, and just under 14 percent of 18- to 25-year-olds have used PCP at least once. PCP is versatile: it can be smoked, snorted, taken orally, or "mainlined." To compound matters, PCP is one of the most commonly misrepresented drugs and is often sold on the street as THC (tetrahydracannabinol, the active ingredient of marijuana), LSD (lysergic acid), cocaine, or amphetamine. Often, people don't know what they are getting when they buy street drugs: recent studies show that when a variety of street drugs are analyzed, up to 50 percent of them are found to be PCP.

Individuals with PCP intoxication have enormous strength, unbelievable paranoid reactions, and they literally feel no pain. PCP is a terrible drug. With one dose, an individual can become violent, destructive, and confused. Many individuals taking PCP have been known to go berserk and kill their friends or loved ones. For example, you might remember reading a few years ago about the 19-year-old boy who went berserk, shot his girlfriend, multilated her body, and repeatedly stabbed himself in the abdomen, apparently suffering no pain. This teenager had not come from the ghetto, but on the contrary had been an outstanding athlete in high school and was attending college on an academic scholarship. His behavior was precipitated by one dose of PCP.

PCP poisoning presents a highly varied and confusing picture: occasionally the individual may be sleepy and calm; and at other times the individual is disoriented and agitated. There is no way to predict the type of reaction that will occur. PCP also produces medical complications—vomiting, seizures, and extremely high blood pressure. Management of PCP abuse requires the most expert care.

Is Marijuana Harmful?

In many ways marijuana is much like alcohol. Used infrequently, the drug causes sedation and a mild euphoric state, so
there appears to be nothing medically wrong with the occasional
use of marijuana. As with alcohol, however, some individuals
can become addicted to marijuana. Chronic daily use of marijuana can produce lethargy, decreased ambition, social deterioration, and moral, mental, and physical sloppiness. Heavy use
can produce paranoid psychosis; in some individuals, there is an
indication that chronic heavy use of marijuana may produce
chromosome abnormalities. Whether marijuana should be legal-
ized is for the courts to determine. As far as scientists can tell
at the present time, there is nothing particularly medically
harmful about marijuana when used in low doses; used in high
doses it is harmful.

Betsy, a 25-year-old woman, came to the campus psychiatric
outpatient clinic after recently divorcing her law student husband. Betsy reported that she had crying spells, feelings of hopelessness and helplessness, lethargy, and poor sleep interrupted
by horrifying nightmares. She had used marijuana heavily since
her college days. When she tried to stop the marijuana she
became anxious and panicky. She protested that there was
nothing wrong with smoking four to five joints a day except that
"it might hurt my lungs." Over the course of a few months, the
psychiatrist was able to convince her to cut back on marijuana
use, and after a year of psychotherapy she stopped entirely. With
the reduction, and finally elimination, of marijuana, her ambition and self-esteem improved. She entered graduate school and
began dating again.

What About LSD?

LSD and mescaline produce visual hallucinations and disorien-
tation. This twilight state can be extremely pleasant—or
extremely upsetting. There is no way to predict which "trip"
will occur.

There has been a long debate about LSD flashback phenomena. Some individuals who have taken LSD claim to have LSD experiences several months or years following the last dose of the medication. No one really knows what causes these "flashbacks," but the possibility of experiencing a flashback is just one of many reasons why it is best to stay away from LSD.

Wesley, a 23-year-old graduate student, entered the hospital emergency room accompanied by three friends. Wesley's mood was labile: staring off into space his grotesque laugh would quickly change to shrieks of horror. He was terrified of the bright lights in the hospital corridors; any noise in the waiting room would seem to trigger a hallucination. He was quickly taken to the back room of the hospital room emergency where there was less environmental stimulation. The nurse "talked him down" by gently telling him where he was and interpreting his environmental misperceptions. The patient would think the doorhandle looked like a face of a witch, the stretcher was an alligator, the patterns in the vinyl floor were crawling snakes, and voices in the corridor were monsters calling from the grave. Within three to four hours, the patient had calmed considerably; before leaving the emergency room he said that he was not going to try LSD again.

What Are the Effects of Opiate Dependence?

Opium (produced from the milky exudate of the unripe seed of the poppy plant) and morphine (a chemical derivative of opium) can produce high physical dependence and addiction. Demerol, dilaudid, percodan, codeine, and heroin are all derivatives of morphine and also have similar addicting properties. With these drugs, tolerance quickly develops so that increasing amounts of the drug are required to produce the same effect. As an individual takes increasing amounts of the drug, the potential for acute overdose occurs. Acute overdose is marked by decreased and slow respiration, constricted pupil size and a rapid but weak pulse rate. Without immediate emergency procedures, death frequently occurs.

Withdrawal from opiates is not as life threatening as opiate overdose. Mild symptoms occur between 12 to 16 hours of the last dose and are characterized by a runny nose, yawning, sneezing, and sweating. Withdrawal from higher doses produces dilated pupils, tremor, goose bumps, muscle cramps, vomiting, and diarrhea. The withdrawal state reaches its height in two to three days but gradually subsides without treatment in five to ten days.

The medication methadone has been used to decrease the severity of the withdrawal symptoms. Methadone is a synthetic opiate that in itself is mildly addicting but fails to produce the pleasures that the other narcotics produce. Methadone, then, has been used as a maintenance narcotic. Although former morphine addicts become addicted to methadone, they are able to function better in society. Methadone maintenance clinics have developed throughout the country to help morphine addicts. People on methadone maintenance come to the clinic each day to receive regulated doses of medication.

The outlook for narcotic addiction is poor: despite the use of counseling, group therapy, and other rehabilitative procedures, 85 percent of narcotic addicts become readdicted. Those on methadone maintenance do somewhat better: 50 to 80 percent of methadone patients remain in methadone programs for five years or more.

Chapter 9
Childhood Emotional Problems
(Mental Health Begins at Home)

Many mental disorders in children are given the same names as illnesses in adults but are very different. Depression or schizophrenia in a child does not look the same as depression or schizophrenia in an adult. Also the diagnosis of mental illness is much more difficult in children than in adults. Psychiatrists have tried to avoid labeling and diagnosing children too soon. That's good—many children have transient situational problems that they "grow out of." I don't want to recommend that you sit back and do nothing when your child appears disturbed, however.

Treatable problems that many parents might ignore as insignificant include thumb sucking, nail biting, temper tantrums, and bed wetting. Symptoms such as seclusiveness, worrying, apathy, shame, guilt, and cruelty may deserve attention. Although all these symptoms may be signs of real disturbance, they're usually not. They are probably merely symptoms of a child's resistance to a move, a school change, or the birth of a new sibling. In this chapter, I am going to help you differentiate those transient childhood problems that you can encourage your child to master without professional assistance from those that need the proper professional attention.

Intellectual Disturbances

What Is IQ?

Intelligence quotient (IQ) is based on tests that measure how your child's intelligence compares with the intelligence of children of the same age. These IQ tests generally make the comparison fairly well. Mistakes can occur, however. No child should be labeled on the basis of an IQ test given to an entire classroom. Sometimes even specially trained psychologists may rank a child as having a low IQ simply because the psychologist has difficulty relating to that particular child.

It's probably best for you not to know your child's IQ because you would have a tendency to label your child and put too much

---

SMART ADULTS WHO HAD PROBLEMS LEARNING AS CHILDREN

Thomas Edison—His teacher told him he was hopelessly stupid; Edison dropped out of school after three months and was educated by his mother.

W. B. Yeats—The painter, John Butler Yeats, became so upset when his son could not learn to read that he threw a book at his head. W. B. recovered and later became the author of the greatest body of 20th Century poetry in England.

Agatha Christie—Author of 68 novels, 100 short stories, and 17 plays, was, as a child, recognized as "the slow one" of the family.

Woodrow Wilson—The 28th President of the United States, didn't learn the alphabet until he was nine years old, couldn't read until he was 11.

Albert Einstein—Was introverted and so slow to learn to speak that his parents wondered if he were abnormal; he soon began to read avidly, however, and by the time he was 13 he had read Immanuel Kant, other philosophers, and all the popular science books available to him.

Source: Simpson, Eileen: *Reversals.* Boston: Houghton Mifflin, 1979.

---

pressure on him or her. Also, don't have an IQ test done on your child unless he or she has continued trouble learning or responds abnormally to normal situations. Finally, don't forget to have your child's hearing tested if he or she is doing poorly in school. Poor hearing is a frequent cause of not doing well.

What Is Mental Retardation?

A diagnosis of mental retardation is based on IQ figures. An individual with an IQ below 70 is classified as mentally retarded; about 3 percent of the population has an IQ below 70. An individual with an IQ below 50 is generally considered uneducable (see the table).

What Causes Mental Retardation?

In about 75 percent of retarded people, no specific biological defect can be found to account for the condition. These cases generally occur in the lower socioeconomic classes, the intellectual impairment is mild (IQ between 70 and 50), and the impairment is probably due to environmental factors. These children are probably simply not getting the environmental stimulation that is needed for the development of intelligence. This lack of environmental stimulation is analogous to a beau-

CLASSIFICATION OF MENTAL RETARDATION

Subtypes	Approximate Incidence	IQ on Stanford-Binet Test	Academic Potential	Social and Work Skills
Mild	5,000,000	70–51	Sixth grade by late teens (educable)	Minimum self-support
Moderate	1,100,000	50–36	Second grade by late teens (trainable)	Unskilled work under sheltered conditions
Severe	300,000	35–20	Able to communicate Trainable in elementary health habits	Partial self-maintenance under complete supervision
Profound	100,000	Below 20	Totally dependent	Need nursing care

tiful plant that isn't getting enough water and fertilization. Soon that plant shrivels and does not grow.

In 25 percent of retarded people—usually those with an IQ below 50—the cause of mental retardation is almost always due to biological defects. Chromosomal abnormalities, infections at birth, birth injuries or hormonal imbalance can all contribute to retardation.

What Can Be Done to Prevent Mental Retardation?

The most frequent cause of moderate and severe mental retardation can be almost entirely eliminated by discouraging pregnancy in older women. As women age, the genes that transfer intelligence to the child become distorted. These distorted genes can produce mongoloid (Down's syndrome) babies. For example, the risk of a mongoloid child being born to a woman under 30 years of age is one chance in 2,000; the risk of a mongoloid child being born to a woman over 40 is one in 50.

Other causes of mental retardation have been virtually eliminated in the United States. For example, the illness phenylketonuria causes mental retardation in children who have inherited a defective gene. This defective gene prevents the metabolism of an amino acid, phenylalanine. The buildup of phenylalanine in the body causes intellectual impairment. Phenylalanine can be eliminated from the diet, preventing the development of mental retardation. The urine of all infants in the United States is tested for this defect on the first day of birth. Thus, the condition is almost always diagnosed early enough to prevent permanent intellectual impairment.

Likewise, hormonal imbalances such as hypothyroidism and hypoglycemia can be detected early in infancy to prevent mental retardation. The discovery of antibiotics several decades ago has helped eliminate infantile infections as a cause of mental retardation.

What Can Be Done for Mentally Retarded Children?

Only about 200,000 of the mentally retarded require institutionalization. The great majority of the approximately 6 million retarded children in the United States respond well to socialization and job training programs. Unfortunately, education facilities are inadequate. The psychologist James C. Coleman estimates that 2 million retarded children fail to receive the training that would allow them to become self-supporting members of their communities.

Developmental Disorders

What Is Autism?

Autism is an extremely rare disorder—two to four cases are found in every 10,000 children. Infantile autism begins prior to 30 months of age and is characterized by a lack of responsiveness to others, gross deficits in language development, and bizarre responses to the environment. The following case is typical.

As an infant, Ralph appeared never to notice the comings and goings of others. At first his mother thought Ralph was deaf, but one day while rocking his lifeless-appearing form, she noticed that he was tracking the sound of an airplane flying overhead. As the hum of the plane engine gradually faded away, Ralph continued to stare glassy-eyed in the direction of the last audible sound. Ralph's attention remained fixed on that solitary spot in space for several hours despite his mother's frantic attempts to distract him. As rudiments of language gradually developed, the parrotlike repetition of the few words that Ralph learned increased the feeling of coldness, almost iciness, that his parents experienced when around him. Hospitalization became necessary when Ralph's severe head-banging and violent temper tantrums became uncontrollable. In the hospital, Ralph would whirl around in circles screaming in a high-pitched voice for hours whenever rocks, bottle caps, keys, or other objects that he liked to collect were taken from his room.

Autistic children are withdrawn and self-absorbed; they pay no attention to what other people say, so that such children are often misdiagnosed as deaf. If they speak at all, it generally isn't related to what other people are talking about. They may sit for hours staring off into space or may collect objects and pile them in neat rows.

Almost all psychiatrists agree that autism is physically caused. No one really knows the exact etiology, but many suspect that the illness is due to infections or genetic defects. Of course, how parents respond to their autistic child does make the condition worse, or better, but autism is not caused by parental mismanagement.

Almost half of autistic children have an IQ below 50. Despite the severe impairment in early childhood, one child in six achieves a good social adjustment by adulthood, and another one in six makes a fair social adjustment. Whether or not an autistic child will have a good outcome depends to a large extent on IQ. The higher the IQ the better chance for a good outcome. Treatment requires the most expert professional help. Several excellent books have been written on autism: two good choices are *Autistic Children: A Guide for Parents and Professionals*, by Lorna Wing, and *The Siege: The First Eight Years of an Autistic Child*, by Clara Claiborne Park.

What Is Childhood Schizophrenia Like?

Children or adolescents with schizophrenia demonstrate the same signs and symptoms as adult schizophrenics (see Chapter 5). Schizophrenic children hallucinate, have active fantasy lives, and are subject to delusions. Childhood schizophrenics do not necessarily grow up into adult schizophrenics, although they usually continue to have some emotional problems. Other symptoms of childhood schizophrenia include excessive anxiety, catastrophic reactions to everyday occurrences, fluctuation of mood, peculiar posturing, self-mutilation, and repetitive behavior. Children who show these signs and symptoms definitely require medical evaluation.

Cindy, an 11-year-old girl, was brought to the Child Guidance Clinic by her parents after they found her slashing her forearms with some scissors. On examination, the girl laughed and cried inappropriately while she sat cross-legged on the floor, her arms extended in front of her and her head cocked to one side.

The parents reported that Cindy had gradually withdrawn from the other children over the course of the past year. She spent most of her time in her room, coming downstairs only for meals. Often they would find her in her room sitting on the floor rocking back and forth and moaning. Cindy reported hearing voices telling her that she was a beautiful princess; she said she slashed her wrists to prove she had the blood of Sleeping Beauty. After long-term hospitalization and psychotropic medication, Cindy was able to return home. She has continued to relate to others superficially and appears cool and aloof.

What Are Learning Disorders?

Three terms are used to describe children who are having trouble learning in school: *learning disabilities, minimal brain dysfunction,* and *hyperactivity*. These conditions overlap. The hyperactive child usually has a learning disability, and both learning disabilities and hyperactivity are thought to result from minimal brain dysfunction. Minimum brain dysfunction means a child has a physical cause for behavioral and learning problems. Minimal dysfunction does not indicate that the condition is trivial, but it means the condition is not as serious as the more severe illnesses, such as mental retardation, cerebral palsy, or childhood psychoses.

Children who are labeled with one of these three conditions may be very bright. There are simply certain things they can't do as easily as other children. Children with the learning disability dyslexia, for example, have trouble learning to read. This difficulty is secondary to defective visual and motor skills—the letter *b* may be confused with *d* and *p* with *g*, syllables may be reversed, and left-right discrimination may be impaired. Another group of learning disabled children may show impaired arithmetic skills (dyscalculia), while still others may have language difficulties: articulation defects, expressive aphasia (delay in learning to speak), or receptive aphasia (a defect in understanding the spoken word). Most children with learning disorders respond well to special education programs.

What Is Hyperactivity?

Hyperactivity is a major cause for poor learning. Hyperactive children can't sit still, are in constant motion, and are easily distracted. Although their intelligence is probably within normal range or better, their school performance is poor. They are difficult to live with at home and at school. They demand more than their share of attention, and can't wait for what they want.

For example, when I was in family practice, Greg—an 8-year-old, engaging, but disruptive boy—visited me for a precamp physical. He created chaos in the examining room, impulsively grabbing instruments off the clinical tray, darting from one end of the room to the other, and interfering with the completion of the examination with a series of jokes, riddles, and long stories. After I was finally able to usher the child out of the room under the watchful eye of my nurse, the mother gave a history of Greg's overdemanding and overactive behavior at school and at home. I was less amazed with the behavior of the child than with the fact that no one had yet diagnosed his hyperactivity—many parents tend to overdiagnose hyperactivity in their rowdy, but normal, children.

TEN MINUTES IN THE LIFE OF A HYPERACTIVE CHILD

8:30	Raises hand to ask teacher if he can go to bathroom
8:31	Throws eraser across room
8:32	Pulls hair of girl sitting in front of him
8:33	Goes to the front of the room to sharpen pencil
8:34	Opens notebook and spills paper on floor
8:35	Gets banana out of lunch box and begins to peel it
8:36	Takes pencil from boy across the aisle
8:37	Fidgets in seat
8:38	Interrupts teacher to ask if he can go to recess early
8:39	Runs to window and looks out
8:40	Goes to principal's office

Hyperactivity occurs in 3 percent of elementary school children and is ten times more common in boys than in girls. Hyperactivity typically begins around the ages of two or three, but generally fails to be diagnosed until school age when the short attention span that marks the illness becomes apparent. The following specific guidelines on the diagnosis of hyperactivity are from the American Psychiatric Association:

1. At least two of the following symptoms of hyperactivity:
   a. Excessive running or climbing
   b. Excessive fidgeting
   c. Difficulty staying seated
   d. Restlessness during sleep
   e. Always on the go
2. At least three of the following symptoms of inattention:
   a. Inability to complete tasks
   b. Inability to listen
   c. Easily distracted
   d. Inability to concentrate at school work
   e. Difficulty sticking to play activity
3. At least three of the following symptoms of impulsivity:
   a. Acting before thinking
   b. Shifting from one activity to another
   c. Difficulty organizing work
   d. Needs for frequent supervision
   e. Calling out in class
   f. Difficulty waiting for turn in group situations

Several factors have been proposed as contributing to hyperactivity: (1) true brain damage (5 percent of patients have a diagnosable neurological disorder), (2) maternal deprivation, (3) cultural deprivation, (4) allergic hypersensitivity, (5) metabolic abnormality, (6) emotional stress, (7) environmental poisoning (such as lead, insecticides, radiation), and (8) genetic predisposition. These multiple possibilities indicate that no one really knows what causes hyperactivity. It's probably best to think of hyperactivity as an inborn temperamental difference in the child.

There are two schools of thought regarding treatment. Some psychiatrists feel that the best and only treatment is drug therapy. The most commonly used drugs, d-amphetamine and methylphenidate (Ritalin), are the drugs that are illegally sold as "speed." These drugs, however, don't speed up hyperactive children; paradoxically, they calm them down. Nevertheless, many psychiatrists question the use of drugs in children. Opponents of drug therapy think that medication may make the child more attentive and manageable in the short run, but in the long run prevent him from developing his or her own capability for coping. If medications are necessary to control the child's behavior in school, it is probably a good idea to reduce the dosage or eliminate the medicine entirely during the summer months because these drugs slow the growth rate.

One important treatment is a firm, consistent, explicit, and predictable home environment. A home disintegrates unless someone in the family sets standards of good taste, good conduct, and simple justice. Establish rules—make them clear and make them specific. Establish rewards and punishments—make them predictable and make them specific. Praise your child's behavior and specifically criticize your child's faults. Although the physician must diagnose and perhaps prescribe, the treatment itself takes place at home and in the classroom. Finally, take heart—for some reason, symptoms of hyperactivity seem to clear up at puberty.

Behavior Disorders

What Causes Behavioral Problems in Children?

Many behavioral problems are caused by economic and environmental conditions. Some children, especially those who come from unstable home environments or from abject poverty, fail to form a normal degree of affection toward others and lack a genuine concern for their companions. Invariably, children with such severe forms of behavioral disorders continue to be symptomatic into adult life and become labeled as antisocial. Some children lie, manipulate, steal, destroy, and even kill because they grew up in a world where violence is admired. Others steal and manipulate because of poverty. These illnesses are more social than emotional, but delinquency, like crime, is a serious problem, as shown in the following examples.

Clara, a 15-year-old girl, was referred to the health department as a carrier of venereal disease. Investigation revealed that Clara began running away from home at the age of 10 years because her stepfather molested and beat her. Before the age of 12 years, she had been picked up on several occasions for shoplifting; on each occasion she reported that she stole because another girl dared her to do it. Clara began having sexual relations to support a drug habit and soon developed asymptomatic gonorrhea. When interviewed, Clara was angry and bitter. She stated that no one could be trusted, that men cared only for sex, and that drugs offered the only pleasure in life.

Leon, a sullen 11-year-old boy, was referred to a child guidance clinic after setting fire to a vacant house. In addition, he had been a chronic truant, had been suspected of purse snatching, and had viciously killed a cat. Leon declared that he trusted no one and felt that others would "use you if you don't use them first." Leon came from a broken home. His father had suddenly left his mother six years before and was living in another state. His mother was often gone, either working in a garment factory or out with men, leaving the child to be raised by his overburdened grandmother. Attempts to help the grandmother set limitations for Leon failed, and he was sent from foster home to foster home, but was unmanageable everywhere he went. After being caught shoplifting, Leon was sent to reform school at age 14 years. He was later arrested on a robbery charge and is currently in prison for a federal narcotics offense.

Obviously, psychotherapy will fail if what's needed is a restructuring of the child's entire environment. Group homes, residential schools, and residential treatment centers of many kinds try to change the environment. They don't always succeed in helping the child but they are far better than the old-fashioned reform schools, whose major accomplishment was to teach the behavior they were supposed to reform. These new residential schools need more money and more public support, but they are actually out of the realm of psychiatry.

Can Delinquent Behavior Be Treated?

Another form of so-called delinquency is found in those children who demonstrate antisocial behavior—vandalism, fire setting, breaking and entering, extortion—but are capable of appropriate friendships. These individuals may feel guilty about their misbehavior and show concern about the welfare of others. It is important to distinguish these aggressive, socialized children from poor-outcome, aggressive, unsocialized children.

Often parents unwittingly encourage the delinquent behavior. Approval of the child's behavior is demonstrated by inconsistent firmness or through indirect encouragement of misbehavior. Inappropriate joking, suggestive remarks, or nonverbal messages such as winks or head nods may encourage the child to act on the parents' unconscious wishes.

For example, a 14-year-old adolescent was brought to his physician by his father because of the child's truancy, vandalism, and drug abuse. The father told, not without pride, of how his son had thrown rocks through school windows, shot out the corner street light with a pistol, and been caught smoking marijuana at school. Despite the boy's flagrant misconduct, he had several enduring friendships and accepted blame for his misbehavior. The father's disciplining was as chaotic as his son's behavior. At times the father would unmercifully spank and restrict the boy; on other occasions he completely overlooked the boy's misconduct. At other times the father would put ineffective restrictions on the boy. The father had been raised in a strict environment. It was apparent after psychiatric interviews that the father was getting vicarious pleasure from the son's activity. The treatment of this boy consisted of helping the father deal with his ambivalence concerning his son's behavior. Realistic expectations were established for the boy, and the father was instructed in methods for establishing firm, consistent discipline. Gradually, with his father's help, the boy learned to become responsible for his own behavior.

What Causes Running Away From Home?

Coleman estimates that at least a million children and adolescents—average age 15—run away from home each year. The vast majority of runaways leave home because of the inability to resolve a family conflict. Family therapy can help solve the lack of communications between the parent and child.

For example, a mature-looking 13-year-old girl repeatedly left home unexpectedly, returning each time after spending a few nights with her friends. In explaining to me why she ran away, it became evident that the girl was trying to get attention from her parents, who were frequently "too busy" with their jobs, friends, and parties to talk to her. I helped the family plan more constructive time together, and as the parents' frenetic social and business life became more reasonable, the girl's running away stopped.

A likely candidate as a runaway is the child starved for attention or some sort of recognition in the home. There are many reasons runaways don't get enough love at home. If the child is from a two-paycheck family, with both parents arriving home exhausted, or from a broken home, there may not be much interaction among family members. This type of situation, compounded with other problems that aren't being dealt with, can drive a lonely, confused child further and further into a world of fantasy, closing out the reality of the world that seems to be rejecting him or her.

There are ways to tell if a child is thinking of running away. Here are some of the warning signs that you as a parent should be on the lookout for:

1. Sudden drop in grades at school
2. New circle of considerably older friends
3. Premature use of heavily applied makeup (other than occasional experimentation)
4. Abrupt change to an inappropriate style of clothes
5. Withdrawal from family activities
6. Behavior problems at school

This list is not intended to strike fear in your heart, and certainly I do not want to arouse an overly suspicious parent or encourage you to discipline your child excessively. But if your child is exhibiting any of these signs of behavior, it may be an indication for a heart-to-heart chat.

To make sure that your child doesn't become a runaway, don't ignore the problem if there is one. Get to know what is going on inside your child's head, even if at first it seems difficult to talk to him or her. If the quantity of time spent with your child is limited, make sure that the hours spent together are "quality" time. Keep communications open and specifically tell the child that he or she can talk with you any time he or she feels there is a problem. Also, tell your teenage children some problems that you are having. Teenagers make good listeners, and such sharing helps them learn adult responsibilities and gives them a feeling of importance.

Emotional Disorders

What Causes Depression in Children?

Depression in children and adolescents, which is probably more common than realized, is usually produced by a stressful situation. Instead of showing adult biological signs (weight loss, decreased appetite, decreased sleep, and decreased sex drive), depressed children often act out their depressed state with destructive anger, withdrawal, running away, psychosomatic complaints (headaches, stomach aches, earaches), or poor school performance. Therefore, it may be difficult to tell if your child is depressed. The best way is to talk with your child. If you notice a change in school performance, or if he or she seems to be withdrawing from his or her friends, try to find out if he or she is feeling sad. A precipitating event for the depression—trauma, separation, illness, death of a loved one, or other environmental stress—is generally present.

For example, a 14-year-old boy with an excellent academic record began skipping school, smoking marijuana, and getting into fights with the neighborhood children. An understanding school principal thought that the child's sudden change in behavior was due to depression over the recent separation of his parents. After consultation with the boy's mother, the principal referred the child to the school counselor. Several sessions, during which the teenager dealt with his anger, frustration, and puzzlement concerning the divorce, enabled him to quickly return to his usual standards of academic achievement.

How Is Depression Treated in Children and Adolescents?

Generally, short-term psychotherapy will help the child deal with the situational stress that is precipitating the depression. If the depression is severe and due to long-standing situational problems, hospitalization may be indicated. Depressed children with the biological signs, namely decreased appetite with weight loss, decreased energy, and poor sleep patterns, respond to the tricyclic antidepressants in a lower dose than that prescribed for adults.

Can Childhood Depression Be Serious?

Suicide, a direct result of depression, is the second leading cause of death in children and adolescents (accidents are first). Some psychiatrists estimate that the actual frequency of suicide attempts may be as much as 100 times greater than is reported. According to one study, approximately half of 3,154 accidental deaths in children were disguised suicide attempts. Furthermore, findings show that children as young as five years old not only have the capacity to be depressed but also can engage in intentional self-destructive behavior.

What Is Separation Anxiety?

Separation anxiety is characterized by morbid fear that something will happen to the mother. Most commonly, separation anxiety appears as a school phobia. Anxiety may be converted into physical symptoms—usually stomach aches, nausea, and vomiting that offer the child an excuse for missing school.

How Can School Phobia Be Treated?

Almost all authorities agree that the best treatment of school phobia involves returning the child to school immediately. As your child begins to realize that you are going to be firm and consistent about the school attendance, he or she usually begins to go to school without complaint.

Fearful parents make fearful children. Children can pick up a parent's apprehension about letting the child venture out in the world for the first time. The child, sensing anxiety, may react by not wanting to go or stay in school. If parents cater to this attitude, they are in effect confirming and perpetuating the fear, while the child becomes further separated from his or her peers. Handling this fear is tricky. The parents should not say, "I don't care whether you are crying or not, but you are going to stay in school." Rather, they should say, "We understand you are frightened and we are not happy you are crying, but we care about you and you are going to have to stay in school anyway." Frank discussions between parents, without the child present, can be helpful in isolating and diffusing their own fears before they pass them on. Older children and adolescents may require psychotherapy to help them overcome their school phobia.

What Causes Timidness?

All young children are afraid of strangers; but timid and shy behavior that continues to occur after 2.5 years of age may slow the child's educational and social development. Unusual inherited sensitivity, early illnesses, early losses, overprotective parents, and poor parental modeling may contribute to the cause of separation anxiety. You can help your child overcome shyness by adopting the attitude that it is proper for him or her to get to know others and meet them. A firm expectation that your child will socially engage with others will gradually help your child give up his or her shyness.

What Causes Frequent Nightmares and Excessive Fears?

Persistent anxiety, excessive fears, nightmares, restless sleep, and physical symptoms such as headaches and stomach aches mark the overanxious child. Often such children come from the upper socioeconomic class, in which love and attention is given contingent on the child's performing well in school and social activities. The child's fear of disappointing the parents leads to chronic anxiety. Other children become anxious about their conscious (and unconscious) desires to outdo their parents. If you have a child who is overly anxious, it could be that you are putting too much pressure on him or her to do well. Take a look at yourself. Perhaps it would be helpful if you told the child that you love him or her regardless of performance in school. You can say directly, "You are special to me, I love you, I want you to do as well as you can, but if you don't make the top grades, or become cheerleader, or make the winning touchdown, I will still love you." It would be well to repeat this message over and over. This kind of message usually helps the child perform better because it relieves the pressure.

How Can I Help My Child Deal with Fears?

In the first place, never try to raise a fearless child. Some fears are survival fear; for example, fear of fire, deep water, heights, and other life-threatening situations. Many fears occur naturally in the growing process and vanish as the child develops. Nevertheless, don't ignore or dismiss a child's fears. Never force children into situations they fear in the misguided belief that it will "toughen" them. However, also never "overprotect" (it's a shortcut to helplessness). Concentrate on creating a normal personality—a child with self-confidence and a true sense of self, and you will have a child with normal attitudes toward fear. The best prescription for helping a child overcome fears consists of love, encouragement, praise for achievement, and understanding in failure.

Parents who allow children to assert themselves and take risks thus help the child deal with fears. Parents should encourage independence, starting with toilet training at about 18 months. A parent should not be too permissive or too strict, but should provide the appropriate opportunities. The trick is a positive and confident attitude. No one can define for you how to walk that thin line between being too soft and too hard. It means setting firm, definite standards of discipline, clearly indicating what is expected of the child. Yet it also means providing democratic authority that can be questioned and discussed.

What Should I Do When My Child Acts Up?

Disobedient, negativistic, and provocative opposition to authority figures is often the only way a child feels capable of exerting control over a situation governed by adults. The appropriate management for disobedient behavior involves refraining from struggle with the child, while reinforcing the child's need to take responsibility for his or her own actions.

Most of the time, a child's aggressive behavior signifies the struggle to develop a separate identity and a sense of control over one's environment. For example, the little girl who throws down a toy that's handed her often is just testing out her new power over her surroundings, flexing her muscles. The intent is to build herself up, not to undermine her parents. She is experimenting with control over objects.

Much misbehavior is caused by the child wanting to have limits set and clearly defined. The child is asking, "What are the rules around this place, anyway?" Provocative behavior usually indicates that the child wants someone to tell him or her how to behave. Problematic behavior begins when parents are unable or unwilling to set limits—the mother who has to tell her child no ten times may not be saying it firmly enough the first or second time.

Children around the age of two go through a phase where they'll say no to just about anything their parents tell them. This automatic stubbornness can drive a parent crazy, but it is a very important phase for children to go through. It means that they are learning to assert themselves without the fear that their parents will desert them—one of the great fears of early childhood. The reason kids say no so often is that they are testing their assertiveness, just as they tested their teeth a year or so earlier.

At the same time that children want to explore and grow, they also want to remain babies. Children have two impulses: to walk away and to cling. In order to overcome that ambivalence, they may have to push their parents away by being stubborn and refusing to cooperate. This negativism is not a power struggle between parent and child, it's a struggle within the children themselves. It's their style of separating.

Instead of retaliating against your child's negative behavior, you have a dual role: (1) to recognize the child's need for self-assertion and (2) to set limits when appropriate. Talking to your child about his or her strong feelings will help the child get a handle on difficult emotions. Parents who squelch their children's ability to express angry feelings run a double risk. First, they may make the child feel guilty about having any anger. Second, they may thwart the child's natural aggression, which is necessary for curiosity and exploration. One way to build strong children is to teach them to express strong feelings appropriately.

Disorders with Physical Manifestations

What Is Anorexia Nervosa?

Characterized by a compulsive drive toward thinness (as noted earlier), anorexia nervosa generally begins between 10 and 15 years of age and occurs predominantly in females (only 5 percent of such patients are males). Behavior directed toward losing weight includes a drastic reduction in total food intake, self-induced vomiting, and prolonged exercise. In some patients, there are episodes of gorging followed by induced vomiting. Death through starvation is common, with morbidity ranging from 15 to 21 percent.

Anorexia nervosa is explained psychodynamically as an impairment of psychosexual development: The adolescent fears developing into a sexually attractive woman and uses a feeding difficulty as a way of clinging to the mother. Treatment consists of behavior modification—with rewards for eating—in a hospital setting. Family and individual psychotherapy aid in over-coming the psychosexual conflicts.

What Is Bulimia?

Bulimia is binge eating. This disorder is seldom incapacitating, but it results in depressive and self-defeating thoughts. Binge eating is a way that adolescents try to handle anxiety. The condition can become chronic if not treated early. The best method of treatment is behavior modification by a skilled psycho-therapist.

What Causes Tics?

Nervous tics result from anxiety. Between 12 and 24 percent of children have a history of such tics. Generally they remit with time and offer no real problem. The best treatment is to ignore them, although it may be a good idea to try to understand the underlying anxiety that is producing the tics.

How Can I Help My Child Overcome Stuttering?

Almost all cases of stuttering occur before the age of 12. In some children, stuttering may represent a conflict over aggression. The child attempts through hesitant speech patterns to control others. Over 50 percent and perhaps as many as 80 percent of children who stutter recover spontaneously. The best treatment, in the majority of cases, is for the parents to ignore the condition, because calling attention to the speech deficiency only increases the problem. For those children who fail to remit spontaneously, speech therapy can help solve mechanical problems, whereas psychotherapy resolves emotional conflicts that contribute to the disorder.

What Can Be Done About Bed Wetting?

One of the most common childhood problems, bed wetting occurs in roughly 10 percent of children age five years, 5 percent of ten-year-olds, and less than 1 percent of adults. Bed wetting (enuresis) may result from a variety of organic causes, including urinary tract infection, diabetes, and structural abnormality of the urinary tract. However, behavioral problems such as faulty learning, immaturity, anxiety, and hostility are commonly thought to be the most frequent causes. A variety of treatments have been used: rewards for dry nights, bladder strengthening by forcing daytime fluids and encouraging retention of urine for as long as possible; setting an alarm clock to go off two hours after going to sleep so that the child can awaken and go to the bathroom, and an electrified mattress that rings an alarm or administers a mild shock at the first few drops of urine.

Because many children seem to use bed wetting as a passive method for demonstrating their fear of growing up, the best treatment method may be for the parents to take a noncritical attitude toward helping the child overcome the problem. Too often parents take a desperate stance, such as saying, "You've *got* to stop wetting the bed" or "Only babies wet their beds." Parents often feel embarrassed about the child's problem, quickly become frustrated, and then angry. Parental frustration and anger only increases the child's bed wetting, and a vicious cycle is established. Parents can pull out of the vicious cycle by giving the child more responsibility in the control of the problem: "It's your bed. If you want to wet it, fine. You will, however, be responsible for washing the sheets and taking care of your clothes. Sooner or later you will be grown up enough to stop. It's just a matter of time for you to learn control."

In resistant cases, referral for a diagnostic workup may be important. After all, bed wetting is a symptom of an underlying problem, just as fever is a symptom of an infection. For those children who have a period of dryness following potty training and then begin wetting the bed later on during school age, a physical workup is probably unnecessary, although it would probably relieve your mind to check with your family physician just to make certain there are no urinary tract infections or physical abnormalities that may be contributing to the bed wetting problem.

An evaluation by a psychiatrist is a good idea if the bed wetting persists more than several months. The psychiatrist may want to see the child for a few sessions to determine whether the condition reflects a severe underlying problem that may benefit from psychotherapy. Occasionally the antidepressant imipramine, given an hour or two before bedtime, may help with the bed-wetting problem. If drugs are used, they should be discontinued after six weeks.

What Can I Do About My Child's Thumb Sucking?

Although not a psychiatric disorder by itself, thumb sucking is considered a sign of continued dependency on the parents and often involves the parent and child in a massive struggle over control. Splints, mitts, and scolding generally prolong the habit. The best treatment, just as for bed wetting, is to pay as little attention as possible to the behavior, perhaps occasionally reminding the child that some day he or she will be grown up enough to stop. Awards for not thumb sucking may be helpful; for example, an ice cream cone if the child does not suck his thumb for a day, or a trip to the zoo if the child avoids thumb sucking for a week.

What Can I Do About My Child's Nail Biting?

Beginning at about five years of age and increasing up to the 12th year, nail biting is a symptom of anxiety and environmental stress. Try to find out what your child is anxious about. The most usual fear is going to school. Treatment consists not of threats to prevent the child from biting his or her nails, but an attempt to understand and to relieve the underlying source of anxiety. The nail biting will gradually disappear as the child talks about what he or she is afraid of.

What Are the Treatments for Childhood Emotional Problems?

Treatment for most childhood emotional problems begins at home. If your child is not severely impaired—if your child does not have schizophrenia, severe mental retardation, or autism—

you can help your child a great deal by teaching him or her responsibility. Reality therapy is a good approach for most children with minor developmental problems.

What Is Reality Therapy?

First proposed by William Glasser, reality therapy is based on the assumption that certain rules of society must be learned to get along in the world, and that to break the social, ethical, and moral rules leads ultimately to self-destruction. Reality therapy teaches the child responsibility. Glasser defined responsibility as the ability to fulfill one's needs in such a way that others are also allowed to fulfill their needs. Using this approach the child is taught that irresponsible behavior is self-defeating. The child is helped to learn behavior that will allow his or her needs to be met more effectively. The following guidelines are used:

1. Communicate verbally and nonverbally to the child that you care enough to be involved in helping your child learn self-discipline.
2. Question inappropriate behavior; for example, say, "What are you doing right now?"
3. Ask your child to evaluate his or her behavior; ask "Is what you are doing helping you?"
4. Ask your child to make a plan that will more effectively get his or her needs met. Several alternatives may be formulated.
5. Ask your child to make a commitment to the new alternatives. A handshake or written agreement helps seal the contract.
6. Give praise for good behavior, because praise solidifies involvement.
7. Use natural consequences as punishment; for example, no television until homework is done, or no use of the car until the car is washed.
8. Stick with the plan. Real changes will take several months to occur (in fact, the behavior will probably get worse for the first few months as the child tests you out).

To be effective, reality therapy requires that the home

1. Be a place of simple justice and good manners.
2. Have children who know the rules.
3. Have children who agree with the rules.
4. Have children who have a say in making the rules.
5. Have children who will know what will happen when they break the rules.

Reality therapy requires a great deal of time and persistence but can be used effectively for almost any discipline and behavioral problem.

Several years ago, Ann Landers printed some rules for parents to live by. These rules were written by boys who were in reform school. Reverend C. Galea, who was assigned to Guelph Correction Center, had asked the boys to think about their lives and figure out why they ended up in an institution for delinquents. These boys drew up a code for parents:

1. Keep cool. Don't lose your temper in the crunch. Keep the lid on when things go wrong. Children are great imitators.
2. Don't get strung out from too much booze or too many pills. When we see our parents reaching for those crutches, we get the idea that it's perfectly OK to go for a bottle or a capsule when things get heavy. We lose respect fast for parents who tell us to behave one way while they are behaving another way.
3. Bug us a little. Be strict and consistent in dishing out discipline. Show us who's boss. It gives us security to know we've got some strong supports under us.
4. Don't blow your class. Keep the dignity of parenthood. Stay on that pedestal. Your children have put you there because they need someone to look up to. Don't try to dress, dance, or talk like your kids. You embarrass us and you look ridiculous.
5. Light a candle. Show us the way. Tell us God is not dead, or sleeping, or on vacation. We need to believe in something bigger and stronger than ourselves.

6. Scare the hell out of us. If you catch us lying, stealing, or being cruel, get tough. Let us know *why* what we did was wrong. Impress on us the importance of not repeating such behavior. When we need punishment, dish it out. But let us know you still love us, even though we have let you down. It'll make us think twice before we make the same move again.

7. Call our bluff. Make it clear that you mean what you say. Don't be wishy-washy. Don't compromise. And don't be intimidated by our threats to drop out of school and leave home. Stand firm. If you collapse, we will know we beat you down and we will not be happy about the "victory." Kids don't want everything they ask for.

8. Be honest with us. Tell the truth, no matter what, and be straight arrow about it. Luke-warm answers make us uneasy. We can smell uncertainty a mile away. This means being generous with praise. If you give us kids a few compliments once in awhile, we will be able to accept criticism more readily. We want you to tell it like it is.

When Should I Seek Psychiatric Help for My Child?

Those children who fail to respond to environmental changes or reality therapy should receive a psychiatric evaluation. Specific indications include

1. Autism
2. Schizophrenia
3. Severe antisocial (sociopathic) disorders
4. Anorexia nervosa
5. Depression with suicidal ideation

Clara Claiborne Park and Leon N. Shapiro, in their excellent book *You Are Not Alone*, point out that although 45 percent of our population consists of children and adolescents, fewer than 10 percent of psychiatrists claim to be specialists in the treatment of children's psychological problems. They give numerous examples of parents desperately searching for professional help for their children, only to be turned away with each inquiry. If your child is seriously disturbed, there is a 448-page directory entitled *U.S. Facilities and Programs for Children with Severe Mental Illness*, compiled by the National Institute of Mental Health (NIMH). Your pediatrician and family physician can also help with a psychiatric referral.

Chapter 10
Emotional Problems
of the Elderly
(Surviving Being Old)

The elderly, laden with stressful situations—retirement, loss of loved ones, slowing of responses, physical disability, and the inevitability of death—experience a high rate of emotional illness. Under the age of 15 there are 2.3 new cases of psychiatric disorders per 100,000 each year, while over 65 there are 236.1 cases per 100,000. With 10 percent of the United States population—23 million people—having celebrated 65 or more birthdays, and the number increasing to 25 percent by 2020, it is important for all of us to understand the special emotional problems of the aging.

What Is Senility?

Almost 3 million Americans, most of them elderly, have symptoms of senility; 1 million are severely incapacitated by these symptoms. The problem, which now costs an estimated 46 billion in nursing home care, is expected to double in size in the next 50 years. At least 40 percent of chronically hospitalized psychiatric patients, and approximately 20 percent of all mental hospital first admissions have some form of senility.

Contrary to what many people think, senility is not an inevitable consequence of old age. Actually, about 90 percent of persons over 65, and many who survive into their 80s and 90s, show no serious mental deterioration. Furthermore, many so-called senile individuals are not really senile at all. Rather, they have underlying and usually treatable problems that cause symptoms similar to senility. Too often, however, doctors fail to look beyond the obvious, and incorrectly diagnose senility. Unless the proper examinations are done, a curable and treatable illness is likely to be overlooked.

Families, too, may assume "senility" to be the cause of personality and behavior changes in the elderly. This assumption may cause family members to accept a superficial diagnosis or perhaps not even consult a physician when such symptoms appear.

What Are the Symptoms of Senility?

Senility, also called *dementia* or *organic brain syndrome*, is characterized by impaired memory resulting from physical

---

FAMOUS PEOPLE WHO SUFFERED STROKES

H. L. Menchen—Literary and social critic, whose stroke incapacitated him from 1948 until his death in 1956. After his stroke, the sage of Baltimore had difficulty remembering proper nouns and names, depriving him of his main source of pleasure—writing.

George Handel—Composed *The Messiah* five years after suffering a stroke.

Louis Pasteur—Despite permanent left-sided paralysis from a stroke, Pasteur developed vaccines for anthrax, chicken cholera, and rabies.

Dwight D. Eisenhower—Completed a second presidential term following a stroke in 1955.

Woodrow Wilson—Recovered from his first stroke, not his second.

Patricia Neal—Stroke in 1965 left her unable to speak. After a long, heroic effort she regained her speech and was nominated for an Academy Award in 1968.

causes. The senile generally forget recent events more easily than remote past events. They forget names, telephone numbers, and conversations. Attempts to cover up intellectual deficits result in social withdrawal, confabulation, and exaggeration of personality traits. Some individuals begin to keep more lists; other individuals become more extreme in dress and mannerisms. Attempting to complete tasks requiring logical reasoning produces anxiety and irritability.

Depression resulting from an awareness of the mental deterioration makes the senile condition worse. Some elderly people, in an attempt to conceal their own diminished capacities from themselves, project their deficits onto others, with angry accusations and suspiciousness. Vulgar language, neglect of personal hygiene, and disregard for conventional rules of conduct mark the progressive downhill course of senility. As the mental functions gradually deteriorate, imprecise vocabulary degenerates to vague, incomprehensible speech.

GRAY PANTHER POWER

Maggie Kuhn, founder and leader of the Gray Panthers, makes these demands for improving the quality of life for all older persons:

1. Allow the elderly the right to be involved in society.
2. Eliminate poverty among the aged.
3. Make the Social Security system more equitable for women.
4. Allow the elderly to work.
5. Improve public transportation.
6. Encourage the development of a health system that fosters preventive medicine.
7. Provide access to safe, decent housing for the elderly.
8. Stop age stereotypes in print, film, and TV.

Source: Kuhn, Maggie: Power to the Elderly People. *Family Weekly* January 3, 1982, pp. 4–7.

What Causes Senility?

About 50 to 60 percent of senile persons are suffering from an irreversible deterioration of the brain called Alzheimer's disease (named for the man who first described it in 1907). Alzheimer's disease is characterized by tangled nerve fibers in the brain and a deficiency of an enzyme essential to the manufacture of acetylcholine, a substance that transmits nerve messages in the brain. Deterioration is progressive, and death generally occurs within ten years. Alzheimer's disease can afflict middle-aged as well as elderly people.

Studies are currently under way to determine if treatment with choline, a substance found naturally in such foods as egg yolks, meat and fish, can reverse some of the symptoms of Alzheimer's disease. Results so far are inconclusive and suggest that, if choline does work, it helps only in the early stages of the disease.

What Are Some Other Causes of Senility?

Another irreversible but perhaps preventable cause of senility is a series of ministrokes, or clots in the small arteries of the brain, that result in the periodic deterioration of brain function. High blood pressure is the usual underlying cause for these ministrokes. Individuals with ministrokes generally have an abrupt onset of confusion followed by a stuttering, but progressive course (rapid changes in the thinking process followed by a leveling off, then more changes, and so on, in a progressively deteriorating steplike manner). Neurological signs such as weakness in the extremities, minor speech disturbances, and a staggering gait may also be present in people who have suffered a series of ministrokes.

Senility can also be caused by chronic alcohol or drug abuse, brain tumors, metabolic diseases (such as thyroid disease), and a variety of rare neurological diseases.

What Should Be Done If Senility Is Suspected?

If you have a family member whom you suspect may be becoming senile, the most important thing that can be done is to get that individual to the physician as soon as possible. Don't accept senility as inevitable, and do not assume that it cannot be treated. The physician can recommend a series of relatively inexpensive tests that will rule out the treatable causes for senility. These tests include a urinalysis, complete blood count, a check for infections, and a standard metabolic screening battery to rule out hormone and electrolyte imbalances. A blood check for serum B_{12} and folate levels will rule out the vitamin deficiencies that can produce senility.

What Is the CAT Scan?

The CAT (computerized axial tomography) scan is a fast, safe, and painless radiological procedure that provides a computerized photograph of the brain structures. Founded on the diverse capacity of various tissues for absorption of photons, computerized tomography works as follows: the head is scanned by narrow x-ray beam in a series of narrow slices; next a computer organizes the information, and finally, the image is recorded photographically. This procedure is especially helpful in detecting brain tumors and other intracranial masses; it is also beneficial in detecting stroke areas and useful in the diagnosis of Alzheimer's disease. Unfortunately, computerized axial tomography is extremely expensive, and only a few of the larger medical universities have a CAT scanner. It is not imperative that everyone with signs of senility receive a CAT scan. Only those individuals with puzzling clinical pictures merit a referral to a large medical center for a CAT scan.

What Is Reality Orientation?

Reality orientation encompasses a specific plan for rehabilitating those senile individuals with confusion and memory loss. Reminding the elderly individual of daily events and restoring information can help the elderly overcome the apathy and withdrawal associated with the deteriorating mental functioning. The following is an example of a method of orienting the confused patient; the speaker is greeting his old uncle early in the morning.

Hi, Uncle Cornel, I'm your nephew, Brad Ingram. Today is Tuesday February 24, 1981, and we are in your home in Lynn Grove, Texas. It is 6:45 A.M. and the sun is just coming up. We are going to have bacon, eggs, toast, and coffee for breakfast this morning and then we are going to town to get a new post hole digger from Richard Weaver, the owner of the hardware store.

When family members begin to use this technique for withdrawn senile patients, the patients become more interested in the environment and begin interacting in relating to others better. Family members should try to feed as much current information to the elderly senile patient as possible, to increase the individual's orientation and memory capacity.

Is Depression Common in the Elderly?

Depression, which is widespread among the elderly, may present the typical signs of sadness, guilt, helplessness, apathy, insomnia, decreased appetite, and suicide ideation. Unfortunately, the characteristic slowing of the physical and mental processes caused by depression may result in an incorrect diagnosis. Experts estimate that hundreds of thousands of otherwise useful lives are tragically wasted because senility is incorrectly assumed or diagnosed in elderly individuals who are actually depressed. Unless the proper examinations and tests are done, the curable depression may be diagnosed as senility, and overlooked. Failure to distinguish depression from senility may lead to placement of the depressed individual in a long-term care facility where, more likely than not, the individual will continue to be neglected.

For example, I was asked to see a patient in a convalescent home, who was called "hopelessly senile." When I approached her, the patient did indeed appear senile. She sat strapped in a wheelchair, her head slumped, and saliva drooled out of the corner of her mouth. I pulled up a chair next to her and began talking slowly and methodically about the beautiful weather we were having and all the pleasant current events I could report to her. When she showed some signs of interest, I gradually began to question her. Her memory proved to be intact; she was oriented and without confusion. On a hunch, I started her on a very low dose of antidepressant medication, which was gradually increased to therapeutic levels. Slowly—almost imperceptively, at first—the patient began to appear more alert. After a while, she began eating better, and she began to sit up and talk spontaneously with other members of the convalescent home. Unfortunately, this misdiagnosed case history is not unusual, although the exact number of depressed patients misdiagnosed as being senile is unknown.

Many of these slowed-down depressed patients may end up in a rest home or in a state hospital with the erroneous diagnosis of senility. They are treated with the wrong medicines (usually Valium), which only causes them to look even more senile. This misdiagnosis is especially unfortunate because almost all of the elderly depressed patients respond to appropriate medical treatment. A 10-point questionnaire by Kahn and associates can help family members distinguish the senile individual from the depressed individual; ask the person the following questions:

1. What is the day of the month?
2. What month is it?
3. What year is it?
4. Where are we now?
5. Where is this place located?
6. How old are you?
7. When was your birthday?
8. What year were you born?
9. Who is President of the United States now?
10. Who was President just before him?

In an individual who has two errors or less, the slowed thinking is more likely due to depression rather than to senility. On the other hand, senility is reflected in eight or more errors. Those individuals with three to seven errors generally have a mild to moderate impairment of intellect that may be made more severe by depression.

Most elderly depressed patients respond well to the tricyclic antidepressant medications, which have been discussed in Chapter 4 and are discussed further in Chapter 14. Doses of tricyclics for the elderly should be lower than for younger individuals.

How Can Hypochondriacal Complaints Be Diminished?

The elderly are especially susceptible to hypochondriasis. Common worries of the elderly—such as failure to accomplish goals, guilt over surviving the spouse, or concerns that their children failed to do as well as was expected—can be displaced into worries over the body. Elderly individuals may worry unnecessarily about cancer. They complain about their muscular aches and pains, or they may be overly concerned about constipation and headaches. These physical complaints are often a statement of disappointment or anxiety.

After a thorough medical check has ruled out any physical illness, you can then help decrease these complaints by getting the elderly individual interested in outside activities. Encouraging the individual to get out of the house, go for walks, visit friends, and get interested in a hobby will gradually, over time, help decrease hypochondriacal complaints.

Emma, a 78-year-old grandmother, who had lived alone in a two-room apartment since the death of her husband five years previously, complained constantly of a variety of ailments: headaches, shortness of breath, palpitations, constipation, stomach pains, muscle aches. These complaints were limited only by her vocabulary and the listener's ear. The family decided to channel Emma's energy into something useful—volunteer work at a local hospital. As Emma began to care for others, her complaints gradually diminished. The most difficult step was getting Emma out of the house. Once this was accomplished, she began to expand her horizons: she went on walks and visited friends in addition to becoming interested in her long-neglected hobby of quilting. Note that this family did not say anything directly to Emma concerning her complaints; instead, the family members ignored the complaints and encouraged her to participate in something productive.

Why Do Paranoid Symptoms Increase with Age?

Suspiciousness increases with advancing age. Paranoid behavior, more common in individuals with hearing or visual difficulties or other physical impairments, develops slowly. Deaf individuals may see other people talking, and because they cannot hear well, think they are being talked about. Occasionally the suspicousness becomes severe enough to develop into a delusional system. The individual may feel that there is a conspiracy against him or her, or, more commonly, may feel that robbers are trying to break into the home. When the paranoid behavior becomes delusional, the patient needs medical treatment. Generally, a low dose of antipsychotic medication such as Haldol can alleviate the paranoid thinking. Also important is including the elderly individual in conversations and trying, as much as possible, to alleviate the elderly individual's physical handicaps.

Mr. Dobbins, an elderly gentleman, was referred by court order for a diagnostic work-up after firing his shotgun during the night at some passing cars. Mr. Dobbins was disoriented, talked mostly of his childhood, and said he thought the cars were people with flashlights trying to get into his house. He had been taking large doses of Valium (supplied by his daughter), which only added to his confusion. In addition, a significant hearing loss contributed to his paranoid ideas. A diagnostic work-up was negative except for an indication of mild cerebral atrophy on the CAT scan. I discontinued the Valium, referred Mr. Dobbins to the otology department for a hearing aid, and prescribed Haloperidol (0.5 mg.) to help control his agitation and paranoid ideas. I also encouraged Mr. Dobbins to participate in a senior citizens' group to increase social interaction. Although Mr. Dobbins remained slightly senile, his chipper good humor always brightened up the clinic when he came for a visit; he could hear and talk better, his delusions remitted, and he became a champion checker player at the senior citizens' club.

What Can Be Done to Help the Elderly?

Rather than writing off the older citizen as a hopeless case, family members that explore ways to improve the plight of the elderly can help most elderly patients lead more satisfying lives. There are several ways that family members can approach the elderly to help them deal with aging; for example,

1. Cultivation of a more involved relationship
2. Increased activity on the part of the family members in talking with the elderly
3. An emphasis on improving the adaptative capacity of the elderly

In attempting to develop a relationship, family members should be more active in talking with the elderly. In addition to inquiring about the elderly's physical health, family members can ask specific questions that will help establish an ongoing relationship: "What have you been doing lately?" "How did you enjoy the ball game?" or "How is your neighbor doing?" (Of course, really *listening* to the answers is also important.) Knowledge of current social contacts, economic status, and living arrangements enable the family member to be more specific in helping the elderly adjust to the changing society.

The family members' emphasis on improving the elderly's adaptive capacity demonstrates the family's optimistic attitude about aging. Many conditions that plague the elderly are reversible. A hearing aid can improve the patient's conversation (and decrease paranoia). Adequate dentures can improve nutrition, special shoes can improve the patient's mobility. The use of community resources can improve the individual's social contacts, and so forth. The family member can act as a catalyst in motivating more social contact and improving the elderly's physical and intellectual function.

One basic prescription for anyone dealing with elderly people, especially the senile, is *Slow down*. Don't try to get an elderly person to respond to more than one thing at a time. Talk slowly and more slowly.

If your elderly relative has trouble reading labels on food packages, mark the packages yourself in large letters. Try to keep the food in a readily accessible place so it is easy to find and reach. Although it might be quicker for you to do everything for such relatives, allowing them to do as much as possible for themselves will help them feel more useful and increase their self-respect.

Try to keep your elderly relatives active and organize their day into an easy-to-follow routine. Have breakfast at one set time; then, perhaps, plan a brief walk. Later in the morning, a visit to the neighbors would be beneficial. Have lunch at a set time, followed by a brief nap and then another walk. After the children return from school, they can visit (one at a time) with Grandma or Grandpa. Again, dinner at a regular time—followed, if it is a pleasant day, by sitting on the porch. Television or a slow-paced game of cards may be appropriate in the evening.

Notice that the emphasis has been on exercise and mental stimulation, albeit at a slow pace. Exercise stimulates the blood cells and muscles, and keeps the joints limber. Metal stimulation keeps the brain active. Studies at Duke University Medical Center have clearly shown that people who keep active—both physically and mentally—live longer and with fewer illnesses. Just as exercising the body keeps it fit; exercising the mind keeps it functioning. The adage "Use it or lose it" is really true. David Wallechinsky and Irving and Amy Wallace, in *The Book of Lists* (pp. 3–4) give ten examples of individuals who continued to "use it" at an advanced age:

1. At 100, Grandma Moses was painting.
2. At 94, Bertrand Russell was active in international peace settlements.
3. At 93, George Bernard Shaw wrote the play, "Farfetched Fables."
4. At 91, Eamon de Valera served as President of Ireland.
5. At 89, Mary Baker Eddy was directing the Christian Science Church.
6. At 89, Albert Schweitzer headed a hospital in Africa.
7. At 88, Konrad Adenauer was Chancellor of Germany.
8. At 85, Coco Chanel was the head of a fashion-design firm.
9. At 81, Johann Wolfgang von Goethe finished his play *Faust*.
10. At 80, George Burns won an Academy Award for his performance in *The Sunshine Boys*.

What Should the Elderly Eat?

Because plasma lipids play a major role in the development of senility secondary to atherosclerosis (hardening of the arteries), saturated animal fats should be eliminated as much as possible from the diet, and foods should be cooked only with polyunsaturated vegetable oils. A low-fat, high-fiber diet is beneficial for the elderly. The high-fiber content of the diet increases intestinal motility so that constipation is alleviated. The low-fat diet will help keep the serum cholesterol below 220 mg percent and the triglyceride level below 150 mg percent. In addition, elderly individuals should eat plenty of green and yellow vegetables. If there is any doubt about the dietary intake, a high-potency multiple pill vitamin is a good idea.

How Can the Elderly's Sleep Patterns Be Improved?

Aging is associated with a decreased need for sleep, so don't think something is amiss if Grandma gets up earlier than you do. However, some elderly individuals may be unable to sleep at night simply because they are failing to get up and around during the day. In this case, increasing the number of walks and daily activities will return sleep patterns to normal.

Another condition that should be seriously considered in the elderly patient complaining of insomnia is the so-called "sundown" syndrome. These episodes occur frequently in the elderly with mild to moderate senility. During the day these individuals function fairly well. But nightfall diminishes the environmental cues, so such individuals become confused, disoriented, agitated, and have difficulty sleeping. A night light or a bedroom closer to the center of household activity may help. If the nighttime confusion becomes severe (with hallucinations and delusions), a very low dose antipsychotic such as Haloperidol (Haldol) may be necessary. Remember that sleeping pills, Valium, and other sedatives make the condition worse.

Finally, if all methods have been tried and your elderly relative still can't sleep, depression is probably the cause. Antidepressant medications in low doses will help.

Chapter 11
Sexual Problems
(Barriers to Pleasure)

Despite the hundreds of books written on the pleasures and problems of sexual activity, individuals continue to have sexual difficulties. One study estimated that one in every ten patients who consulted a physician have a significant sexual problem, while Masters and Johnson estimated that 50 percent of all married couples have sexual difficulties. In this chapter, I answer some of the frequently asked questions about sexual problems.

What Are Some Physical Problems That Cause Sexual Dysfunction?

Although the majority of sexual problems are emotionally based, about 15 percent of patients seeking relief from sexual dysfunctions have physical causes for impaired sexual response. Some of the more common causes include venereal disease, prostate disease, thyroid dysfunction, diabetes mellitus, spinal cord disease, high blood pressure, atherosclerosis (hardening of the arteries), liver disease, and diseases secondary to alcohol.

SEXUAL PRACTICES THROUGHOUT HISTORY

Ancient Greece—The Greek's believed that a wife's place was in the home. Her task was to obey her husband who was absolute master. Women for hire were divided into 3 categories:

> pornae—common prostitute
> auletrides—flute players who entertained with dance or music
> hetaerae—women who served as companions

(No one asked women what they thought of this system).

The Greeks also believed that homosexuality enabled a boy to "take in" the manly qualities of an elder teacher. The boy's homosexual relationship terminated when he began to grow a beard; he was then expected to have full heterosexual relationships with women.

Ancient Rome—As long as good manners were observed, any Roman gentleman could pursue any Roman wife without being subject to reproach. Men were often bisexual. Julius Caesar was known as the Queen of Bithynia because of his homosexual relationship with the King of Bithynia.

Early Christianity—Sexual pleasure was considered evil; women were condemned as temptresses. The Council of Macon (585 A.D.) debated the proposition that women did not have immortal souls. The Council finally decided women had souls only because they became sexless at the Resurrection.

The Reformation—Mixed messages about sexuality were delivered from the pulpit: Martin Luther believed that celibacy was an invention of the devil (he fathered six children); John Calvin, on the contrary, extolled asceticism and preached against sexual depravity.

The Victorian Period—Open mention of anything remotely related to sex was a social taboo. It was inelegant to offer a lady a leg of chicken rather than one of the upper parts. Some librarians separated books by male authors from those written by women.

The Scientific Revolution—Sigmund Freud broke the bonds of Victorian repression. While Freud's work related to the psychological factors of sexual expression; Masters and Johnson scientifically studied the physiology of sexual activity.

Source: Dickes, Robert. Adult Sexuality, Historical & Cultural Perspectives. In *Understanding Human Behavior in Health and Illness*: 2nd edition, ed. R.C. Simons & H. Pardes. Baltimore: Williams & Wilkins, 1981.

What Are Some Medications
That Cause Sexual Dysfunction?

A large number of drugs can cause intermittent sexual dysfunction by acting either to interfere with the function of the sexual organs or by decreasing sexual desire. Some of the more common drugs that interfere with sexual function include alcohol, sedative-hypnotics, morphine, codeine, estrogens, cortisone, antihistamines, most "cold" preparations, and many antihypertension medications.

How Can You Tell If an Emotional Problem
Is Causing Sexual Difficulties?

A situational pattern of sexual dysfunction generally indicates an emotional problem. For example, a man who experiences impotence when attempting sexual intercourse with his wife, but who has consistent erections during the night or early in the morning, usually has an emotional conflict as the source of the impotence.

What Are Some Emotional Causes of Sexual Dysfunction?

Anxiety is probably the most common cause of sexual dysfunction in the male. Fear of failure (called *performance anxiety*) is probably the most prevalent cause of impotence and is discussed

---

TWO FAMOUS PEOPLE WHO SUFFERED EMOTIONAL CONSEQUENCES FROM SYPHILIS

Guy de Maupassant—French writer of short stories and great lover who developed delusions and hallucinations from syphilis of the brain. He felt that an imaginary creature, the Horla, was trying to kill him. In an attempt to escape the Horla, de Maupassant set fire to his house and later tried to commit suicide by cutting his throat.

Henry VIII—His wenching led to destroyed brain cells from syphilis. The cultured, handsome, and accomplished young prince became increasingly confused and belligerent. He died fat, ugly, demented, and impotent.

---

in greater detail later. Other individuals have a fear of sexuality because of sexual misinformation. Others feel guilty about their sexuality; the guilt interferes with normal sexual functioning. Failure of communication is another prime source of sexual dysfunction. Occasionally anger, sometimes hidden, toward the partner can interfere with sexual functioning. Sexual acrobatics or trying to outperform everyone else can interfere with the pleasure of the sexual experience and produce sexual problems.

Can Masturbation Cause Problems?

Some people still believe that masturbation causes physical and mental illness. Masturbation is practiced to some extent by almost all children and by many adults. The act is considered abnormal only if performed in a compulsive manner several times a day for long periods—a sign of obsessive anxiety, psychosis, mental retardation, or an underlying resentment toward parents. Occasionally parents, either because of misconceptions or as an attempt to discourage the child, tell the child that masturbation will lead to insanity or stunted growth. This statement is not true. On the contrary, massive attempts to thwart the masturbatory act may interfere with the child's healthy personality development by causing the child to feel guilty about a universal process.

Isn't the Public Well Enough Informed About Sexual Problems?

Over half a million teenage pregnancies, a quarter of a million of which terminate in abortion, show that young people are *not* well informed concerning sexual matters. In addition, 10 million Americans contract venereal disease each year—400,000 are afflicted by syphilis, 3 million by gonorrhea, and 6.5 million by some other form of sexually transmitted disease—indicating the need for more extensive sexual education.

Does Penis Size Affect Sexual Functioning?

Some men believe that penis size is related to sexual adequacy. Most women contend, however, that sexual satisfaction is related to quality rather than quantity. Some women fear that penetration by an extra-large penis can cause pain. Studies have shown, however, that with sexual excitement the vagina has an almost limitless capacity for accommodation.

Do Men Have a Greater Sexual Need Than Women?

No. The belief that men have greater sexual needs than women is quickly being challenged in the age of sexual revolution.

Is a Simultaneous Orgasm Necessary for Sexual Pleasure?

No. Simultaneous orgasms are found with regularity only in romantic novels and sex manuals.

Will Aging Interfere with My Ability to Perform Sexually?

The notion that old age will be sexless has been proven false in study after study. Provided that they are healthy, elderly people are capable of an active sex life into their 80s and 90s. Sexual performance may be slowed somewhat with aging, but sexual pleasure and capacity remain intact.

What Is a Sexual Deviation?

Sexual deviation refers to atypical sexual behavior that fails to conform to prevailing social patterns. Generally, sexual deviation develops as a learned response in early childhood. Treatment most commonly involves behavior modification techniques—aversion therapy, desensitizations, and counter-conditioning—but success rates are low.

Is Homosexuality a Sexual Deviation?

Homosexuality is considered a psychiatric disorder only in those people who are disturbed by their own deviant sexual orientation. According to Kinsey, approximately 37 percent of males and 13 percent of females have had at least one homosexual experience to the point of orgasm. Female homosexuality is known as lesbianism.

What Is Pedophilia?

Pedophilia is sexual activity by an adult with a child. This deviation reflects psychosocial immaturity. The adult is generally afraid of sex with someone his or her own age and seeks out a child because he or she feels more secure with a child. The prevalence of the disorder is unknown, but the disorder constitutes a significant proportion of criminal sexual acts.

What Is Fetishism?

Fetishism is the use of inanimate objects, such as clothing, as a method of producing sexual excitement. It is related to fear of rejection by members of the opposite sex.

What Is Transvestism?

Transvestism is cross-dressing by a heterosexual male. Transvestism is a learned response. In childhood those individuals were encouraged to dress in feminine attire by females in the family who thought it cute.

What Is Zoophilia?

Zoophilia is sexual gratification through contact with an animal. It is extremely rare.

What Is Exhibitionism?

Exhibitionism is repetitive exposure of the genitals to an unsuspecting stranger for the purpose of sexual excitement. This disorder constituted one-third of all charges in apprehended sex offenders. Commonly possessing strong bonds to an overly protective mother, exhibitionists demonstrate shyness, immaturity, and a strong need to demonstrate masculinity and potency.

What Is Voyeurism?

Voyeurism—obtaining sexual gratification from looking at the genital or sexual behavior of others—is to be distinguished from sexual excitement from visual stimulation that may be a prelude to normal sexual activity. Voyeurs, feeling shy and inadequate in heterosexual relationships, substitute looking for normal sexual contact.

What Is Sexual Masochism?

Sexual masochism—sexual gratification obtained through suffering physical or emotional pain—results from earlier experiences associating pain with sexual pleasure. For example, a young adolescent was having his fractured arm set without anesthesia. He was comforted by the physician's attractive nurse. She caressed him and held him tightly against her breasts. As a result, the adolescent experienced a powerful combination of pain and sexual stimulation, which led to masochistic behavior in later sexual relations.

What Is Sexual Sadism?

Sexual sadism—sexual gratification obtained through inflicting physical or emotional pain on others—may be a learned response in which an individual, while inflicting pain on another person, experiences unexpected sexual excitement. In other cases, sadistic behavior may arouse sexual excitement in otherwise timid, undersexed individuals. Severe forms of sadistic sexual behavior may be associated with schizophrenia.

What Is Transsexualism?

Transsexualism—a reversal of gender identity and the wish for surgical transformation in order to live as a member of the opposite sex—develops in the context of a disturbed parent-child relationship in early life.

What Are Some Sexual Problems That Can Be Treated?

Since the pioneering research by Masters and Johnson, many sexual clinics have been established for the treatment of sexual problems. Common sexual difficulties that can be treated include premature ejaculation, impotence, retarded ejaculation, painful intercourse, and frigidity.

How Is Premature Ejaculation Treated?

Technically, the diagnosis of premature ejaculation can be made if a man reaches orgasm before his wife more than half the time. In more practical terms, however, premature ejaculation consists of sexual dissatisfaction resulting from early male orgasm. There have been many attempts to explain this phenomenon: some authorities believe that premature ejaculation can be a learned response; others attribute it to fear, guilt, or hostility. Whatever the cause, the condition is probably the most common sexual dysfunction found in men. More importantly, the disorder is relatively easy to treat.

A middle-aged couple reported to a sexual dysfunction clinic with the main complaint of the husband's premature ejaculation. During the interview, it became apparent that the wife was extremely dominating. She accused her husband of being weak and ineffectual, and bemoaned the fact that she had not married a "real man." The interviewers thought the husband's premature ejaculation was a response to his wife's domination. His premature ejaculation was the only way he could get even. This case was a complex situation that called for individual psychotherapy for both husband and wife, as well as training in sex therapy techniques. The couple's sexual dysfunction was relatively easy to alleviate using the technique discussed as follows, but several years of intensive therapy was needed to help them resolve their personality differences.

The "squeeze technique" involves manual stimulation of the penis by the woman until imminent ejaculation, at which time the woman applies pressure on the penis. A firm squeeze causes the penis to lose 30 to 40 percent of its volume and prevents ejaculation. This procedure is repeated until stimulation can be maintained without ejaculation for 15 to 20 minutes. Intercourse is then practiced with the woman in the superior position (above the man). When ejaculation seems imminent, the penis is withdrawn and the squeeze applied. Masters and Johnson report a failure of only 2 percent in patients using this technique.

How Is Retarded Ejaculation Treated?

Retarded ejaculation, defined as a psychological block to ejaculation when the penis is in the vagina, most commonly results from moral inhibition or fear of causing pregnancy. This disorder can be treated by having the woman manually stimulate the male until ejaculation is inevitable, when the penis is quickly inserted into the vagina where ejaculation occurs. Generally a single intravaginal ejaculation is sufficient to break the block.

A 28-year-old married male reported to the sexual dysfunction clinic with the complaint of being unable to ejaculate with sexual intercourse. The patient's problem had begun six months before his visit to the clinic when he had attended a convention in another city. At that time, the patient attempted intercourse with a prostitute but was unable to ejaculate. On returning home, the patient still had the problem. Short-term psychotherapy relieved the patient's guilt, and within a few weeks he resumed normal sexual intercourse with his wife.

How Can Impotence Be Treated?

Impotence—defined as the male's inability to maintain a sufficient erection to complete sexual intercourse—may result from fear of the female genitals, moral prohibition, or physiological conditions, but more commonly impotence results from a fear of failure. For example, an intoxicated male attempting to have intercourse may be unable to maintain an erection, precipitating a performance anxiety. In other words, the man becomes afraid that he will not be able to perform sexually. With his next attempt at intercourse, his fear of failure prevents the ability to maintain an erection. Subsequent failures create additional anxiety. Soon the male becomes more concerned about his ability to perform rather than with his sexual pleasure. Many cases at sexual dysfunction clinics read like the following one.

A 36-year-old white man complained of impotence of five years duration. The patient clearly remembered the precipitating event. Returning home intoxicated late one night, he became incensed when his wife refused to cook him dinner. He beat her severely and attempted to rape her but could not achieve an erection. Since that time, although he and his wife have reconciled their differences, he has remained impotent.

Performance anxiety can develop secondary to many conditions. Stress on the job can prevent the male from having an erection: occupational stress, the length of time after a heart attack, depression, and financial worries can all produce the inability to maintain an erection. This transient inability to maintain an erection can develop into performance anxiety if the man doesn't understand that almost all men have difficulty maintaining an erection during certain stressful situations.

The first step in overcoming impotence is understanding that the most common cause is performance anxiety. Next, the sexual partners need to focus more on having fun rather than concentrating on the man's attempt to maintain an erection. The couple should practice touching and being touched. Gentle caressing of the feet, legs, arms, and body proceeds to touching the genital areas and then manipulative play of the sexual organs until a moderate, nonthreatening level of arousal is reached. When an erection occurs, it is allowed to recede and then the cycle of touching is repeated until erection again occurs. Proceeding through several arousal-resolution cycles builds confidence in the ability to maintain an erection. After the man has been able to produce an erection several times, the woman then assumes the kneeling superior position and the penis is inserted into the vagina. Gradually thrusting is begun, eventually leading to complete sexual activity and ejaculation. If the man loses his erection during intercourse, the cycle is repeated beginning with gentle caressing. It generally takes a couple of weeks of romance and gentle caressing before the performance anxiety can be overcome.

How Is Painful Intercourse Treated?

Painful intercourse (dyspareunia) can be caused by local infection of the sexual organs or genital tract, surgical scars, vaginal ulcerations, endometriosis, or tumors of the genital organs. If physical causes of painful intercourse have been ruled out, the problem is most often due to lack of vaginal lubrication resulting from inadequate sexual excitement. Treatment consists of improving sexual communication between the partners and of gentle caressing and foreplay before intercourse, as discussed in the section on impotence.

For example, after the birth of her first child, a 25-year-old woman reported to the sexual dysfunction clinic complaining of painful intercourse. A pelvic examination showed entirely normal functioning, without evidence of trauma or vaginal ulcerations. The patient reported that whenever she had sex with her husband, she remembered the painful birth of her son. This memory made her tense and took away her desire for sexual intercourse. Treatment consisted of helping the patient deal with her ambivalence concerning the possibility of having another child, as well as helping her husband to improve his love-making techniques.

What Is Frigidity?

Frigidity—the female's inability to reach orgasm during sexual intercourse—can be caused by several conditions: inadequate sexual techniques by the male partner, fear of failure, strict religious views, early family conflicts, hostility toward men, and double standards of sexual morality. Therapy consists of improving communication between the partners and the sexual exercises, as discussed in the section on impotence. Some individuals with severe sexual inhibitions may benefit from intensive psychotherapy.

A 27-year-old woman reported to the sexual dysfunction clinic with the complaint of "frigidity." The patient reported that she had always been popular. She had been head cheerleader in high school and homecoming queen in college, and was currently secretary of her garden club. From the many men that she had dated, she finally chose to marry a handsome, athletic banker, whom she thought could give her security and happiness. Soon after their marriage, however, the couple began to fight. Their arguments primarily centered on what the patient regarded as "excessive sexual demands" and what the husband regarded as his wife's lack of interest. Both individuals were, in part, correct. The husband was demanding and boorish with his sexual advances; the wife was inwardly hostile toward men. Therapy involved helping the husband and wife become more sensitive toward members of the opposite sex, as well as improving communication between the husband and wife. As the personalities of both individuals became more flexible, they were able to benefit from the sexual exercises discussed in the section on impotence.

Who Benefits From Sexual Therapy?

Many sexual problems can be overcome without formal treatment. Most cases of performance anxiety and frigidity remit with sexual education. Once the couple understands the cause of the problem and begins to get some romance back into their lives, sexual pleasure returns. There are many good books written to help individuals with sexual problems. The one that I generally recommend to my patients is the *Joy of Sex*, By Alex Comfort, M.D. A more technical book, but still good for the general public, is *The New Sex Therapy: Active Treatment of Sexual Dysfunction*, by Helene Singer Kaplan, M.D., Ph.D. Masters and Johnson's books *Human Sexual Response* and *Human Sexual Inadequacy* are also excellent reference sources. Couples who continue to have sexual problems after reading and practicing the recommended techniques would benefit from therapy at a sexual clinic.

Chapter 12
Sleep Problems
(To Sleep, Perchance to Dream)

Between 12 and 15 percent of the U.S. population—about 30 million people—have sleep complaints. Two major surveys found sleep disturbance to be second only to anxiety among mental symptoms. Clearly, sleep disturbance is a major health problem, but only in the last two decades has sleep research allowed a beginning knowledge of sleep disorders. This chapter reports some of the exciting findings in sleep research and discusses some of the common problems of sleep.

What Is Normal Sleep?

Until the early 1950s, little was known about sleep. Then Nathaniel Kleitman discovered that rapid eye movements of the sleeping person were associated both with dreaming and brain wave changes. This discovery launched a surge of remarkable research. Since that time, dozens of sleep research centers have documented the basic pattern of sleep.

During a typical night, the individual moves from the awake state into deeper and deeper sleep. During periods of restful sleep, the heart rate, blood pressure, and respiratory rate diminish, and the brain wave patterns slow rhythmically. About every 90 minutes throughout the night, this peaceful rest is interrupted by increased brain wave frequency, heart rate, and respiratory rate; by elevated blood pressure; and by more body movements. It is during this time that dreaming occurs. During dreaming, the eyes of the sleeping individual dart about rapidly behind closed lids—hence the term *rapid eye movement* (REM) *sleep.*

ABRAHAM LINCOLN'S CATAFALQUE DREAM

A few days prior to his assassination Lincoln recounted the following dream:

"About ten days ago I retired very late. I had been up waiting for important dispatches from the front. I could not have been long in bed when I fell into a slumber, for I was weary. I soon began to dream. There seemed to be a death-like stillness about me. Then I heard subdued sobs, as if a number of people were weeping. I thought I left my bed and wandered downstairs. There the silence was broken by the same pitiful sobbing, but the mourners were invisible. I went from room to room; no living person was in sight, but the sounds of distress met me as I passed along. It was light in all the rooms; every object was familiar to me; but where were all the people who were grieving as if their hearts would break? I was puzzled and alarmed. What could be the meaning of all this? Determined to find the cause of a state of things so mysterious and so shocking, I kept on until I arrived at the East Room, which I entered. There I met with a sickening surprise. Before me was a catafalque, on which rested a corpse wrapped in funeral vestments. Around it were stationed soldiers who were acting as guards; and there was a throng of others weeping pitifully. 'Who is dead in the White House?' I demanded of one of the soldiers. 'The President,' was his answer; 'he was killed by an assassin!' Then came a loud burst of grief from the crowd."

Source: Oates, Stephen B: *With Malice Toward None—The Life of Abraham Lincoln.* New York: Harper and Row, 1977, pp. 425–426.

Does Everyone Dream?

Everyone dreams. Some people just don't remember their dreams. Research laboratories have documented that approximately one-fourth of sleeping time is spent in dream sleep. Waking in the middle of a dream allows an individual to remember dreams more clearly. Thus, an individual who is depressed or anxious may report more dreams because he or she is probably waking up more during the middle of the night.

How Can Dreams Be Understood?

As Dr. Elliott Hammett at the Durham Veterans Administration Medical Center likes to tell his patients, dreams can be thought of as a story with a beginning, middle, and end. Each dream offers an intuitive solution to a current real-life problem. The dreamer's job is to understand the dream's problem and the solution offered by the dream. For example:

A surgeon dreamed he was a robot. As the dream progressed he became more and more mechanical; finally he was thrown on a junk heap by his partner. The surgeon had been having problems with elbow pain. He was concerned that the pain would cause him to be unable to work and would take away his freedom (hence the dream of becoming a robot and eventually being discarded). The surgeon's solution to the problem in the dream was to seek treatment for his elbow pain.

Insomnia

What Is the Most Common Cause of Insomnia?

Probably the most common cause of insomnia is a conditioned sleep disturbance. After a few weeks of poor sleep, insomnia can develop into a conditioned response that may persist for decades. For example, you may develop difficulty falling asleep because of a transient stressful situation and may quickly learn to associate the simple process of going to bed and turning off the light with frustration and sleeplessness. You then take a sedative, but the effects of the sedative soon fail, which perpetuates the frustration-insomnia cycle, prompts a search for another pill, and so on.

Unfortunately, you may believe (and be able to convince your physician) that your insomnia can be easily treated with a sedative medication. Sedatives may work for one or two weeks, but eventually they will cause serious trouble. Barbiturates suppress dream sleep and lead to drug dependence and tolerance, so that you will need to take increasing doses to get to sleep. Eventually you will be unable to sleep despite high doses of sedatives. Not only is there a danger that you may take an overdose of sedatives in an attempt to get to sleep, but the sedatives decrease

FAMOUS INSOMNIACS

Ernest Hemingway—For a period of 42 days, while a correspondent during World War II, slept only two and one half hours a night.

Howard Hughes—The eccentric millionaire couldn't sleep so he purchased a TV station to entertain himself with old movies throughout the night.

Roman Poet Horace (65–8 B.C.)—Wrote the classic line: "I cannot sleep a wink."

Thomas Edison—Known for his inexhaustible tenacity, Edison, on one occasion, worked continuously for five days with no rest. Edison rarely slept more than five hours a night.

Irving Berlin—Popular song writer who constantly complained of not getting enough sleep. One morning while lamenting about his lack of sleep the previous night, he was told that there had been a fire in his hotel. Although the blaze had been nearby with fire engines and noise all around, Berlin never heard a thing, he was sleeping so soundly.

Hugh Hefner—The Playboy magnate works, thinks, makes love, and sleeps in his tremendous round bed, which he uses as a desk. Hefner, who wears pajamas most of the time, has been known to work for 36–48 hours nonstop before drifting off to sleep on his "desk."

dream sleep. This decrease of dream sleep produces irritability, anxiety, and depression.

For example, Mr. Conners, a 56-year-old executive, entered my office requesting a refill of Placidyl, which he had been taking since his promotion a year and a half ago. At that time Conners was excited about his new position, which demanded considerable decision making and independence. Conners thrived on this responsibility, but, at the same time, he couldn't shut off his executive engine at night. The company physician had given him a prescription for 100 mg of Placidyl, which helped temporarily. But Conners eventually required increasing amounts to get the rest he felt he needed. Rather quickly he had increased the nighttime dose to 500 mg; occasionally he would take as much as 1500 mg of Placidyl—without sleeping well.

Treatment was not as difficult as I had imagined it might have been. Conners listened carefully to what I had to say and followed instructions explicitly. He said he would do anything to get some sleep: he was tired of the nightmares he had when he did fall asleep, and he felt so groggy during the day he could not function well.

The first task was to gradually decrease the Placidyl dosage. To prevent seizures from drug withdrawal, Placidyl was discontinued slowly over the course of three weeks. Next I gave Mr. Conners the following prescription:

1. Divert your attention from your business activity an hour before going to bed by reading a novel, preferably a dull one.
2. Go to bed only when you feel sleepy, and if you fail to go to sleep in five to ten minutes, get out of bed and return only when sleepiness recurrs.
3. Set your alarm clock for six o'clock each morning and no matter how sleepy or tired you are, get up at this time.
4. Do not take daytime naps.
5. Don't watch TV or read *in* bed.

Conners followed this prescription faithfully, and within a week after stopping the Placidyl, he was sleeping soundly.

What About Early Morning Insomnia?

Waking in the middle of the night can also be a conditioned response. If you have this problem, getting out of bed on awakening and returning only when sleepy may break this pattern. The most common cause of waking in the middle of the night or early morning awakening is depression. If this early morning awakening persists, see your physician. He or she will probably be able to help you by prescribing a tricyclic antidepressant medication.

Can Drugs Cause Insomnia?

If you take a sedative or minor tranquilizers, you will initially experience an increase in sleep, but within a couple of weeks your total sleep time will decline, escalating the need for higher doses of the sedative medication. If you stop the medication abruptly, sleep will be even more disturbed, with an increase in nightmares and unpleasant dreams.

For example, a 29-year-old editor complained of nightmares. She would frequently dream that she had fallen into a vat of red ink; this red ink would turn to blood and she would awake screaming. She revealed that she had been taking large quantities of Seconal at bedtime. After a few weeks on Seconal, instead of sleeping better she experienced restlessness and nightmares.

You may be tempted to go from doctor to doctor in the hopes of finding the magical pill that will help you sleep. This strong belief in medication puts pressure on doctors to prescribe a medication that they realize will not help in the long run. I hope that if you are an insomniac, you will give up your search for the magic pill and will instead follow the prescription I gave earlier in this chapter. And remember: if you have been on sedatives for a long period of time, you need to gradually withdraw the medication. If sedatives are not withdrawn gradually, seizures and other disturbing symptoms will occur.

For example, Mrs. Davis, a 28-year-old housewife, was seen in consultation because of a sudden onset of seizures that could not be explained. The initial fear that Mrs. Davis had a brain tumor had been ruled out. Now her physicians considered she might have a conversion disorder with psychological symptoms causing her symptoms. A detailed history revealed that the patient had been taking increasing doses of the sedative Nembutal for several months. When she had stopped the medication abruptly, she had begun to have withdrawal seizures.

Does Alcohol Produce Sleep Problems?

You bet. Many people use alcohol as a sedative because after a couple of drinks it produces relaxation, peaceful feelings, and sleepiness. Unfortunately, the effects of alcohol wear off in three or four hours, and a rebound hyperalertness is produced. This explains why after drinking alcohol you can sleep soundly for a few hours and then wake up in the middle of the night and can't go back to sleep. Alcohol withdrawal produces difficulty going to sleep, an increase of dream sleep (usually nightmares), and frequent awakenings during the night. Here's another important tip: insomnia and sleep disturbance may persist as long as six months after withdrawal from alcohol if you have been a heavy drinker.

For example, Paul, a 42-year-old textile sales representative, complained that when he went on sales trips he could only get a few hours' sleep. He reported that he drifted off to sleep without any difficulty, but a few hours later he would awaken with anxiety and agitation and be unable to return to sleep. While at home, he slept soundly. A detailed interview revealed that Paul drank heavily when on the road; at home he had no more than two drinks nightly, and often did not drink at all. Cutting back on his drinking while traveling alleviated Paul's sleep disturbance.

Can Coffee Cause Insomnia?

Caffeine is probably the most overlooked cause of insomnia. Caffein causes a decline in total sleep time, decreased deep sleep, and a decrease in dream sleep. The poor sleep at night results in daytime grogginess and a tendency to drink more and more coffee during the day, increasing the vicious cycle. If you are having difficulty sleeping, always consider your caffeine intake. Caffeine is found in a variety of preparations:

Freshed brewed coffee, 125 mg per cup
Instant coffee, 90 mg per cup
Colas, 50 mg per 8 oz.
Fresh brewed tea, 45 mg per cup
Decaffeinated coffee, 2 mg per cup

Count the number of beverages you drink a day. If you are a heavy coffee or cola drinker, begin to keep a chart of your consumption. Reduce your consumption by one cup or one cola every third day until you are below two cups or two colas daily. If you get to three or four cups and can't go any further, congratulations anyway—four cups of coffee is much better than ten cups or so a day.

For example, Rose, a 26-year-old secretary, complained of daytime grogginess and poor sleep at night. She reported that she could hardly keep her eyes open while typing during the day; she attributed this sluggishness to the boring reports that she typed. While the reports that she typed were indeed boring, her main sleep problem was a high coffee intake. She drank three cups of coffee for breakfast, a couple of cups of coffee during the morning and afternoon breaks, and one or two cups of coffee with lunch. In addition, she was constantly sipping from a cup of coffee next to her typing stand, and she would supplement her caffeine intake with several cola drinks during the day. The stimulus she received from the caffeine during the day prevented her from sleeping well at night, while the boring reports that she typed during the day induced her to drink more and more coffee. After Rose realized the cause of her grogginess, she began to reduce her consumption, methodically using a chart to help her. For one week she documented the cups of coffee she drank. She then reduced this amount by eliminating one cup of coffee every third day until she was down to one cup of coffee in the morning and one cup for each break period during the day.

Her grogginess abated and her sleep at night improved. The reports remained boring.

Review the list of caffeine contents. It is extremely important. Caffeine is a drug that can cause sleep disturbance, and it is often the cause of generalized anxiety. If you are anxious and can't find the reason, always think about how much coffee you've been drinking.

What Causes Difficulty in Waking Up?

If you have difficulty falling asleep and then once asleep are exceedingly difficult to wake up, you may have what is known as a *phase-lag syndrome.* In other words, your sleep pattern may be out of synch. If you have this condition, you should adhere to a strict 24-hour cycle of work, play, and sleep in an attempt to restore the normal sleep rhythm. To get your sleep pattern back in rhythm, you should arise early in the morning—no matter how sleepy—and avoid naps. By arising early in the morning—say, 7 A.M.—you will gradually train yourself to be able to go to sleep earlier in the evening. By the way, trying to go to sleep earlier at night just won't work; you'll just toss and turn until your biological clock tells you it is time to go to sleep. To repeat myself, you must wake up early in the morning to overcome this problem. Buy a fire whistle or get someone to drag you out of the bed, but get up early.

For example, Blake, a 21-year-old college student, complained that he slept through his early morning classes. Often he would not hear the alarm clock. When he did, he would groggily turn it off, roll over, and go back to sleep. Blake's sleep patterns were reinforced by his weekend activities. Over the weekends, he would frequently party until 3 and 4 A.M., falling into bed exhausted and not awakening until around noon. After a detailed history and physical examination revealed no emotional or physical abnormalities, Blake was diagnosed as having a phase-lag syndrome. He was instructed to get out of bed, no matter what, every morning at 7 A.M. For the first few weeks, they would literally drag him out of bed and push him into the shower. Soon his sleep patterns converted to a normal expected time for his age group: 11 P.M. to 7 A.M.

What Causes Heavy Snoring?

Some people have a floppy trachea (windpipe). During sleep the windpipe gets obstructed and breathing stops, resulting in what is known as *sleep apnea* ("without breath"). The individual struggles to overcome this obstruction, thrashing about in bed and snoring loudly. Interestingly the individual, who for some reason is almost always a male, is usually unaware of the breathing difficulty. His wife, however, definitely knows about it. Often the snoring is so loud the wife moves to another room so that at least she can get some sleep. In addition to loud snoring and violent thrashing in the bed, as many as 600–800 episodes of cessation of breathing may occur during the night. As you may imagine, sleep apnea can cause numerous problems with oxygenation of the blood. Irregular heartbeat and high blood pressure is also common.

Don't equate loud snoring alone with sleep apnea. To have sleep apnea, the individual must have long pauses in breathing during the night. If, however, you have a husband that does snore exceedingly loud, complains of feeling groggy on awakening, and has no pep and energy during the day, then have him see his physician. If your husband does have sleep apnea, he will need a surgical procedure called a *tracheotomy*, at which time a small cut is made in the trachea and an apparatus is inserted to keep the windpipe open. A tracheotomy prevents heart disease and high blood pressure associated with sleep apnea, but it shouldn't be performed until a thorough evaluation is done at a sleep evaluation center.

For example, Mr. Mullins, a 67-year-old obese retired hardware store owner, reported to the sleep evaluation clinic with the complaint that his grandchildren refused to travel with him. Mr. Mullins enjoyed going on cross-country trips in his mobile home with his wife and grandchildren. After their first trip, the grandchildren refused to go again: they said their grandfather snored too loudly. His wife said that Mr. Mullins did snore loudly, but she learned to sleep through it. Associated with this snoring were long pauses in his breathing during the night and violent thrashing in the bed. Mr. Mullins said he felt groggy during the day and he had no pep or energy, but felt that this was due to "old age". Physical examination revealed an irregular heart rhythm and high blood pressure. A detailed study in the sleep laboratory documented that Mr. Mullins had sleep apnea. Following a tracheotomy, his hypertension and irregular heartbeat returned to normal. At last report Mr. Mullins was going on a trip to Red River, New Mexico, with his wife and grandchildren.

My Husband Thrashes Around in Bed While Asleep. Is This Normal?

Everybody moves at night when they are sleeping. There are, however, some individuals who move around much more than normally accepted. Although the afflicted individual is unaware of his abnormal movements, the bed partner can usually describe the disturbance in full detail. This abnormal movement is characterized by jerks that last for a few seconds and occur in episodes that last for a few minutes to more than an hour. These jerks are so violent that the bed covers often come off and the bed shakes as if an earthquake had struck. This condition is known as nocturnal myoclonus (muscle jerks at night). Although we have a fancy name for this affliction, we don't really know what causes it and we have even more difficulty treating it. Valium sometimes seems to diminish the severity of the jerks.

A condition that is closely related to nocturnal myoclonus is known as *restless legs syndrome*. This problem is marked by a disagreeable but rarely painful creeping sensation that occurs deep inside the calf and occasionally in the thighs and feet and causes an almost irresistible urge to move the legs. About a third of these patients have a family history of the disorder so that the condition is probably inherited. I have had some success in treating patients with restless legs by putting them on an exercise program coupled with the relaxation techniques described in the chapter on anxiety. Valium also seems to help some individuals with this condition.

My wife and I once went sailing with our neighbors Mark and Pam. Mark had mentioned that he would like us to join them for a long weekend sailing trip down a part of the intercoastal canal in North Carolina but he was concerned that he might keep us awake with his irregular sleep patterns. When falling off into sleep, he would experience an irresistible urge to move his legs. He would have a bothersome creeping sensation inside the calf of his legs, which made him thrash about, kicking his covers off the bed. His sleep disturbance was so bad that his wife refused to share the same bed with him. I asked about his family: he said that his mother had the same problem and that his brother was beginning to show signs of the problem. In brief, I placed my friend on a daily exercise program and taught him the relaxation response (Chapter 3). His symptoms diminished, and everyone was happy. His wife returned to their bed, my friend had an unusual syndrome he could talk about at cocktail parties, and my reputation as an astute clinician was enhanced.

What Causes Excessive Sleepiness During the Day?

The most common causes of excessive daytime sleepiness are narcolepsy, sleep apnea, and drug dependency. As you can imagine, individuals with sleep apnea have such a restless sleep during the night that they are groggy during the day. If I see someone in the office who complains of daytime grogginess and has no history of drug abuse, the first question I ask is "Does your wife report that you snore a lot?" If the answer is yes, I suspect sleep apnea. Of course, I also ask questions to make certain that the patient doesn't have narcolepsy.

What Is Narcolepsy?

Narcolepsy is characterized by profound sleep attacks and a sudden paralysis of the muscles. Whenever an individual with narcolepsy is presented with an emotional situation, whether it be laughter, joy, fear, or anger, he or she becomes weak and falls down. At other times, the individual has an irresistible urge to sleep.

Narcolepsy is an interesting disease. Research centers have found that the narcoleptic attacks are brought on by sudden dream (REM) sleep. In other words, individuals with narcolepsy have a defect in their brain wave patterns so that the brain goes into dreaming and sleeping episodes spontaneously. The diagnosis of narcolepsy can easily be made in the sleep laboratory by monitoring the sleep patterns.

Narcolepsy is fairly common (there are four cases for every 10,000 people), is found equally in both sexes, and is probably an inherited disease. Narcolepsy can be fairly well treated with a combination of a tricyclic antidepressant such as imipramine (the imipramine decreases the dream attacks) and amphetamine (amphetamine decreases the sleep attacks).

Hank, a vigorous truckdriver, lost his job because, when driving, he had an irresistible impulse to pull over to the side of the road and sleep. In addition, when his friends learned that he was easily startled, they took pleasure in jumping out from behind doors, saying, "Boo", and watching the big truckdriver fall to the floor. Studies in the sleep laboratory confirmed the clinical impression of narcolepsy. After Hank was placed on a combination of imipramine and amphetamine, he was able to return to work and friends no longer had fun startling him.

Drugs Again?

Yes, drugs again. I can't overemphasize the seriousness of drugs in causing sleep disturbance. Excessive sleepiness can be caused by withdrawal from caffeine (coffee and colas). Also, because caffeine interferes with sleep at night, it causes a rebound increase in sleepiness during the day, which results in a need to take a stimulant to stay awake. A vicious cycle develops.

Don't forget the sedatives. They can cause you to be groggy and sleepy during the day and get you to drink more coffee, which causes you to have difficulty going to sleep, which causes you to take more sedatives, which causes you to drink more coffee, and so on. Again, probably one of the worst things that you can do is ask your doctor for a sedative. Sedatives almost always end up causing you problems.

What Can I Do About Jet Lag?

Individuals who fly around in jet airplanes a lot have trouble regulating their sleep patterns, resulting from rapid change of multiple time zones. These changes in time zones cause the individual to attempt to continue sleeping and waking on the schedule of his or her usual environment. This attempt to continue sleeping on the old clock results in marked sleepiness during the wake period and insomnia during the sleep period. Fortunately, the disturbance generally remits after two days in the new location. Eastward flights upset the sleep pattern more severely than westward flights. There is not much you can do about "jet lag" except wait it out. However, you can really mess yourself up by taking naps during the day in an attempt to make up for lost sleep.

I Go To Sleep Too Early and Awaken Too Early; What Can I Do?

It will do you no good to try to sleep later in the mornings. You will just toss and turn in bed and have a generally miserable time. The only way to overcome this problem, known as *advanced sleep phase syndrome*, is to force yourself to stay awake later in the evenings. If you are typically going to bed at 8 P.M., then gradually try to go to bed later. The first night try to stay up until 8:30, the second night stay up until 9, the third night up until 9:30, and so forth until you are going to bed around 11 P.M.

Other Sleep Problems

What Can I Do About My Child Who Sleepwalks?

Sleepwalking commonly occurs between the ages of 6 and 12, and most children grow out of it. The best thing that you can do for a sleepwalker is to make certain the walker does not hurt him- or herself. Sleepwalkers generally do not have full consciousness. Their coordination is poor and they are likely to stumble or lose balance despite open eyes.

Adults who have problems with sleepwalking generally have some personality disturbances or emotional conflict. If you are an adult sleepwalker, you would probably benefit from talking with a physician about your problems. He or she can refer you to a psychiatrist if necessary.

What Is Sleep Terror?

Sleep terror is a sudden arousal from the deepest sleep, associated with extreme panic. Typically, such people sit up in bed, looking frightened. Their pupils may be dilated; generally they are sweating profusely and their hearts thump rapidly. Although they have their eyes open, they are confused and dazed. Most frequently there is amnesia for the entire episode the next morning. This condition is thought to be due to a disturbance of deep sleep and is not associated with psychiatric illness. Probably the best treatment is the reassurance that the condition will gradually go away.

What Causes a Nightmare?

Nightmares usually occur in the middle or the later third of the night and are associated with less confusion than someone who is having a sleep terror. An individual with a nightmare usually recalls his or her dream. Frequent nightmares usually signify a stressful situation that can be cleared up with psychotherapy.

What About Bed Wetting?

Bed wetting has plagued people ever since we discovered the mattress. No one knows the cause of bed wetting, and no one has a definitive treatment. Bed wetting usually occurs during the first third of the night, during deep sleep. Those individuals who are deeper sleepers than the normal population have a tendency to wet their beds more frequently. Bed wetting, then, can be an indication of a mild sleep disturbance that will remit as the child gets older, or it can be an indication of an emotional stress. Almost invariably, bed wetting clears up with puberty.

About 10 percent of all children at the age of seven wet their beds. About 5 percent of children occasionally wet their beds at age 11 or 12. About 1 to 3 percent of men age 18–20 sometimes wet their beds. Most people who wet their beds beyond age 20 have a serious psychiatric disturbance.

Many treatments have been tried for bed wetting and many of them work. But they don't work universally. One technique might work for one child; another technique might work for another. Back in the frontier days, they used to throw kids in cold spring water to stop bed wetting. We now have electrically wired blankets that sound a loud alarm when a person begins to wet the bed.

I personally feel that more harm can be done by getting upset and overwhelmed about bed wetting than can be done by doing nothing. If a child does have a bed wetting problem, talk to him or her about what's going on at home or school. Perhaps the child is upset with a teacher or mad at a sister or is afraid that a parent is leaving him too much. Simply letting the child talk about fears and angers will help. You might try rewarding the child for not wetting the bed by giving him or her a quarter every time the bed is not wet or giving a star or some token of merit. This works occasionally.

If the child has some other symptoms—for example, difficulty at school, starting fires, running away from home, or throwing temper tantrums—then you would do well to talk with your physician about the problem. Very rarely children who wet their beds have some physical cause for wetting. Children who were toilet trained and appear to have good bladder control until age five or six and then begin wetting their beds are usually under some kind of emotional stress that has precipitated their bed wetting.

Remember, this condition always clears up. The best treatment is probably no treatment except talking with the child and helping him or her through the stresses of growing up.

For example, a nine-year-old boy had a three-year bed wetting problem until his parents finally learned to stop struggling with him. This delightful boy, apparently normal in all other respects, began wetting the bed when his father received a promotion and the family moved to another neighborhood. The enuresis upset the entire family. The father felt he was a weakling because he couldn't get his son to stop wetting the bed. The mother was angry because of the extra washing she had to do. The sister teased the boy about his problem. And the boy felt helpless, unloved, and frightened. The family tried all sorts of techniques, none of which worked. Monetary awards, a star-chart system for dry days, spankings, setting an alarm clock in the middle of the night, lectures, medication, and brief psychotherapy all eventually failed. Finally the entire family gave up. The bed wetting became "no big deal." The boy was expected, however, to change his own sheets. A few months after the family became reconciled that there was nothing they could do for the bed wetting, the enuresis stopped.

What Is a Sleep Evaluation Center?

Since the mid-1950s there has been a great interest in documenting normal sleep patterns and trying to find out the cause of sleep disturbances. A dozen or so sleep evaluation centers located in the large cities around the country have done some remarkable research and contributed tremendously to the treatment of sleep disturbances. Individuals that have puzzling sleep problems are often referred to one of these sleep evaluation centers.

If you go to one of the sleep centers, you will find a professional group of men and women who will ask you a series of detailed questions about your sleep disturbance and do a thorough neurological and medical examination. Following these procedures, you will be asked to complete a detailed sleep diary, at which time you record your sleep patterns over a two-week period. In addition, you will probably be asked to take a few psychological tests to round out the evaluation. By the time that this evaluation has been completed they will know you like a book, and they have only started.

Next you will go to what is known as the sleep laboratory. About one to two hours before your usual bedtime, they will prepare you for your sleep evaluation. Tiny wire electrodes and sensors will be applied to the scalp muscles and two tying electrodes will be applied to the outer eyelids to record eye movements. Next, two electrodes will be placed on your chin, and a couple of reference electrodes will be applied to the earlobes. In addition, a sensor that is used to measure the respiratory rate and air flow will be attached to your chest and electrocardiogram leads will be attached to measure your heart rate and rhythm. Finally, electrodes to measure the muscle tone will be placed over both legs.

They will then take you to a comfortable bedroom from where a technician in a separate room monitors the electronic leads. A continuous reading of your sleep patterns throughout the night is recorded and is studied the next day by the sleep team. Because of all the electrodes that are hooked up to you it might be necessary for you to spend two to three nights in a sleep laboratory before a proper reading can be obtained. Using these procedures, the sleep researchers will be able to pinpoint the particular sleep problem that you have.

Who Should Go to Sleep Evaluation Centers?

People who have puzzling sleep patterns should go to a sleep evaluation center. Also, people who are strongly suspected of having sleep apnea should go, because often correcting their sleep apnea requires a rather radical surgical procedure—and you don't want to be cut unless you are absolutely sure that it's necessary.

Chapter 13
Overwork
(The Forgotten Mental Illness)

Certain groups of individuals—business executives, lawyers, doctors, accountants, and housewives—are subject to what is known as the overwork (burnout) syndrome. This syndrome is characterized by the inability to maintain work performance and a decline in efficiency and initiative. Individuals with this syndrome typically become increasingly cynical about their work, and their negativistic attitude leads to a rigid, inflexible outlook. Although such people may spend increasing amounts of time at work, their productivity declines. Accompanying poor work performance is the inability to relax and enjoy recreational pursuits. This chapter discusses ways to be more productive at work while at the same time enjoying yourself more.

Are Certain Personalities Prone to the Overwork Syndrome?

To contrast those who suffer from overwork with those who thrive on work, Duke University psychiatrist John Rhoads studied 15 successful, effective, and healthy professionals who worked at least 60 hours weekly. The healthy professionals were able to recognize and respond promptly to evidence of fatigue: most responded by quitting work early or taking time off within one week of indications for the need for rest. All 15 of the healthy successful professionals had the ability to suppress thinking about problems until an appropriate time to deal with them. In addition, they engaged in regular exercise, avoided drug or alcohol abuse, scheduled and enjoyed vacations, had stable family situations, and possessed the ability to maintain friendships (see the boxed list).

Paradoxically, individuals who have the overwork syndrome almost never complain of being overworked. They complain instead that they are unable to work as well as they would like. Symptoms include fatigue, irritability, sleep disturbance, difficulty concentrating, depression, and physical complaints. Alcoholism and drug abuse may result in attempts at self-treatment.

DIFFERENCES BETWEEN PROFESSIONALS WHO THRIVE ON LONG WORK HOURS AND THOSE WHO EXPERIENCE OVERWORK SYNDROME

Professionals Who Thrive on Long Work Hours	Professionals Who Experience Overwork Syndrome
Ability to postpone thinking about problems	Rumination about work problems
Ability to respond promptly to evidence of fatigue	Lengthening workday to compensate for diminished productivity
Avoidance of drug and alcohol abuse	Use of alcohol or drugs as an escape from stress
Enjoyment of scheduled vacations	Tendency to postpone vacations
Stable domestic situation	Chaotic family life
Ability to maintain friendships	Loners
Engagement in regular exercise	Sedentary lifestyle
Varied interests outside work	Narrowed interests
Sense of humor	Inability to laugh at self

What Causes Overwork Syndrome?

Several factors are associated with the overwork syndrome. Some individuals attempt to overcome insecurity and fear of failure with work; others identify with a demanding, unpleasant parent, making that parent's demands a part of their own conscience. And for still others, overwork appears to be an attempt to make up for physical limitations such as poor health or aging. Almost all individuals who overwork (1) attempt to solve problems of aggression and guilt by excessive work done in a compulsive manner (found in the Type A personality), and (2) need approval.

How Does Need for Approval Cause Overwork?

Some people, seeking approval from almost everyone, may use work as a primary method to enhance self-esteem and gain social approval. Unable to say no to demands of others, these

---

WORKAHOLICS

James B. Duke—Founder of the American Tobacco Company, he was a fervent advocate of the gospel of work. He said: "No man ought to be allowed to live if he will not work." He followed his own advice, working 12 hours a day, six days a week.

Henry Ford—With single-minded purpose while developing a low priced motor car, he worked in a machine shop during the days and as a watch repairman in the evenings. During slack times he assisted his father in farming and lumbering. Work left Ford isolated and prejudiced. He said, "I don't like books; they mess up my mind. I wouldn't give five cents for all the art in the world. History is more or less bunk."

James Edgar Hoover—Without vices or a sense of humor, the "complete bureaucrat" through a spartan regimen and incessant hard work, devoted all his energies to the growth and enhancement of the FBI.

Gerald Ford—Reportedly worked 16 hours a day for 25 years of his life on the way to becoming 38th president of the United States.

Thomas Edison—Owner of 1,093 U.S. patents, the inventor rarely left his laboratory.

OH, YOU'RE JUST A HOUSEWIFE
OR
SCHEDULE OF A MAD HOUSEWIFE

6:15	Rise, dress
6:45	Wake children and husband
6:50	Fix breakfast
6:55	Wake children and husband again
7:15	Make lunches for children
7:30	Send children off to catch school bus
7:35	Get husband off to work
7:40	Take children to school after they miss bus
8:15	Return home—feed dog, wash dishes, make beds, put load of clothes in washer
8:40	Take dog to Vet
9:15	Volunteer work at school library
11:00	Return home; pick up trash that dog turned over
11:15	Prepare for Garden Club luncheon
12:00–2:00	Garden Club meets at house
2:00	Clean-up house mess Garden Club made
2:30	Pick-up children at school
3:00	Prepare snacks for children
3:15	Take son to basketball practice
3:45	Take daughter to dancing
4:00	Grocery shopping
4:15	Pick up son at basketball and take to orthodontist
5:00	Jog around parking lot while son is at orthodontists
5:30	Prepare supper
6:05	Husband calls (too late) to offer to take you out to dinner
6:30	Serve dinner
7:00	Wash dishes
7:30	Fold clothes
8:00	Help son with homework
8:30	Call teacher about daughter's missing homework assignment
9:00	Call guests for husband's dinner party
9:30	Read book for book club
10:30	Make invitations for son's birthday
11:00	Sew buttons on husband's shirt
11:30	Go to bed with headache

individuals cultivate few activities that bring pleasure or satisfaction to themselves. Because these individuals put excessive demands on themselves, they eventually become burdened by fatigue, which in turn leads to decreased effectiveness. Lengthening their work day to compensate for a diminished ability to produce efficiently, these individuals may become tired. Instead of taking a break, they eliminate exercise and recreational time in a desperate attempt to meet the demands placed on themselves, which only tends to further decrease their work capacity. Escalating frustration produces more frenetic activity, and the resulting vicious cycle tightens to produce symptoms of overwork.

The increased workload these individuals impose on themselves causes a deterioration in their marriage and family life, undermining their main source of non-work related support. Likewise, trying to crowd more work into an already overloaded schedule causes their employers or the public they serve to complain about the inefficiency of their work. Paradoxically, overwork—rather than resulting in approval—eventually causes the individual to be criticized by his or her family, colleagues, and employers.

For example, Dr. Lakein, a 38-year-old physician, was admitted to the psychiatric unit suffering from a severe depression. His father had abandoned the family when the boy was seven years old. As a young boy, Lakein felt responsible for his mother's happiness and did everything to please her, including going to medical school. This early childhood pattern continued throughout Dr. Lakein's life. He simply could not say no. He continued to take on ever increasing numbers of patients, even when his books were full. In addition, because he wanted to be thought of as a flexible, cheerful boss, he had difficulty managing his employees. For example, whenever they wanted to take time off, no matter how inconvenient, he would always let them. He also permitted his partners to take advantage of him—he was always available to take their calls, and he always allowed them first choice of vacations. Eventually Dr. Lakein's workload became so overwhelming that he could not please everyone, although his attempts to make everyone happy increased. His frenetic activity on the job decreased his ability to work effectively. He became more and more overwhelmed, eventually requiring hospitalization for a depression. Treatment consisted of helping Dr. Lakein understand his abnormal patterns of behavior and changing his activities to a more reasonable level.

How Does Type A Personality Contribute to Overwork?

The predilection to overwork is probably related to many of the qualities of the Type A personality discussed in Chapter 6. These highly competitive individuals are more preoccupied with quantity than quality, and are fascinated with the accumulation of material objects. They work fast and frenetically, but they may never be completely satisfied with themselves no matter how well they do.

How Can I Avoid Overwork?

Hans Selye, the foremost authority on stress, contends that a certain amount of stress is beneficial. Selye cites several examples of the healthy aspects of stress:

1. The benefits of strenuous exercise
2. The benefits of concentrated study
3. Work as a benefit outlet for aggression
4. The satisfaction one gets out of meeting a challenge
5. The physical or mental growth that occurs when a difficult task is accomplished

Selye goes on to say that there are individual differences in the amount of beneficial stress a person needs to assure security and happiness. However, when so much stress occurs that tasks cannot be successfully completed, frustration (distress) results. To prevent frustration, Selye offers these suggestions:

1. Strive for the optimal stress level that allows the successful completion of tasks. Don't put unattainable demands on yourself. When you finish a particular task, take a break before going on to another one.
2. When completion of one task becomes impossible, change activity. Stress on one system helps relax another. Most people cannot work efficiently at one task for longer than 90 minutes—if you haven't finished by then, go on to something else for a while.
3. Substitute demands made on the mind for demands on the body, and alternating cycles. The human body wears longest when it wears evenly.

How Can I Relax?

The unavoidable frustrations of work produce diffuse anxiety and physical tension that interfere with productivity and the pursuit of pleasure. The remedy for excess tension is the ability to relax as quickly and completely as possible. Although a number of techniques successfully produce relaxation, perhaps the most popular has been Transcendental Meditation. Transcendental Meditation has been discussed earlier in Chapter 3, as has another approach for overcoming tension, the relaxation response. If you are unduly tense, practice Transcendental Meditation or the relaxation response at least once or twice daily. Although you will be unable to eliminate many of the situations that produce tension and mental fatigue, practicing the relaxation response is an effective mechanism to counteract some of the harmful psychological and physiological effects of a stressful occupation.

A friend of mine recently told me how he had benefited from practicing the relaxation response. This friend, a hard-driving, energetic editor, did not seem to have enough time in the day to get all his work done. When he got to the office, he was flooded with telephone calls from writers, agents, book dealers, salespeople, and businesspeople. After the morning staff meeting, he tried to read and respond to his mail, but kept getting interrupted by members of the staff and more phone calls. He usually

had two or three drinks at lunch to help him relax. Unfortunately, these drinks made him sleepy in the afternoon so that
he could not get as much work done as he would have liked.
Driving through the traffic in the evening exhausted him and
made him tense. He had a few more drinks on arriving home
and was useless for the rest of the evening. Not until his boss
challenged him concerning his decreased productivity, did the
editor begin to change his habits. He decided to get to work an
hour before everybody else so that he could work on his staff
reports and mail without being interrupted. He then instructed
his secretary that he would take telephone calls for one hour in
the morning and would return calls at 4 P.M. each day. He did
not allow himself to be interrupted during the day. In addition,
the editor began practicing the relaxation response twice daily.
With daily practice of the relaxation response, he noticed no
need for alcohol; with better organization, he felt less tense and
got more work done.

How Can I Take Care of Myself?

In caring for others, we often neglect our personal needs for love,
warmth, and understanding. It makes no sense for you to be nice
to others but ignore your own needs. There are several ways to
avoid self-neglect:

1. Attend professional meetings for the social and supportive
   aspects, as much as for the learning component.
2. Share interests with people outside your own profession.
3. Share feelings with others.
4. Ask others for help.
5. Have periodic life-planning sessions with the family.
6. Consider entering into a business partnership.
7. Take stock in what really matters—faith, loved ones, freedom,
   and friends.
8. Study the methods for overcoming Type A personality (see
   Chapter 6).
9. Cultivate those traits that successful executives use to combat
   overwork (see the table presented earlier in this chapter).

To combat the tendency for overwork, then, requires that you be able to set limits for yourself. Combatting overwork does not mean that you cannot become the best that you are capable of being, but that you need to know your own limitations. By refusing tasks that are beyond your time allotment, you can avoid frustration and the escalating spiral leading to overwork.

Some factors that contribute to emotional problems are the lack of leisure time, the incessant seeking for approval, and Type A personality traits. The following methods can help reduce tension in work stress:

1. Exercise vigorously for at least 20 minutes each day (physical exercise produces relaxation, which combats mental frustration).
2. Practice relaxation response 10 to 20 minutes daily, which diminishes mental and physical tension.
3. Be aware of muscle tension throughout the day (stretch, breathe in deeply, and out slowly; relax).
4. Read for inspiration (the classics).
5. Laugh loudly (at yourself and with others).
6. Talk about ideas, events, and feelings (not about others).
7. Become completely involved in a hobby (diversion prevents fatigue).
8. Limit yourself to two alcoholic drinks daily (alcohol in moderation increases longevity).
9. No smoking (increases blood pressure and pulse).

If you follow these methods for reducing stress, you will cultivate a measure of equanimity that will enable you to take better care of your family, while at the same time preventing personal emotional problems.

Part III
Getting Help:
Psychotherapy and
Psychotropic Medication

Chapter 14
The Uses and Abuses
of Psychiatric Drugs
(Help But No Cure-All)

In the mid-1950s, before the use of psychiatric drugs, 500,000 patients were hospitalized in the United States for mental illness. By 1973, the number of hospitalized mental patients had fallen to 250,000, largely due to the use of psychoactive drugs. In addition to playing a major role in reducing the number of hospitalized mental patients, psychopharmacology (drug therapy) has revolutionized prescription practices. Approximately one in five adults in the United States receives a prescription for a psychoactive drug during the course of a year. Two-thirds of these drugs are for the minor tranquilizers or sedatives, 14 percent are for stimulants such as amphetamines, antipsychotic agents account for 10 percent, and antidepressants for 9 percent.

Over 128 million prescriptions are written for sedative-hypnotics or minor tranquilizers each year. These figures clearly indicate tranquilizer overusage in the United States.

Who's to blame? Both physician and patient. Physicians find writing a prescription for Valium much easier than arguing the patient out of his or her demands. Recently, I saw a patient who was on seven different drugs. I began to eliminate them. She said, "You will not take me off my Valium! If you do, I will get it elsewhere." Doubtless she could—I knew several Valium-pushing physicians in the community. I elected to keep her on the Valium, temporarily, in hopes of gradually helping her get off the drug. I'm still trying, without much success, to talk her out of her demands. What should I do? Stop the medication and have her go elsewhere? The crime was committed when she was placed on Valium—but I am perpetuating it.

This chapter, then, is dedicated to the Valium lady. Maybe by reading these words, she will heed them more readily than when I speak them to her. Perhaps others reading this chapter will refuse Valium when it is offered for the first time. I hope still others will feel more comfortable taking appropriately pre-scribed psychoactive drugs.

HEAD MEDICINE

Drug	Number of Prescriptions Per Year
Valium (tranquilizer)	60 million
Dalmane (sedative)	13 "
Librium (tranquilizer)	10 "
Elavil (antidepressant)	9 "
Miltown or Equanil (tranquilizer)	8 "
Phenobarbital (sedative)	7 "
Mellaril (antipsychotic)	6 "
Tranxene (tranquilizer)	6 "
Triavil (antidepressant and antipsychotic)	5 "
Thorazine (antipsychotic)	4 "
Serax (tranquilizer)	3 "

Source: Graedon, Joe: *The People's Pharmacy—2.* New York: Avon, 1980, p. 409.

Are Psychoactive Drugs Harmful?

Yes. Given inappropriately and indiscriminately, any drug is harmful. Given appropriately, however, the benefit of medications far outweigh the hazards. Certain fairly well-defined indications for medications will be discussed under the individual drugs. Side effects cannot be ignored, and they also will be discussed. A word of warning: drug therapy is not the entire answer. When you, the patient, have been brought to your usual level of function with medications, psychotherapy is important to help you adjust to your illness and to make social and personal advances. Although medications can stabilize erratic behavior, they do little or no good for "neurotic" behavior, nor will they help you with the everyday problems of living.

What Are Antipsychotics?

Antipsychotic medications, also called *neuroleptics* or *major tranquilizers*, have been an effective treatment for schizophrenia and other psychotic disorders since the drug chlorpromazine (trade name Thorazine) was developed in France in the early 1950s. The antipsychotics have been used in treatment of organic brain syndromes, schizophrenias, and other psychotic disorders characterized by hallucinations, delusions, and bizarre, erratic behavior.

Are There Different Brands of Antipsychotic Medications?

Over 20 antipsychotic medications are sold under various brand names. The most common of these, with their usual dosage range, are listed in the table. The generic name of the drug reflects the chemical structure; the trade name is the name chosen by the drug company to help distinguish their particular drug from chemicals with identical structures. For example, aspirin is a generic name while the trade names, St. Joseph and Bayer, distinguish two brands of aspirin made by different drug companies. Fluphenazine is the generic name for the trade drugs Prolixin and Permitil.

Because of changes in the chemical structure, each generic drug varies in potency and side effects. For example, it akes a larger dose of Thorazine to have the same antipsychotic effect as Haldol. Likewise, Thorazine has more sedative side effects, whereas Haldol may cause muscle stiffness as a side effect. Psychiatrists understand the differences between the medications and may use a particular antipsychotic drug because of the side effects or lack of side effects that it produces. For example, a person who has trouble sleeping may respond best to the drug Mellaril because of its sedative effects, while a malnourished elderly individual might suffer from the side effects of Mellaril because it would make that particular individual too groggy. Similarly, Stelazine, a drug that has more energizing effects, may be useful for the person who is apathetic and withdrawn.

EQUIVALENT DOSES AND DOSAGE RANGE OF COMMONLY USED ANTIPSYCHOTIC AGENTS

Generic Name	Trade Name	Approximate Equivalent Daily Dose (mg)	Dosage Range (mg per day)
Phenothiazines			
Aliphatic			
Chlorpromazine	Thorazine	100	50–1,000
Piperidines			
Thioridazine	Mellaril	100	50–800
Piperazines			
Fluphenazine	Prolixin, Permitil	2	5–40
Perphenazine	Trilafon	10	2–64
Trifluoperazine	Stelazine	5	2–60
Dibenzoxazepine			
Loxapine	Loxitane	15	20–250
Indolones			
Molindone	Moban	10	5–225
Thioxanthenes			
Thiothixene	Navane	5	5–60
Butyrophenones			
Haloperidol	Haldol	2	2–60

How Do Antipsychotics Work?

Biological research done in the past few decades has fairly well established that dopamine, a normally occurring chemical in the brain, plays a large part in producing psychotic thinking. Dopamine helps regulate movement of nerve impulses in the area of the brain that controls emotion. If there is too much dopamine in the brainstem, nerve impulses are transmitted faster than normal so that an individual becomes flooded with strange thoughts, begins to hallucinate, and acts in a bizarre manner. The antipsychotic medications help relieve the psychotic thinking by blocking the activity of dopamine so that thoughts and behavior return to a more normal level.

What Types of Psychotic Behavior Do Antipsychotics Prevent?

Antipsychotic medications can stabilize and normalize erratic behavior. They can reduce racing thoughts and can make unusual thoughts less distressing. Antipsychotic medication does not cure social withdrawal, apathy, and interpersonal difficulties that are found in schizophrenics and other psychotic individuals. Psychotherapy is needed to help with these problems. There is no doubt, however, that the antipsychotic medications can prevent relapse in the bizarre thinking and rehospitalization. Studies have shown that over 70 percent of schizophrenic patients who take their medications regularly can remain out of the hospital.

What Is Prolixin?

Prolixin is a long-acting antipsychotic medication that can be given every two to three weeks by intramuscular injection. Because Prolixin is long acting, your psychiatrist may choose to use this medication if you have a tendency to forget to take your medicine.

Do Antipsychotics Need to Be Taken Regularly?

Yes. It has been conclusively shown that antipsychotic medications can prevent relapse into bizarre erratic thinking and behavior if they are taken regularly. Almost all schizophrenics who stop taking their medication end up back in the hospital. However, it's all right to reduce the dosage of the medication with the help of your doctors. After your thinking returns to normal, your doctor may elect to lower the dose. If you begin to feel symptoms returning you can tell your physician and he or she can gradually increase the dose until your bizarre thoughts diminish. Schizophrenia is a lifelong illness but with proper medication combined with psychotherapy you will be able to function without hospitalization and perhaps be able to return to work. A cooperative and friendly relationship with your doctor can make the difference between a life of productiveness or an existence in the back wards of a mental hospital.

What Are the Side Effects of Antipsychotic Medications?

Antipsychotic medications have several side effects. The so-called high-potency antipsychotic medications can cause muscle stiffness in some individuals. Occasionally people who take antipsychotic medications develop motor restlessness, with the inability to sit still. Such people pace the floor a lot or when they are sitting move their legs back and forth as if they were trying to walk. Other common side effects are a fine tremor of the extremities and slow movements. All these side effects can be reversed with the medication Cogentin or Artane.

Individuals who take the so-called low-potency drugs such as Thorazine and Mellaril have a tendency to develop a different set of side effects—blurred vision, dry mouth, constipation, urinary retention, and irregular pulse rates. The low-potency antipsychotic medications also produce more grogginess and sleepiness than do the high-potency drugs.

What Is Tardive Dyskinesia?

It has been recently discovered that some individuals who have been taking antipsychotic medications for 10–15 years or less develop a movement disorder known as *tardive dyskinesia*. *Tardive* means "late"; *dyskinesia* means "abnormal (*dys*) movements (*kinesia*)". These abnormal movements are characterized by jerking around the face and neck, involuntary protrusions of the tongue, and chewing activity of the mouth. Probably only 1 to 2 percent of people who take antipsychotics for a prolonged period of time develop tardive dyskinesia, but because the symptoms are so bizarre they are well worth watching for. Once these symptoms occur, the antipsychotic medication should be radically reduced in dosage or stopped entirely. After the medication dosage has been reduced, the tardive dyskinesia generally goes away. But then the physician has another problem—what to do to prevent another schizophrenic episode from occurring? This question is not easily answered. Unfortunately, there is no treatment for tardive dyskinesia except stopping the antipsychotic medication.

For example, Larry, a 35-year-old man, was initially admitted to a psychiatric hospital in 1968. At that time Larry had been walking up and down the road of the business section of his home town. He kept warning people that there was going to be a robbery of the local drugstore, organized by the Mafia. He said that he was afraid to go home because his house was bugged and the Mafia leaders were trying to kill him. He felt as if people were controlling his thoughts by equipment in his head. Larry responded well to antipsychotic therapy, and within a few months was able to return home. Over the next dozen years, whenever the medication was discontinued the patient became paranoid and psychotic. A few months ago, Larry was noted to have signs of tardive dyskinesia. He had involuntary chewing activity of the mouth, and every few seconds he would protrude his tongue. Larry's medication was gradually discontinued, and thus far Larry has had no flare-up of his schizophrenic symptoms. If Larry does have a return of psychotic symptomatology—which, given his history, he probably will experience—then it will probably be necessary to place him back on antipsychotic medications despite their side effects.

How Can Antipsychotic Drugs Be Taken Safely?

Since the antipsychotic medications need to be taken for a lifetime and they have some rather serious side effects, it is essential that you, as a patient, maintain an ongoing relationship with your physician, letting him or her know of any changes in your condition or life style and having an annual physical examination. Understanding as much as possible about your medication and your illness will help your doctor take care of you. If you and your doctor work well together, the antipsychotic medications can be the most effective way of preventing rehospitalization. Here is a checklist for you to keep in mind:

1. It is important to take your medicine regularly as prescribed by your physician.
2. Notify your doctor whenever you notice any unusual side effect of the drug.
3. Let your doctor know if you are taking other medications, because these can change the amount of antipsychotic you need.
4. It is important to have an annual physical examination.
5. If you plan to become pregnant, tell your doctor, because your medication may have to be reduced or changed.
6. Remember—antipsychotic medications help control bizarre behavior but they are not effective in helping you develop (or relearn) social skills. It is important, then, for you to have regular psychotherapy sessions to help improve your productiveness and dignity.
7. Occasionally patients have mild schizophrenic episodes despite adequate dosage levels of the antipsychotics. It is essential, however, that you keep taking your medication, regardless of a relapse, to prevent major attacks in the future.

What Are the Tricyclic Antidepressants?

Since their development in the late 1950s, the tricyclic antidepressants have become the most frequently used drugs for the treatment of depression. There are currently eight tricyclic compounds marketed under various brand names in the United States (see the table). Soon there will be a new generation of antidepressants that will not have as many side effects as the tricyclics.

THERAPEUTIC DOSE RANGE OF TRICYCLICS

Generic Name (Brand Name)	Dosage Range
Amitriptyline (Elavil, Endep, Amitril)	75–300 mg
Doxepin (Sinequan, Adapin)	75–300 mg
Imipramine (Tofranil, Imavate, Presamine)	75–300 mg
Desipramine (Norpramin, Pertofrane)	75–200 mg
Nortriptyline (Aventyl, Pamelor)	40–100 mg
Protriptyline (Vivactil)	30–60 mg
Trimipramine Maleate (Surmontil)	75–200 mg
Amoxapine (Asendin)	100–400 mg

How Do the Tricyclic Antidepressants Work?

Most depression is caused by a deficiency in one of two chemicals, called *neurotransmitters*, that carry messages from one nerve cell to the other nerve cell. A deficiency in either chemical can produce depression. The tricyclic antidepressant medications keep the neurotransmitters in the space between the nerve endings so that messages can be transferred easily. Some of the tricyclic antidepressants increase the level of one chemical (serotonin), while the other tricyclic antidepressants work to increase the level of the other chemical (norepinephrine). The choice of medication depends on which chemical your physician thinks is deficient in the nerve endings.

What Symptoms Do the Tricyclic Antidepressants Help Relieve?

Individuals who have the following symptoms respond well to the tricyclic antidepressants:

1. Disturbances in sleeping habits (usually sleeplessness during the night but sometimes excessive sleepiness)
2. Loss of appetite
3. Loss of sex drive
4. Feeling tired most of the time despite adequate rest

5. Irritability
6. Sadness
7. Feeling worthless and unwanted

Are Tricyclics Alone Enough to Fight Depression?

Although the tricyclic antidepressants are extremely effective medications (they work to relieve symptoms in over 85 percent of depressed patients), it will also be necessary for you to have psychotherapy sessions. Depressed patients have problems with adjusting to stress that can be treated with psychotherapy. Occasionally a depression may be so severe that tricyclic antidepressants do not help. It will then be necessary for you to take another medicine like an MAO inhibitor—or, if your thinking becomes so disturbed that you are out of touch with reality, the antipsychotics. Electroshock therapy is reserved for those patients who are extremely suicidal and unresponsive to medications.

What Precautions Should Be Taken With Tricyclic Antidepressants?

Tricyclics are contraindicated during the acute recovery period of a heart attack. During pregnancy and lactation, tricyclics should be avoided unless the potential benefits of the medication outweigh the possible hazards to the patient and the infant. Tricyclics should be used cautiously if you have a heart abnormality, glaucoma, prostate problems, a thyroid condition, seizures, or schizophrenia. It is all right for you to take the tricyclics if you have any of these conditions; you just must be more careful of the side effects.

What If Tricyclic Medication Does Not Work?

As was mentioned earlier, there are two chemicals that are believed to cause symptoms of depression. Some tricyclics work to elevate one of these chemicals, other tricyclics work to elevate the other. At present, there is no standard laboratory test that determines which chemical is deficient in the brain. The physician chooses the drug empirically. If you have failed to respond to a particular tricyclic after three to four weeks, the physician may decide to switch to another tricyclic that works on the opposite chemical.

What Are the Side Effects of Tricyclics?

The most common side effects from the tricyclics are dry mouth, possibly some minimal blurred vision, feelings of grogginess, perhaps a little difficulty with urination, and constipation. Because of these side effects your physician will start you off on a low dose and gradually increase the dose to a therapeutic level. It is important for you to continue to take your medicine even though you have these side effects. If you continue to take the medicine, then eventually your body will adjust and the side effects will diminish. The most common cause of failure of the tricyclic medications to work is failure to take your medications.

In many ways, the side effects of the tricyclics are a good sign. The side effects indicate that the medicine is getting into the bloodstream and soon will work its way into the brainstem and begin working for you. Because of the side effects, your physician may want to have you take most or all of the dose of medication at bedtime. The side effects wear off while you are sleeping but the antidepressant effect continues to work the following day.

Are the Tricyclics Addicting?

No. The tricyclics are not tranquilizers, sedatives, hypnotics, or narcotics. They are not addicting, although some patients who have a chronic deficiency in the neurotransmitters need to take the tricyclics for a long period of time.

How Long Will I Need to Take the Medication?

Although you will begin to feel much better two to three weeks after you begin taking the tricyclic medication, it is very important for you to continue to take your medication for at least six months. Just as an individual who is anemic needs to take iron for a long period of time to build up the chemical stores, so you need to take the tricyclic for a six-month period to return the neurotransmitters to completely normal levels. Once the symptoms of depression have remitted and you have been maintained on medication for six months, your physician will gradually reduce your medication. If your symptoms return, your physician can add medication again. Some individuals who have a chronic deficiency of the neurotransmitters may need to be on a low maintenance dose to prevent symptoms from recurring. Most patients, however, do very well after six months of therapy and can go off their medicine without difficulty.

Should I Avoid Other Medication When Taking Tricyclics?

Alcohol, the minor tranquilizers, sedative drugs, and over-the-counter sleeping pills, in addition to making depression worse, add to the sedative effects of the tricyclics. You should avoid these drugs. The antidepressant drugs interfere with certain high blood pressure pills. If you have high blood pressure, you and your doctor can work together to choose the correct antihypertensive.

What Are the Monoamine Oxidase Inhibitors?

The monoamine oxidase inhibitors (MAOI) are antidepressants that work by preventing the metabolism of the neurotransmitters. These medications, too, are effective in treating depression, but because of rather rigid dietary restrictions the MAOIs are used less frequently than the tricyclics.

What Symptoms Do the MAOIs Relieve?

The MAOIs seem to work more efficiently in individuals with an unusual cluster of depressive symptoms. These symptoms include

1. Depression associated with acute anxiety attacks or phobic attacks
2. Depression associated with a great deal of physical complaints such as headaches, backache, constipation, and so forth
3. Those patients who fail to respond to the tricyclic anti-depressants

Many patients have what physicians call a "masked depression," which is merely a way of saying that physical complaints predominate when the cause of these complaints is actually a depressed mood. If your physician has given you a complete and thorough physical examination and can find no cause for your physical complaint, he or she will probably want to try you on the tricyclic antidepressants or one of the MAOIs to see if they can alleviate some of your physical symptoms.

What Problems May Arise When Taking MAOIs?

Although the MAOIs are extremely effective medications, it will be necessary for you to carefully watch your diet when you are taking these medications. The most dangerous side effect from the MAOIs results from extremely high blood pressure that can result when the medication is taken in combination with food or drugs containing tyramine. Medications to be avoided while taking MAOIs include

1. Any over-the-counter "cold" preparation
2. Nasal decongestants
3. Hay fever medications
4. Sinus tablets
5. Weight-reducing preparations or "pep" pills
6. Antiappetite medicine
7. Asthma inhalants
8. Certain prescription drugs

Foods to be avoided include

Cheese	Chopped liver
Wine	Chocolate
Beer	Sour cream
Pickled herring	Yogurt
Yeast extracts	Fruits

How Long Will It Be Necessary to Take MAOIs?

As with the tricyclics, the MAOIs need to be taken at least six months to build up the neurotransmitter stores. The MAOIs are not addicting; they are not tranquilizers, sedatives, or narcotics and are safe and effective if you are careful of your diet and medication intake.

What Precautions Should I Take If MAOIs Are Prescribed?

Here is a checklist for patients taking MAOIs:

1. It is important to take your medicine regularly as prescribed by your physician.
2. Notify your doctor if you notice any unusual side effect of the drug.
3. Carry the name of the MAOI with you at all times so that if an emergency arises hospital personnel will know what medicine you are taking.
4. Whenever you consult a doctor or dentist, notify him or her that you are taking a MAOI.

What Is Lithium?

Lithium has been an effective treatment for manic-depressive illness for over 25 years. It was first used in 1949 by the Australian psychiatrist Dr. John Cade. Because of the success that he had in treating patients, it was next tried in Europe, with similar outstanding results. After extensive tests for its effectiveness and safety, lithium was finally approved by the Food and Drug Administration (FDA) for use in this country.

How Does Lithium Work?

Biological research done in the past few years indicates that manic-depressive illness is related to biochemical factors. Chemicals known as neurotransmitters regulate movement of nerve impulses in the area of the brain that controls emotions. A decrease in the activity of the transmitters seems to be related to depression, while an increase in transmitter activity is related to mania. There is also evidence that mood swings have something to do with the sodium balance in the body. Sodium, a major electrolyte that regulates impulses along the nerve cells, has been found to increase in concentration in the nerve during mania. It appears that lithium works in at least two ways: by leveling out the activity of the transmitters and by helping to maintain a constant sodium concentration in the brain. There may be additional explanations of how lithium works, and scientists are continuing to investigate the precise mechanism of its action.

What Types of Manic-Depressive Illness Does Lithium Help?

Lithium is effective in controlling mania in a few days. But more important, continuous use of this drug prevents recurrent episodes of mania or depression in the three different types of manic-depressive illness. In the first, classic type (called *manic-depressive illness—circular* by psychiatrists), there is a circular swing of mood that may take any number of patterns. Periods of elated mood, continuous speech, and hyperactivity may alternate cyclically with periods of depression, despondency, and mental dullness. There may be several episodes of mania and only one of depression, or just the opposite. Mood swings may occur rapidly or over long periods of time. Often the mood changes become so severe that the person is not in control of his or her behavior and has to be hospitalized.

Second, the person with manic-depressive illness, manic type, has periods of normal or slightly energetic moods alternating with elated phases of overactivity. During the elated phase, the person never sleeps, talks excessively, and becomes impulsive, impatient, and impersonal. Worse yet, he or she can enter into a state of acute mania that is totally out of touch with reality. It may become impossible to understand what he or she is talking about. The patient may begin to hear voices or to have delusions of having special powers or abilities. He or she becomes acutely dangerous to him- or herself and to others.

The third type of patient with manic-depressive illness has a normal or quiet temperament alternating with periods of depression. The depressed period involves restless sleep, decreased appetite, weight loss, and diminished sex drive. Such people may begin to hear voices criticizing them and calling them unforgivable sinners, and may become so despondent as to indulge in thoughts of suicide.

Does Lithium Need to Be Taken Regularly?

Although lithium usually begins to level out mood swings in a few days after it is first taken, some patients respond slowly to treatment with moderate mood swings weeks or months after therapy is started. However, these episodes usually become less and less severe and gradually die out completely. It is essential that you understand that attacks may occur for several months after initiation of the drug, so that you will not neglect to take the most effective drug for your illness. Thus you should continue taking your lithium despite an occasional relapse.

Does Lithium Interfere with Normal Thoughts?

Lithium does not prevent a patient from having normal thoughts, feelings, or emotions. To determine whether lithium has any effect on normal mood or mental ability, scientists asked students to volunteer to take either lithium or placebo (sugar pills) for a week and then take the opposite pill for another week. At the completion of the study, it was clear that the students' feelings were the same whether they were taking lithium or placebo.

What Happens When Lithium Medication Is Stopped?

Some patients do interrupt their lithium treatment, however, when they find that it takes away their feelings of well-being that they experienced when they were in a mildly excited state. Most of these patients return to taking their medication when they find that if they do not, they will begin to have disabling manic episodes again.

It is understandable that if you remain well for week after week you might forget how bad you once felt and either not remember to take your medication or feel that you are completely well and need no more treatment. There is little doubt, however, that if you were to stop taking your medication, the probability of having another manic or depressive attack would be just as great as before you started taking lithium, no matter how long you had been on it.

How Is the Dosage of Lithium Regulated?

Just as insulin does not cure diabetes mellitus, neither does lithium cure manic-depressive illness; lithium regulates mood swings just as insulin is used to regulate the blood sugar level. The dosage of lithium varies greatly from patient to patient depending on the amount of lithium your body needs. Your doctor will determine how much lithium you need by drawing a sample of your blood from time to time to determine how much lithium is present. This is called a lithium blood level. If you stop taking your medicine for only one day, then your blood levels will be half what they should be for effective therapy. However, if you forget to take a dose, don't double the next dose—it might cause your lithium level to go too high. You can see that it is necessary to be constantly alert to taking your medicine regularly. Likewise it is important that lithium levels be drawn on a routine basis so that your physician can recommend the proper lithium dosage.

Because the blood levels of lithium rise rapidly for a few hours after you swallow a lithium pill and then slowly level off, having your blood drawn right after taking the medicine might mislead your doctor into thinking that your dosage was too high.

To give an accurate idea of the steady state blood level, it is important to have your blood drawn 8 to 12 hours after your last dose. Most patients take their nighttime dose of lithium and then come to the doctor's office the next morning to get their blood drawn before taking their first pill of the day.

What Are Some Dangers and Side Effects of Lithium?

Lithium is not digested in the body and is excreted unchanged by the kidneys. Several factors alter lithium excretion. The more sodium a person has in his or her body, the more lithium is excreted. The less sodium in the body, the greater the chance of lithium buildup, resulting in possible lithium poisoning. Diuretics (medications for high blood pressure) cause the kidneys to excrete sodium, thus causing lithium levels to rise. Increased sweating, a low-salt diet, and diarrhea all result in less sodium present in the body, thus producing higher lithium levels. Naturally, a high-salt diet causes lower lithium levels.

Because of these factors, lithium should not be used in the presence of severely impaired kidney function. Patients with heart diseases and others who have a change in sodium in their diet or periodic episodes of heavy sweating should be especially careful to have their lithium level monitored regularly. Lithium should probably not be used in the first three months of pregnancy, unless strongly indicated. Women should not breastfeed when they are taking lithium.

Most patients experience a minimum number of side effects while starting lithium therapy. Initially, the patient may have nausea, stomach cramps, thirstiness, muscle weakness, and slight feelings of being tired, dazed, or sleepy. A mild hand tremor may be present. These effects are normally minimal and usually subside after several days of treatment.

Some of the initial side effects may carry over into long-term therapy. A few patients will continue to have a slight hand tremor, others will drink more water than usual, while still others may put on a few extra pounds. Patients with low amounts of thyroid hormone might be expected to develop an enlargement of the thyroid gland, but this is generally not serious if followed closely by a physician.

Like almost any drug, lithium can be poisonous if taken in excessive doses. Toxic doses cause vomiting, diarrhea, extreme thirst, weight loss, muscle twitching, abnormal muscle movement, slurred speech, blurred vision, dizziness, stupor, and pulse irregularities. However, with regular blood-level checks these problems can almost always be avoided.

Many patients have been taking lithium for over 20 years without chronic side effects, addiction, or withdrawal symptoms. The only serious side effect is acute poisoning and that usually occurs only if the patient develops some other illness, takes the lithium sporadically, or fails to get regular lithium blood checks.

How Can Lithium Be Taken Safely?

Because lithium does not cure manic-depressive illness, you will probably be on the medication for a long time. It is essential, then, that you maintain an ongoing relationship with your physician, letting him or her know of any changes in your condition or lifestyle, getting your regular blood checks, and having an annual physical examination. Understanding as much as possible about lithium and your illness will help your doctor take care of you. If you and your doctor work well together, lithium can be one of the safest and most effective medications available. Here is a checklist for patients taking lithium:

1. It is important to take your medicine regularly as prescribed by your physician.
2. Frequent blood samples for lithium levels are essential.
3. Blood for lithium levels should be drawn at least eight hours after the last dose was taken.
4. Notify your doctor whenever you have changed your diet, because this may cause the lithium level in your body to change.
5. Let your doctor know if you are taking other medications because this can change your lithium levels.

6. Women taking lithium should not breastfeed their infants.

7. Notify your doctor when you have an illness or loss of appetite, because adjustment of dosage may be necessary.

8. If you plan to become pregnant, tell your doctor.

9. It is important to have an annual physical examination.

10. Remember—it takes time for your mood swings to be completely controlled by lithium. It is important not to get discouraged but to continue taking your medicine until the episodes are regulated.

11. Occasionally patients have mild episodes of depression or mania despite adequate lithium dosage. It is essential, however, that you keep taking your medication regardless of a relapse to prevent major attacks in the future.

What About Shock Treatment?

Electroshock therapy or electroconvulsive therapy (EST or ECT), was first used in 1937 by two Italian psychiatrists, Ugo Cerletti and Lucio Bini, to treat schizophrenia. They had such remarkably good results that they next used ECT for depression with even greater benefits (remember, this was before the modern drug treatments). When it was initially used, ECT was a violent treatment. There was no predrug sedative, and assistants had to hold down the patient's arms and legs during the treatment process. The convulsions were sometimes so severe that they broke bones.

Shock therapy continues to be a highly controversial subject. Many people object strongly to its use. These opponents believe that it is inhumane and degrading. In an emergency, however, ECT works faster than anything else. Most psychiatrists reserve ECT for those patients who are so depressed that they are out of touch with reality and suicidal.

It generally requires six to eight treatments for a patient to receive full benefits. These treatments generally are spaced out, every other day; for example, on Mondays, Wednesdays, and Fridays. Prior to receiving ECT, the individual has a thorough physical workup including a heart, lung, and bone examination.

On the day of the treatment the patient receives no breakfast and is given an injection of medication to help dry up body secretions. The patient is then taken to the ECT room and given an injection of Brevitol, which rapidly puts him or her into a sleep that lasts for approximately two to three minutes. During this time, the patient is given an injection of Succinylcholine, which produces total muscle paralysis to prevent severe muscle contractions. After this injection, the patient is given a few breaths of oxygen with an ambu bag. Two electrodes are then applied to the temples and a current (100 or so volts at 200 to 1600 milliamps) passes through the brain for less than a second. Usually the only indication of a seizure is a slight toe twitching or finger twitching or perhaps some goose bumps. The electrical impulses produce a seizure in the brain, however, that changes the neurotransmitters to relieve symptoms of depression.

About a half hour after ECT, the patient wakes up, groggy and confused. Usually, past memories come back gradually over a few weeks, although many patients never recover a memory of the time immediately surrounding the treatment. Permanent, disabling memory loss can happen occasionally, but no major medical treatment is without risk.

Severe depression is the major indication for ECT, and ECT remains the fastest and most reliable treatment. ECT may occasionally be used in individuals with acute psychotic episodes who fail to respond to the antipsychotic medications. It should not be used routinely for schizophrenia, and it never should be used for mild depressions.

What Are the Uses of the Sedatives and the Minor Tranquilizers?

The minor tranquilizers (benzodiazepines) are the most frequently prescribed medications. In the United States, approximately 100 million prescriptions a year have been written for benzodiazepines, at a cost approaching $500 million. Because of their abuse potential, the minor tranquilizers and sedative hypnotic agents, such as the barbiturates, should only be used for a short period of time, say one or two weeks.

Are the Sedatives Dangerous?

Yes. Although sedatives are widely used, their potential for tox-ification, abuse, and lethal overdose renders them obsolete as antianxiety agents or as sedatives except in extremely unusual circumstances. Avoid them.

Sleeping pills—Doriden, Luminal, Placidyl, Quaalude, Val-mid, Noctec—account for 27 million prescriptions in the United States each year. These drugs are directly implicated in 5,000 drug-related deaths and many more nonconfirmed drug-related deaths each year.

What Are the Benzodiazepines?

The benzodiazepines include Librium and Valium (see the table). These drugs work selectively on the limbic system in the brain, while essentially sparing the cerebral cortex and reticular acti-vating system. The limbic system is responsible for emotions such as rage and anxiety, whereas the cerebral cortex and the reticular activating system are responsible for thinking and alertness. These medicines are by far the most prescribed drugs in the United States, mainly because they produce tranquiliza-tion without producing as much sedation as other medications do. These medications have an extremely long half-life (they are slowly metabolized in the body) so that it is unnecessary to take more than one to two pills a day to feel tranquil all day and all

THE BENZODIAZEPINES

Generic Name	Representative Brand Name
Chlordiazepoxide	Librium
Diazepam	Valium
Oxazepam	Serax
Clorazepate	Tranxene
Lorazepam	Ativan
Prazepam	Centrax
Clorazepate	Azene

night. The half-life of these drugs is so long (70 hours or more, in some cases) that there can be quite a buildup of drug effect in the brain.

Now that I have given you the scientific facts about Valium, Librium, and the other benzodiazepines, allow me to make this dogmatic statement: these drugs are bad for you. In contrast to the tricyclic antidepressants, the MAO inhibitors, the antipsychotics, and lithium, all of which have specific indications and are necessary for specific disorders, the benzodiazepines are simply tranquilizers—they numb the emotions. They are the drugs that take away the zest and enthusiasm for life. They will make you a zombie.

The drug companies stress that the benzodiazepines have low abuse potential. They say that you can take these drugs for long periods of time and get along fine. They're right, if you don't mind missing out on the richness of life. What's more, if you take Valium for several months in doses of 40 mg or more a day and then stop the medication abruptly, you can have seizures and die. Valium in combination with alcohol has killed many people.

Not only do these drugs interfere with the normal coping mechanisms, but they have been shown to increase irritability, hostility, and agressiveness when taken over long periods of time. Other reports indicate that these drugs increase the chances of depression.

As long as I am on the bandwagon, let me go on. Remember Aldous Huxley's *Brave New World*? As the story goes, people in this new world had lost their individuality. The new society used every effort to make completely true its motto, "Community, identity, stability." John, the protagonist of the novel, was called a savage because he continued to champion tears, inconvenience, God, and poetry. In this new society, art was stifled completely; science was dominant. People took **soma** holidays, **soma** being a drug which induced forgetfulness and dulled human emotions. Is Valium our first step toward **soma**? I think so.

I prescribe Valium very infrequently—only for individuals with acutely debilitating anxiety—and, except for the Valium lady, I never allow any of my patients to take it for longer than two weeks. A little unhappiness, a little instability, a little anxiety are part of the human condition. I'm for being human, not for being **soma**-tized.

More Preaching?

Please allow me to preach a little more against drug overuse. We seem to be conditioned from infancy to believe there is a pill for every ill. This belief in jet-age pharmacology—the idea that total comfort rests in having the right drug connection—will, in the end, leave us emotionally bankrupt. Good times are made, not ingested. We need to remember Winston Churchill's axiom that "most of the world's work is done by people who do not feel very well."

Chapter 15
Psychotherapy
(Helping Yourself Get Help)

More than 70 well-designed clinical studies have demonstrated the effectiveness of a wide range of individual and group therapies in helping people with emotional problems. With an encyclopedic variety of treatment choices and a heated debate about which therapy is best, how can you choose the appropriate psychotherapy for you? That's what this chapter is about. I make no statement about "This is the best," or "This treatment is no good." I start with Freud, the beginning of modern psychotherapy, and progress to some of the newer treatment methods. First a few introductory remarks.

Can Psychotherapy Cure?

It's probably best to think of psychotherapy as a teaching process rather than a curing process. There is no such thing as perfect emotional health, just as there is no such thing as a perfect physical specimen. Psychotherapy helps a person learn, and with new insights about him- or herself, perhaps adopt better ways of handling problems in living.

Who Practices Psychotherapy?

You may get psychotherapy from an analyst, a psychiatrist, a psychologist, a social worker, or your medical doctor (see Chapter 2). Occasionally, bartenders and beauticians make fairly good psychotherapists. An interesting study done at Duke University Medical Center found that 15 percent of the United States population suffers from a major mental disorder. Of these people, 60 percent are treated by their family physicians, 18 percent are treated by psychiatrists or other mental health workers, and 22 percent have no professional treatment at all. Think of it—22 percent. That's more than 7.5 million people who rely on their neighbors, bartenders, beauticians, mailmen, or whatever to get by. And these "patients" have a major mental disorder—schizophrenia or a severe depression or anxiety that interferes with their ability to function in daily tasks. This figure is even more startling when you consider that it does not include those people with problems of living.

We have a paradox here. Many of the people (22 percent, to be exact) who need psychotherapy do not get it whereas the rich, the educated, and the comparatively healthy obtain a large share of the psychotherapist's time. Psychotherapy for the rich is a status symbol; for the poor it is a social stigma.

What Is Psychoanalysis?

Psychoanalysis, based on the theories of Sigmund Freud, is a long, expensive, but extremely worthwhile method for helping an individual understand more about him- or herself and, through this understanding, perhaps change some maladaptive patterns of behavior. Freud found that if a patient talks in an uncontrolled and spontaneous manner (which he called "free association"), the patient will reexperience in the analytic hour the major developmental influences in his or her life. To encourage free association, the patient lies on a couch. The analyst, seated behind the couch and out of sight of the patient, points out resistances that the patient uses to prevent remembering emotional conflicts from childhood.

Psychoanalysis delves into the past—the forgotten images and the long-repressed fears and anxieties of childhood. The more inactive the analyst, the easier it is for the patient to relive these experiences. Merely remembering the experiences is not enough; the patient must reflect, over and over again, thinking about the past and reliving the past during the analytic hour. The analytic setting encourages reexperiencing the fantasies, dreams, and realities of childhood with very strong emotions so that what was once emotionally harmful can be safely relived and understood.

Psychoanalysis is lengthy (four 45-minute sessions weekly for three to five years or longer) and costly ($50 to $60 or more a session). Nevertheless, it is of great benefit to psychologically minded patients who have the capacity to form warm relationships with other people but are plagued with neurotic conflicts. In other words, individuals who need psychoanalysis the least benefit from it the most.

To be a psychoanalyst in the United States, one must first have an M.D., or occasionally another advanced degree, and take extensive coursework to learn the analytic process. The coursework includes a personal analysis and direct supervision by a practicing analyst on four controlled cases. It generally requires the candidate to have eight to ten years of training following medical school before certification by an analytic institute.

What Is a Typical Psychoanalytic Session Like?

The typical psychoanalytic session is like solving a mystery. You enter the analyst's office, nod a cursory greeting, and then lie down on the couch. Generally there is a cushion for your head, with a disposable cloth napkin and a small mat at the foot of the couch. You lie on the couch, look up at the ceiling, and then you begin to talk. You talk about your dreams, what happened to you the day before, what you have been worrying about, what your best friend just told you, or whatever else comes in mind. The analyst will help you understand your conflicts and ambitions better by making interpretations connecting your childhood emotion pattern with the present situation. You will gradually develop a profound understanding for yourself and a deep appreciation for yourself and others.

What Is Psychodynamic Therapy?

Psychodynamic therapy, psychoanalytically oriented psychotherapy, insight psychotherapy, and uncovering psychotherapy are all based on psychoanalytic theory. This therapy can be practiced by a psychiatrist, a psychologist, a social worker, or a physician.

With typical psychotherapy, the patient will sit on a chair facing the therapist. The therapist talks more and is much more active than in classical psychoanalysis. There is more give and take, and the sitting position encourages conscious rather than unconscious processes. Psychotherapy tends to focus on specific problems rather than on thorough exploration of childhood conflicts.

What Is Jungian Therapy?

When Freud first began developing his theories of psychoanalysis, his primary follower was Carl Gustav Jung. Over the course of time, Freud began to believe that basic human problems were due to conflicts over sex and aggression. Jung and Freud began to argue; eventually they completely split up. Jung didn't like the emphasis on sex and aggression. Jung, more optimistic than Freud, believed in the collective unconscious—a deep reservoir of energy and potential creativity, present in every individual and passed on from generation to generation.

The technique in Jungian treatment differs vastly from classical Freudian psychoanalysis. The patient and therapist sit face to face; practical advice is dispensed; and a warm, positive relationship with the analyst is encouraged. Neurotic conflicts are handled in a matter-of-fact way, and the Jungian analyst is more friendly and self-revealing than the Freudian analyst. A great emphasis is placed on dream analysis in an attempt to strengthen the patient's energy and creativity.

What Is Family Therapy?

Family therapy aims to open up communications and teach healthy interactions to the family. Family therapy is recommended when a key member suffers from a chronic illness and this illness tears apart the emotional fabric of the others, creating turmoil and hostility. Family therapists occasionally use unusual approaches. For example, during a session a daughter may be asked to assume the role of the mother while the mother takes the daughter's role. These acted-out role changes helps each family member empathize more with the others as they begin to experience a new set of responsibilities and difficulties. The therapist attempts to show family members what they are doing to each other and to teach them how to get along better.

What Is Group Therapy?

Group therapy offers the individual a chance to examine his or her interactions with the help of the group members and the group leader. The individual is able to learn and practice techniques for successfully relating to others while at the same time exploring inner emotional conflicts. In addition, group psychotherapy offers a model of self-disclosure, contact, and intimacy, while at the same time allowing an individual to learn that others have the same fears, angers, and wishes that he or she does.

Although no iron-clad rules prevail, most groups meet once weekly for 1.5 to 2 hours. The optimal number of group members is generally felt to be seven or eight patients. Group therapy is the most practical and least expensive way of offering psychotherapy. There are groups for children, for parents, for couples, for adolescence, for alcoholics and for people with assorted problems with living. Some of the most effective groups are run by laypeople and cost nothing; for example, Alcoholics Anonymous.

What Are Encounter Groups?

Encounter groups are for healthy people who want to increase their potential for intimacy, openness, genuineness, and self-realization. Encounter groups are not for sick people. Sometimes an overenthusiastic "therapist" uses outrageous techniques that can cause severe emotional damage. In a carefully controlled study by three well-regarded clinicians and researchers, 10 percent of healthy students who volunteered for an encounter group research demonstrated severe psychological damage following the encounter group training. This serious psychological harm was present six to eight months after the group ended. Considering the effect of encounter groups on college students who were apparently well, it is probably best to avoid these groups, especially if you have a history of emotional problems.

What Is Transactional Analysis?

Transactional analysis (TA) is a therapy founded by the late Dr. Eric Berne, author of *Games People Play*. Transactional analysis combines psychoanalytic and interpersonal insights presented with a commonsense approach. TA concentrates on people's interactions (transactions) with each other. These transactions are analyzed in terms of the parent-adult-child parts of each person's personality (other names for Freud's superego, ego, id). TA therapists concentrate on here-and-now change; they may use behavior therapy, roleplaying, and reality therapy to achieve their means.

What Is Behavioral Therapy?

Behavioral therapy, derived from laboratory investigations of learning, focuses on modifying behavior by manipulating the environment. Behavioral therapists believe that to change behavior the environment can be arranged to give rewards for good behavior in progressively small steps so that deviate behavior will disappear. As the patient begins to act differently, feelings and attitudes will change. The rewards the patient obtains by achieving goals will continuously provide what he or

A GLOSSARY OF PSYCHOTHERAPY TERMS

abreaction—emotional release after recalling a painful experience

acting out—expressions of unconscious emotional conflicts in actions rather than words

anima—in Jungian psychology, a person's inner being as opposed to the character (persona) presented to the world

anniversary reaction—an emotional response to a previous event occurring at the same time of year as that of event

aversion therapy—a behavior therapy procedure in which stimuli associated with undesirable behavior are paired with an unpleasant stimulus, resulting in the suppression of the undesirable behavior

behavior therapy—a mode of treatment that focuses on modifying observable behavior by means of systematic manipulation of the environment

biofeedback—the use of instrumentation to provide information (feedback) about physiologic processes not ordinarily perceived (for example, muscle tension or blood pressure)

catharsis—the healthful release of ideas through a "talking out" of conscious material accompanied by an appropriate emotional reaction

cognitive therapy—a treatment method that emphasizes the rearrangement of a person's maladaptive processes of perceptions, attitudes, and thinking

collective unconscious—in Jungian theory, a portion of the unconscious common to all people

crisis intervention—a form of psychotherapy that emphasizes identification of the specific event precipitating the emotional trauma and uses methods to neutralize that trauma

defense mechanism—unconscious intrapsychic processes serving to provide relief from emotional conflict and anxiety

dynamic psychiatry—the study of psychiatry emphasizing both psychological meaning and biological instincts as forces relevant to understanding human behavior

ego—in psychoanalytic theory, the mediator between the demands of primitive instinctual drives (the id), of internalized social prohibitions (the superego) and of reality

existential psychiatry—a school of psychiatry that stresses the way in which a person experiences the world and takes responsibility for existence

flooding (implosion)—a behavior therapy procedure in which anxiety producers are presented in intense forms, either in imagination or in real life free association—in psychoanalytic therapy, spontaneous, uncensored verbalization by the patient of whatever comes to mind

holistic—an approach to the study of the individual in totality, rather than as an aggregate of separate physiologic, psychologic, and social characteristics

id—in Freudian theory, the part of the personality structure that harbors the unconscious and instinctual desires

insight—self-understanding

integration—the useful organization and incorporation of both new and old data into the personality

neurosis—emotional disturbances of all kinds other than psychosis; implies subjective psychological discomfort beyond what is appropriate

primary gain—the relief from emotional conflict and the freedom from anxiety achieved by a defense mechanism

reciprocal inhibition—in behavior therapy, the hypothesis that if anxiety provoking stimuli occur simultaneously with relaxation, the bond between those stimuli and the anxiety will be weakened

reinforcement—the strengthening of a response by reward or avoidance of punishment

repetition compulsion—the impulse to reenact emotional experiences

repression—a defense mechanism operating unconsciously that banishes unacceptable fantasies, ideas, feelings, or impulses from consciousness

resistance—one's conscious or unconscious psychologic defense against bringing repressed thoughts to light

secondary gain—the external gain derived from any illness such as personal attention, disability benefits, and release from unpleasant responsibility

somatic therapy—the treatment of mental disorders with drugs or electroconvulsive therapy

superego—in psychoanalytic theory, that part of the personality structure associated with standards, ethics, and self-criticism

supportive psychotherapy—a type of psychotherapy that aims to reinforce a patient's defenses and help suppress disturbing psychologic material

systematic desensitization (desensitization)—a behavior therapy procedure involving the construction of a hierarchy of anxiety producing stimuli by the subject and gradual presentation of the stimuli until they no longer produce anxiety

transference—the unconscious assignment to others of feelings and attitudes that were originally associated with important figures in one's early life she needs to continue with more effective activity. There are a variety of behavioral techniques:

1. Assertiveness training is a form of behavioral therapy in which people are taught appropriate interpersonal responses involving frank, honest, and direct expression of their feelings, both positive and negative.

2. Aversive control, used only with the consent of the patient or his or her guardians, uses unpleasant stimuli to change inappropriate behavior. For example, an individual who is a child molester may be placed before a video screen; as pictures of nude children are flashed on the screen he or she is given an unpleasant electrical shock.

3. Operant conditioning is the process whereby an individual is given reinforcement (either through money, praise, or rewards of any kind) for good behavior.

4. Extinction by negative reinforcement is a fancy term that simply means, "Ignore bad behavior and it will go away." Remember: attention—even unfavorable attention—may be reinforcing, so to get bad behavior to go away, ignore it. Praise good behavior and it will increase.

5. Shaping consists of giving a reward for each small step that is taken to master new problems. Sometimes it is helpful to keep track of changes using a progress chart, a feedback device that in itself reinforces behavioral change.

6. Systematic desensitization, developed by Dr. Joseph Wolpe, gets rid of fears by accustoming patients, in a progressive step-by-step manner, to what they fear. Patients are first taught ways of relaxing deeply while imagining what they fear as vividly as they can. Say, for example, that a woman is afraid of driving in automobiles, because she has been involved in an automobile accident. She is first taught relaxation techniques and then is asked to imagine seeing an automobile at a distance. The individual then gradually approaches the automobile in her imagination, imagines getting into the car, and finally imagines driving off in the automobile. Whenever the patient becomes anxious, she is asked to divert her attention and relax again. She goes through this hierarchy until she is able to master the imagined scenes without anxiety. Next the patient goes through the hierarchy in reality. These tech-

niques are practiced until she is actually able to drive in an automobile without fear.

7. Implosive therapy, or flooding, is the opposite of systematic desensitization. With this method patients are exposed, in their imaginations, to what they are afraid of, as vividly as they can imagine it.

What Is Cognitive Therapy?

Cognitive therapy and rational emotive therapy are based on the notion that by changing our thoughts we can change our feelings and behavior. These therapists challenge negative beliefs and persuade their patients to think positively. By thinking positively, a patient begins to feel better. This therapy is good treatment for depression and adjustment difficulties.

What Makes Psychotherapy Work?

Regardless of the type of psychotherapy, each school seems to have three broad goals:

1. To reduce suffering of the patient
2. To smooth the patient's social functioning
3. To improve the patient's performance

Likewise, although the various forms of psychotherapy differ in their conceptual framework, they all seem to have several elements in common that produce emotional change. They are:

1. The therapist-patient relationship
2. Release of tension by talking about problems
3. Insight and understanding the source of the problem
4. Reinforcement from the therapist when appropriate behavior patterns are tried
5. Identification with the therapist
6. Suggestions from the therapist
7. Practice of new coping techniques
8. Consistent emotional support from the therapist

How Do I Find the Right Therapist?

Several months ago, just as I was getting up from the dinner table, a neighbor called. He said that he had recently been promoted to a managerial position, and, although happy about the increase in salary and power, he was having difficulty dealing with giving orders and delegating authority. He had a nagging idea that something was wrong. He knew he needed help, but didn't know where to get it. In quick succession, he asked, "Do you think I need psychotherapy? Where can I go to get help? How long will it take? Do you really think it will help?"

We had a long conversation, but in essence I told him that with the proper therapist, psychotherapy can help just about everyone. Psychotherapy, after all, is finding out more about yourself. Naturally, the better you understand yourself, the better you can deal with everyday problems of living. The major part of the conversation dealt with my steering my neighbor in the right direction and referring him to a therapist whom I thought would be right for him.

Although no part of psychotherapy is easy, picking the right therapist is probably the hardest part of therapy. Choosing a therapist from the Yellow Pages could be hazardous to your mental health. The best way to pick a therapist is to be well informed about the various schools of psychotherapy and the variety of psychotherapists. The next thing you should do is talk to someone who has had psychotherapy and ask your family physician for some names of therapists. Then you need to consider exactly what you want to work on, how much time you want to spend in therapy, and how much money you can afford to pay. If you have the time, visit with several therapists before you choose one. Probably the most important criteria for a good therapist are these questions: (1) "Is the therapist professionally trained and certified?" and (2) "Is the therapist empathetic and warm, without being smothering?"

Once you have made your choice and you are satisfied that it has been a good one, stick with it. As with all close relationships, there will be good times and rocky times. Psychotherapy is difficult and you will want to quit many times during the procedure. Keep going and you will get something out of it. The psychotherapeutic process is hard work, agonizing work, but in the long run rewarding work.

What Can I Do to Improve My Chances of Getting Help From Psychotherapy?

A favorable outcome in psychotherapy correlates with what is known as the therapeutic triad: empathy, nonpossessive warmth, and genuineness on the part of the therapist. So if you want to have successful psychotherapy, try to pick a therapist who genuinely wants to help you; one who is emotionally warm, but not smothering; and one who will allow you and encourage you to grow and change. For emotional change to occur, you will need encouragement and consistent (neither too much or too little) emotional support. Your therapist's belief in your worth as a person will enhance your self-concept and strengthen your confidence so that you will gradually develop a sense of mastery and control over your impulses and feelings. You benefit from warm understanding and unwavering respect, but overkindness and overprotectiveness are detrimental to your development of independence.

These three factors—empathy, nonpossessive warmth, and genuineness—can be thought of as the therapist's contribution to your getting better. Your contribution is the motivation to change—not merely to get rid of symptoms, but to make some basic change in adaptational patterns. This means that you must be willing to understand the source of the emotional problems, actively participate in the treatment process, and make a reasonable sacrifice in terms of time and fees.

The opportunity to talk to an authority about your anxieties, frustrations, and concerns allows for emotional relief through the release of tension. This unburdening process strengthens the relationship that you will develop with your therapist and will contribute to your expectation for improvement.

As the psychotherapeutic process evolves, the therapist will help you become aware of some of the reasons and causes of your problems. The therapist will attempt to help you clarify your problems, confront you with self-defeating behavior, and review your previous life experiences. Only after reworking and reworking the difficulty in therapy can you begin to make some definite changes in everyday living and perceptions. Just as it takes many hours of practice to change an errant golf swing, to change old patterns of personality requires repeated working-through (going over and over the same conflicts again and again) before new techniques can be mastered.

Naturally, the therapist has his or her own set of ideas about behavior. He or she will explicitly and implicitly approve of certain behavior and disapprove of other behavior. The therapist's approval serves as a reward; disapproval serves as a punishment. These responses will gradually encourage you to change to more appropriate behavior. Of course, there can be problems with this type of behavioral change. What if your therapist's idea of behavior differs from society or from your own cultural and social background? That's one of the reasons it's vitally important for you to pick a therapist you feel comfortable with. You will tend to model yourself consciously and unconsciously after the therapist. So pick a therapist who behaves maturely and appropriately.

How Do I Go About Getting What I Want From Psychotherapy?

From the very beginning of therapy, you must be completely honest in the presentation of thoughts and problems. The therapist must agree to protect the confidentiality of your revelations. In addition, stipulations of the treatment process need to be established from the onset. You need to have a clear understanding of the times that you will meet and the cost of therapy. You should also have a rough grasp of how long the therapy is going to take. Is the treatment process going to be short term— only 10 to 20 sessions—or is it going to last for several years?

The time limit and frequency of the visits should be strictly followed. Most therapist will charge for unexcused missed appointments unless they have been caused by circumstances clearly out of your control. There are a couple of reasons for doing this. In the first place, the therapist can be expected to want to get paid—after all, this is how he or she makes a living. In the second place, therapy can be emotionally upsetting, and it will not be unusual if you would want to miss some meetings. Knowing that you are going to have to pay for $50 or $60 if you miss a meeting will probably inspire you to attend even though you would rather be doing something else. Attending when you don't want to will help you change quicker. Likewise, you should expect that your therapist see you punctually and give you undivided attention during the sessions.

It is essential that both you and your therapist try to focus on your major conflict. It is easy to digress and talk about things that really don't bother you too much. Because you are paying for the therapy, you should try to get the most out of it by staying on the subject of your problem. Of course, this is a major part of the therapist's job—he or she will help you deal with your resistance to talk about those things that are bothering you. Your job will be to do most of the talking, while the therapist's main tasks is to keep you on the subject of your problem. Basically, the therapist will assume the responsibility of helping you overcome resistance to improvement, and you will assume the responsibility to improve.

The therapist will repeatedly link the specific stress factor in your present situation to childhood problems and feelings. You will invariably ruminate over things that really aren't important, forget appointments, forget what was said in previous sessions, become silent, and so forth. The therapist will nonjudgmentally point out these resistances to change and try to find out what is causing them.

Transference is another inevitable phenomenon of therapy. You will develop feelings about your therapist based on reaction that you had for significant people in childhood. Thus, if you felt criticized in your childhood you will perceive the therapist as critical. Anger, fear, affection, and sexual attraction may be a result of transference distortion. The therapist's task is to recognize these transference phenomena and interpret them to you.

When the time comes to end therapy, you will be surprised how difficult it will be to give up the therapeutic relationship. You will not end your therapy abruptly, but, instead, over the course of a few sessions or a few months, depending on how long you have been seeing your therapist, you will gradually work through what it will mean to you to be on your own.

Part IV
For Family and Friends:
How to Help

Chapter 16
Making Behavior Change Possible
(What To Do Before the Psychiatrist Arrives)

Actually, the title of this chapter is misleading. If you have a friend or relative with an emotional problem, you will be working closely with that person both before and after the psychiatrist is called on to help. You, the family member, will often be called on to do much of the therapy. For example, if you have a loved one who needs medication, the psychiatrist will ask you to help make sure that the patient takes the drug at the appropriate time periods.

Not only will you be called on to help in the therapy of the loved one, but you, the family member, will also need some reassurance and assistance from your physician. This book was written to help you deal with problems that may arise when you have a loved one with an emotional disorder. But don't rely solely on this book; feel free to call on your physician for further guidance. In this section, I will specifically apply what I have already said in previous chapters, reiterating what you as a family member can do to help both yourself and your loved one.

How Can I Help the Anxious Individual?

If you have read the chapter on anxiety, you will understand that anxiety can be caused by a variety of conditions. If your friend or relative is anxious because of unconscious conflicts, about the only thing you can do is make certain that that person sees a therapist regularly. Making interpretations yourself, naturally, won't work. However, if your relative or friend has a phobia, there is a great deal that you can do. Perhaps, for example, your husband has a fear of riding elevators but has just landed a job with an office on the thirty-sixth floor. In all probability, you could help decondition his phobia simply by having him practice riding the elevator, much as was described in the section on systematic desensitization.

One of the best methods of helping someone deal with panic attacks is to pay as little attention to them as possible. Someone who has hyperventilation attacks, for example, will have these attacks reinforced if someone pays attention to them. If the only time you pay attention to your wife is when she is having a hyperventilation attack, naturally—if she cares for you—she will hyperventilate just to get your attention. For a hyperventilator, then, you might say in a calm, reassuring voice, "The doctor has told us that this attack you are having is caused by anxiety. This anxiety causes you to overbreathe, which is causing your symptoms of dizziness. Why don't you lie down for a while and practice your relaxation techniques?" Then go about your business. When your wife is not hyperventilating is the time to pay attention to her. Which brings up the adage: ignore bad behavior and it will go away; pay attention to good behavior and it will increase.

For the special problem of posttraumatic stress disorder secondary to the Vietnam War (which, I have already said, plagues at least 500,000–700,000 combat veterans), you can be of great assistance. Convince, conjole, persuade your husband (or other loved one) to see someone at one of the "storefront centers" or, better yet, to visit a psychiatrist at the mental hygiene clinic in the Veterans Administration hospital nearest you. Don't take no for an answer. Have your husband read the section on the

Vietnam problem earlier in this book. Let him know that the VA is to be trusted. If, despite your most heroic efforts, your husband continues to resist seeking help, then visit the social worker at the mental hygiene clinic—he or she will probably be able to help you.

How Can I Help Someone Who Is Depressed?

Again, ignore the depressive behavior as much as possible, while paying attention to normal behavior. For example, if your husband has developed a chronic depressive character, try not to pay too much attention to him when he is especially despondent and blue (unless of course, he is suicidal, which we will cover later). Instead, the time to take your husband out for a surprise dinner is when he is already happy. This reinforces the cheerful feeling and, over a period of time you can help your husband learn that he gains nothing from being despondent.

If your spouse has sleep disturbance, decreased appetite, decreased sex drive, decreased energy, and loss of interest in activities, a major depression is probably brewing and merits prompt medical treatment, usually with tricyclic antidepressants. Your family physician will be completely familiar with these medications and can prescribe them correctly. The most important thing you can do in this case is to make certain that your spouse takes the medication. Unfortunately, the tricyclics have side effects, which, for the first few days they are taken, cause some people to resist them. Explain to your spouse that the dry mouth, blurred vision, dizziness, and grogginess which he or she is feeling when taking this medication will gradually go away as the body adjusts to the drug. Encourage your spouse to stay away from work for a week until the side effects from the medicine become more tolerable. After a week or so, your spouse will be feeling much better and the side effects will diminish.

If you understand the symptoms of depression (see Chapter 4), you can help your relative overcome the illness. If your depressed wife awakens early in the morning, for example, train yourself to get up at the same time. Fix breakfast and chat with her. This concern will help dispel some of her sense of doom and will help her relax. If, on the other hand, your wife is using sleep as an escape, encourage activities to create wakefulness.

In his book *Up From Depression*, Leonard Cammer, M.D., suggests an appropriate approach for encouraging the depressed individual to eat. Cammer correctly points out that the patient's loss of appetite is due, in part, to an inner desire to be punished. Telling your depressed relative, "Eat so you can get well," will not help, but on the contrary, will tend to make the relative become more obstinate in his or her refusal to eat. A better approach, as Dr. Cammer suggests, would be to say, "By not eating, you are taking something out on yourself. Maybe you are right to want to punish yourself, maybe not. But starving won't help solve your problem. Let's figure out some other way to deal with your depressed feelings. But first let's sit down and eat together." Praise the depressed relative for what is eaten, but make no comment on the food left untouched. (Again remember the axiom: "praise good behavior and it will increase, ignore bad behavior and it will diminish").

Gradually help the depressed patient become interested in former activities. For example, a symptom of one of my depressed patients was his loss of interest in tennis. Formerly an avid tennis player who participated in matches at least three or four times weekly, the patient's enthusiasm for tennis waned as his depression increased. Finally, he stopped playing altogether. After the diagnosis had been made and he had been started on the appropriate medications, I sought the assistance of his wife in encouraging him to get back on the tennis court. She managed, with a great deal of prodding, to get her husband to attend the weekly club tennis league. The following day the patient appeared a little brighter, talked more, and ate better. Before long he began to look forward to his tennis engagements.

Almost every depressed patient loses sexual desire. Rather than ignoring this loss of interest in sexual drive, the spouse should approach the subject openly. Reassure your spouse that sex is a way to exchange affection. Express your confidence that the sexual drive will return as your spouse begins to feel better.

If your depressed relative is becoming neglectful of his or her personal appearance, insist that your relative bathe, comb his or her hair, and brush his or her teeth regularly. Firmly direct your relative to dress appropriately and behave in a civilized manner. After all, a person who looks better will feel better.

For a depressed individual who has lost self-confidence, the important task is, as the song says, "accentuate the positive." For example, a salesman became depressed over his loss of several promising contracts. He began to say, "I'm not good at anything anymore. My ability to sell is gone." His wife reminded him of the other contracts that he had signed. She praised him for his ability to get up and go out again and again despite his recent setbacks. She praised his efforts and his ability to keep at it. Little by little, the patient began to develop belief in himself again. Every small step that the depressed patient makes toward recovery can be reinforced by praise.

When an individual begins to complain of physical ailments, instead of calling the complaint imaginary concede that that symptom must be real. Reassure your relative at the same time that the physician has done everything that he or she can to alleviate the discomfort. Encourage your relative to do something to help get the aches and pains off of his or her mind. For example, you might say, "I know your pain is real, but the doctor has told us that there is nothing we can do about it. Let's sit down and play a hand of gin rummy. Perhaps that will help take your mind off your pain, although we will not be able to make it disappear completely." Alternatively, you might suggest a walk, a visit with friends, or a movie. At the conclusion of the activity, you can say, "I admire your fortitude in playing gin (or going for a walk, movie, visiting friends or whatever) despite your pain. Your internal strength amazes me."

For individuals with an agitated depression—such people can't sit still, are restless, wring their hands, pace the floor, and seem in a state of hyperalertness—plan brief activities. A stroll around the block, a brief shopping trip, or a short visit with a friend will help work off some of the hyperactivity.

For relatives with slowed-down symptoms of depression— boredom, complaints of being tired and weak, and sluggish thoughts or feelings—your task is to find something to interest them. In the first place, people who are slowed down have difficulty dealing with others who talk fast and do things quickly. Your first task then is to slow down yourself. Talk slowly and deliberately. Next, probe for a spark of interest by opening up a conversation on general topics. Start with the current national affairs (if they are not too tragic) and move on to family affairs (if they are not upsetting). Talk about what you have been doing. Dr. Cammer suggests that you deliberately give some incorrect details on a subject that you are certain that your relative knows something about. This may prompt your relative to correct you and stimulate his or her interest in talking. Once your relative begins to talk, then it is easier to mobilize activity.

For example, a depressed patient of mine wouldn't talk. Therefore, I began to ramble on, talking on just about anything pleasant that came into my mind. I happened to mention that I had seen a fantastic catch on a televised baseball game. This triggered the patient's memory, and he suddenly began talking about the catch that he saw Willie Mays make in the World Series game against Cleveland. That's about all he said that day, but on the following day we talked more about baseball. Soon the patient began to watch baseball on TV. He then became motivated to play catch with his son, and gradually he became more interested in other family activities.

Another aid in stimulating the slowed-down depressed patient is to organize his or her day. Put up a schedule that will include daily tasks and gradually draw him or her back into previous obligations. Encourage activity with praise for any activity that shows a glimmer of initiative.

One day at a time is a good rule for dealing with the depressed individual. Relatives often make the mistake of trying to cheer the depressed person by talking of future plans. The more elaborate and pleasant the plans sound, the more your relative will contrast them with his or her own sad condition. Defer discussions of the future; deal only with the present.

What Should I Do If Someone I Know Is Suicidal?

This answer is simple but sometimes more difficult to accomplish than it sounds: get that person to the doctor. Also, make certain that there is nothing around the house that might be used in a suicide attempt. Guns, for example, should be removed from the house and hidden away or locked in a safe place. I never cease to be surprised by the number of patients I have seen who are talking of shooting themselves, yet their loved ones allow them to keep loaded weapons around the house. Just yesterday a patient and his wife came into my office. The patient was unequivocally suicidal. His wife mentioned that she had allowed him to continue to keep his handgun in his desk drawer beside their bed, despite his repeated threats to take the gun and blow his brains out. When I asked her why she had not taken the gun away earlier, she said that she was afraid she would make her husband angry.

The most common suicide weapon is medication. If your spouse is potentially suicidal, take all the medicines and lock them up. If the spouse is potentially suicidal and is being treated with medication, it would be best for you to administer the drug. Keep the antidepressant medications with you, and when the time comes for your spouse to take the medication give him or her the correct dosage. Usually your physician will prescribe less than a week's supply of tricyclics—a sublethal dose—until the suicidal danger is over.

What Is Commitment to a Hospital?

Hospital commitment is a privilege that allows a family member and physicians to protect an individual from self-harm. Although state laws differ slightly concerning commitment, typically a person can be detained in a hospital against his or her own will if that person is dangerous to him- or herself or others and out of contact with reality. People who are definitely suicidal should be committed for their own protection. Again, I am constantly surprised by the reluctance of family members to commit acutely ill patients to a hospital out of fear that they will anger them. I say, in as kind a way as possible, "better angry than dead." Granted, it is a major step to commit someone that you love to the hospital. The act of taking charge, however, when your loved one has decompensated, is an act of love.

For most states, the commitment procedure involves something like this: a relative (wife, mother, father, brother, sister, son, or daughter) goes to the magistrate's office in the county courthouse to file a petition for commitment to the hospital. You will tell the magistrate exactly what causes you to believe the individual is out of touch with reality and dangerous to him- or herself and others. The magistrate fills out the papers, and a sheriff seeks out the ill individual. The sheriff then takes the individual to be examined by one or more physicians. The physician then fills out a form stating his or her findings and the reason the physician feels the patient is or is not dangerous and psychotic. If the physician thinks the patient need not be committed, the patient is released. If, on the other hand, the physician feels the patient is psychotic and dangerous, the patient is taken to the hospital designated by the magistrate. The patient can then be released, at any time, by the hospital physician. Within a period of seven to ten days, the patient is entitled to a hearing before a judge. The judge then determines whether the patient needs further hospitalization. He or she can release the patient or commit the patient for a period up to 90 days in a hospital.

In most states, physicians can release the patient as soon as they feel that the patient is capable of caring for him- or herself appropriately outside the hospital. If the patient remains in the hospital for the entire length of time designated by the judge, then another hearing is scheduled at the end of the commitment time and the case is reevaluated. To me, this law seems as fair as possible for both patient and family. Many lives have been saved, and many people have been returned to being useful citizens, because of it.

How Can I Help the Schizophrenic?

With the recent trend to discharge the schizophrenic patient from the hospital as soon as possible, the role of family plays an important part in rehabilitation. Whereas psychotherapy helps the patient become aware of the reasons for his or her feelings and actions, rehabilitation facilitates the patient's relating normally to others—the family can be of immense aid in this process.

Living with a schizophrenic day by day is not an easy task. The family must make the patient feel accepted even if his or her behavior is a little unconventional. However, the schizophrenic should be expected to conform to the general rules of society: that is, get up at a reasonable time, eat three meals with the family, be involved in routine housework (and, later, productive work outside the home), and go to bed at a regular time. Some schizophrenics like to stay up late at night watching TV and then sleep half the morning. This pattern should not be tolerated. Also, schizophrenics like to use their illness as an excuse from helping around the house; this, too, is unexcusable. If a patient is well enough to be out of the hospital, that patient is well enough to participate, at least minimally, in daily chores. Pampering the schizophrenic just adds to his or her social withdrawal.

Scientific research has shown that a schizophrenic patient has a much better chance of staying out of the hospital if he or she helps around the house. It is beneficial for the schizophrenic to remain occupied; it makes the person feel like a contributing member of the family and takes his or her attention away from delusional beliefs. After the patient has adjusted to daily household chores, he or she can be encouraged to participate in a vocational rehabilitation service, offered by most mental health centers.

A schizophrenic's delusions, no matter how bizzarre, are real to him or her. These delusional beliefs must be listened to and evaluated with respect, but it does no good to challenge them directly. If a family member does not understand what the patient is talking about, he or she should at least respond to the schizophrenic's request for attention and conversation. Delusions are false beliefs that cannot be reasoned or reckoned with; they can, however, be modified. When the schizophrenic seems to be upset concerning his or her delusional beliefs, the relative can encourage participation in something else to get his or her mind off the delusions.

The schizophrenic is frightened by too much emotional closeness. Don't smother the schizophrenic. Treat the schizophrenic with genuineness, respect, and try to convey a sense of nonpossessive warmth. Rather than focusing too much attention on the schizophrenic, try to simply include him or her in the family. Try to avoid overstimulation on the one hand and environmental understimulation on the other. Neither expect too much or too little. Finding this perfect balance isn't easy. Scientific research has shown, however, that more than 15 hours a week of face-to-face contact between a schizophrenic patient and a relative carries a strong risk of rehospitalization. A private room, responsibility, recreational activities, and a job can aid the schizophrenic in developing self-reliance and prevent relapse.

In summary: give a schizophrenic a place to withdraw to and don't force him or her into social gatherings. At the same time, expect the person to conform to the basic rules of society. Make certain that your relative takes medications as prescribed and sees a doctor regularly. Don't hesitate to consult with the physician about how you can help, and give the physician factual summaries concerning the patient's progress.

How Can I Help the Alcoholic?

First, take comfort in the fact that there is hope and help for the alcoholic. Among those who accept treatment, the recovery rate from active alcoholism is now higher than from any other chronic illness. Second, remember that alcoholism is a disease—an illness from which the compulsive drinker can find no release. Once you have accepted the idea that alcoholism is an illness, you can give up the false beliefs that alcoholism is caused by weakness of will, immorality, or a desire to hurt others—beliefs that prevent the alcoholic from getting the appropriate treatment he or she needs.

Don't wait for the alcoholic to seek help before you take action on your own behalf. You can get valuable firsthand knowledge about alcoholism and relief from the constant emotional strain and pressures of living with an alcoholic by attending the open meetings of Alcoholics Anonymous. AA is usually listed in the telephone directory; if not, ask your doctor or clergyman, or call the Alcoholism Information Center nearest you. Don't hesitate to attend AA meetings; the members will welcome anyone interested in the problem of alcoholism. If you are lucky, there will be an Al-Anon Family Group in your community. Take advantage of these meetings also. Finally, read everything you can find on alcoholism: the more you know, the better you will be able to help your relative or friend.

You will soon learn that the alcoholic suffers from extreme guilt. Harassing him or her about neglect of family and friends, failure, and social errors only makes the situation worse. Likewise, the "if you love me, don't drink" approach magnifies the alcoholic's guilt. Arguments, coaxing, threats, and promises fail to influence the compulsive drinker. The World Service Conference of Al-Anon Family Groups has approved the following list of don'ts for relatives and friends of alcoholics:

1. Don't treat the alcoholic as if he or she were a naughty child.
2. Don't check to see how much the alcoholic is drinking.
3. Don't search for hidden liquor.
4. Don't pour liquor away; the alcoholic always finds ways to get more.
5. Don't nag the alcoholic about drinking.
6. Never argue with the alcoholic while he or she is under the influence of alcohol.
7. Don't preach, scold, or enter into quarrels.

Often it takes a crisis—an accident, an arrest, or the loss of a job—to convince the alcoholic of the need for help. It's best to do nothing to prevent such a crisis from happening. Talking with the boss, paying bad checks, or arranging for special privileges with creditors only puts off the inevitable. The consequences of drinking will eventually help the alcoholic realize the seriousness of the situation.

Be ready when the alcoholic asks, "What can I do?" Give the telephone number of Alcoholics Anonymous—but let him or her make the call. The step toward treatment should be taken freely, without coercion from you or anyone else.

In acute withdrawal, immediate medical care or even hospitalization may be necessary. Occasionally psychiatric consultation may be helpful. Allow your physician to make these medical decisions. Whatever treatment is decided on, don't expect immediate, complete recovery. Just as alcoholism takes a long time to develop, convalescence will be a slow process, too. Extreme fatigue for a year or more after drinking stops may be one of the symptoms of withdrawal. The mood swings and emotional tensions in the abstaining alcoholic may temporarily make you think things are worse than they were in the drinking days. Patience and understanding on your part will help these difficult times to pass.

Both you and the alcoholic may have slips and setbacks. Learn from your mistakes, skirt around the disappointments, and push forward. The road to sobriety, although not easy, is worth traveling.

What Is Al-Anon?

Al-Anon is an anonymous self-help program for family and friends of the alcoholic. The only qualification for membership is that their lives have been or are being deeply influenced by a close relationship with an alcoholic. In the September 5, 1977, edition of *JAMA* (the Journal of the American Medical Association), Dr. Anthony M. discussed how he became involved in Al-Anon:

Dr. M. and his wife, Helen, were hardly married before problems began. There would be long, loud arguments about Helen's heavy drinking. The more Helen drank, the more vehement the arguments became. It was not unusual for Doctor M. to return home to find Helen semiconscious on the floor. Arousing her would bring on a vitriolic tongue-lashing. These episodes of irrational behavior were interspersed with periods when Helen was remarkably well.

The family became isolated. Helen did not want to see family or friends because they might impede her drinking. The children were concerned that their mother might "get sick" and did not want their friends over. Dr. M. wanted no visitors because he felt as if he should be controlling the problem and he could not.

Over the course of 11 years, Helen was attended by eight psychiatrists and five consultants who at one time or another labeled her as diabetic, hypothroid, hypercholesterolemic, and Addisonian—but never alcoholic. Dr. M. described the first ray of hope as coming when the ninth psychiatrist told Helen, "I can't do a thing for you. You're a drunk. Why don't you get into AA?" That night Dr. M. took Helen to her first AA meeting. The second ray of hope came when two Al-Anon members persisted in encouraging Dr. M. to attend Al-Anon meetings.

Al-Anon introduces each member to the fact that alcoholism is a disease. This acceptance of alcohol as a disease offers the family members freedom from guilt and blame. Because members of Al-Anon learn that they cannot cause the disease, they can begin to feel better about themselves and their self-worth increases.

Al-Anon works to help family members to increase their personal peace and serenity rather than teaching ways of controlling the alcoholic. The program demands that family members take a hard look at themselves. In this difficult task, the new member is supported and directed by the caring, concerned members of Al-Anon. The meetings are not for sympathizing or socializing, but for encouragement, understanding, and emotional growth.

What Are Some Other Self-Help Groups?

Here are some addresses of "anonymous" self-help organizations for people with problems:

Narcotics Anonymous	2335 Crenshaw Blvd. Los Angeles, CA 90017
Parents Anonymous (child abuse)	250 West 57th St. New York, NY 10019

Schizophrenics Anonymous	Huxley Institute 114 First Ave. New York, NY 10021
Recovery, Inc.	116 S. Michigan Ave. Chicago, IL 60603
Gamblers Anonymous	P. O. Box 17173 Los Angeles, CA 90017

With the exception of AA, by far the most successful emotional self-help organization is Recovery, Inc., founded in 1937 by Dr. Abraham Low. Recovery has 7,000 members, 1,025 chapters, and weekly meetings in every state. Meetings are highly structured and relentlessly practical. The majority of the members have been hospitalized at least once, but deeply disturbed people are not accepted at meetings. Recovery (as the name implies) is for people who are partly well already—individuals with anxiety, depression, stabilized schizophrenia, or other chronic recurrent illnesses.

The National Association for Mental Health (1800 North Kent St., Rosslyn, VA 22209) was organized by former mental patient Clifford Beers in 1908. NAMH works for better mental health programs, more research funding, improved hospitals, increased public understanding of emotional illnesses, and patient rights. It's a good organization to join.

What Have You Learned From This Book?

The most important thing I hope you have learned from this book is this: you are not alone. We all have emotional problems, to a lesser or greater degree, and I hope that the knowledge that no one is perfectly emotionally sound will take away some of the stigma of mental illness. This stigma has probably prevented more people from getting the appropriate help than any other factor. If you know of someone who would benefit from therapy, please do not hesitate to insist that they seek help. If you need help, the biggest favor you can do for yourself is to talk to someone.

Researchers estimate that almost one-fourth of patients with a major mental disorder receive no professional treatment at all. Countless thousands of others with less severe emotional disturbances fail to seek help. Many people lack confidence in the effectiveness of psychiatric treatment. Granted, psychiatry is an inexact science, and unfortunately there are some quacks in the field. Carefully checking out a potential psychotherapist can help prevent quackery, however. Furthermore, cooperating with the psychotherapist (including learning as much as possible about your or your relative's illness) can aid in obtaining emotional maturity. To paraphrase psychoanalyst Milton L. Miller, M.D., if we are to develop more effective social attitudes we must do so with gradual understanding of our innermost emotions.

Other Questions

I have tried to answer the questions that people most frequently ask me about psychiatry. I'm sure you have some that I didn't answer. If so, check with the representative from your local or county mental health society or your area's medical association. Also read as many books as you can about your particular problem. Be well informed, and if you need professional help please seek it out.

References

Al-Anon. *The 12 Steps and Traditions of Al-Anon Family Groups.* New York: Al-Anon, 1973.

Alexander, F. *Psychosomatic Medicine: Its Principles and Applications.* New York: Norton, 1950.

American Association of Mental Deficiency. *Manual on Terminology and Classification in Mental Retardation* (rev. ed.), ed. H. J. Grossman. Special publication, series No. 2. Washington, D.C.: American Association of Mental Deficiency, 1973.

American Psychiatric Association. *The Diagnostic and Statistical Manual of Mental Disorder.* 3rd ed. Washington, D.C.: American Psychiatric Association, 1980.

Arieti, S. *Interpretation of Schizophrenia.* 2nd ed. New York: Basic Books, 1974.

Arnold, L. E. Disorders of childhood and adolescence. In I. Gregory and D. J. Smeltzer, eds., *Psychiatry: Essentials of Clinical Practice.* Boston: Little, Brown, 1977.

Baldessarini, R. *Chemotherapy in Psychiatry.* Cambridge, Mass: Harvard University Press, 1977.

Beck, A. T. *Cognitive Therapy and the Emotional Disorders.* New York: International Universities Press, 1976

Beecher, H. K. Pain in man wounded in battle. *Annals of Surgery,* 1946, *123*: 96–105.

Benson, H. *The Relaxation Response.* New York: Morrow, 1975.

Birk, A. W. Sex therapy: A behavioral approach. In A. M. Nicholi, Jr., ed., *The Harvard Guide to Modern Psychiatry.* Cambridge, Mass: Harvard University Press, 1978.

Blazer, D. G. Psychopathology of aging. *Monograph of American Family Physician,* 4:6–16, 1977.

Boekelheide, P. D. Evaluation of suicide risk. *American Journal of Family Practice,* 1978, *18*:109–113.

Bootzin, R. R. *Self-Help Techniques for Controlling Insomnia.* New York: Biomonitoring Applications, 1976.

Bort, R. F. Ambulatory management in alcoholism. *American Family Physician,* 1977, *16*(5):131–134.

Brenner, C. *An Elementary Textbook of Psychoanalysis.* Rev. ed., New York: International University Press, 1973.

Bruch, H. *Eating Disorders.* New York: Basic Books, 1973.

Brutten, M., Richardson, S., and Mangel, C. *Something's Wrong with My Child: A Parent's Book About Children with Learning Disabilities.* New York: Harcourt Brace Jovanovich, 1973.

Burton, A. Behavior change through love and suffering. In A. Burton, ed., *What Makes Behavior Change Possible?* New York: Brunner/Mazel, 1976.

Butler, R. N. The geriatric patient. In G. Usdin and J. M. Lewis, eds., *Psychiatry in General Medical Practice.* New York: McGraw-Hill, 1979.

Cammer, L. *Up From Depression.* New York: Simon & Schuster, 1969.

Campbell, Robert. *The Enigma of the Mind.* New York: Time-Life Books, 1976.

Cannon, W. B. *The Wisdom of the Body.* New York: Norton, 1932.

Cassem, N. H., and Hackett, T. P. Psychological aspects of myocardial infarction. *Medical Clinics of North America,* 1977, *61*(4):711–721.

Cocaine: Middle-Class High. *Time Magazine,* July 6, 1981, pp. 56–63.

Coleman, J. C. *Abnormal Psychology and Modern Life.* 5th ed. Dallas: Scott, Foresman, 1976.

Cousins, N. *Anatomy of an Illness.* New York: Norton, 1979.

Dement, W. L. Normal sleep and sleep disorders. In G. Usdin and J. M. Lewis, eds., *Psychiatry in General Medical Practice*. New York: McGraw-Hill, 1979.

DiCicco, L., Unterberger, H., and Mack, J. Confronting denial: An alcoholism intervention strategy. *Psychiatric Annals*, 1978, *8*(11):54–64.

Dickes, Robert Adult Sexuality: Historical and Cultural Perspectives. In Understanding Human Behavior in Health and Illness: 2nd ed., ed. R. C. Simons & H. Pardes Baltimore: Williams & Wilkins 1981.

DiPalma, J. R. Phencyclidine: Angel dust. *American Family Physician*, 1979, *20*(1):120–122.

Eimers, R., and Aitchison, R. *Effective Parents/Responsible Children: A Guide to Confident Parenting*. New York: McGraw-Hill, 1977.

Ewing, J. A. Recognizing confronting, and helping the alcoholic. *American Family Physician*, 1978, *18*(5):107–114.

Fieve, R. R. Moodswings: The Third Revolution in Psychiatry. New York: William Morrow, 1975.

Frank, J. D. An overview of psychotherapy. In G. Usdin, ed., *Overview of Psychotherapeutics*. 6th ed. New York: Brunner/Mazel, 1975.

Frazier, Shervert H. (editor). *A Psychiatric Glossary*, 4th edition. Washington, DC: American Psychiatric Association, 1975.

Freedman, A. M. Drug dependence. In A. M. Freedman, H . I. Kaplan, and B. J. Sadock, eds., *Comprehensive Textbook of Psychiatry*, vol. 2. 2nd ed. Baltimore: Williams and Wilkins, 1975.

Friedman, M., and Rosenman, R. H. *Type A Behavior and Your Heart.* New York: Knopf, 1974.

Freud, S. *The Ego and the Id* (Standard ed.), ed. J. Strachey. Vol. 19. London: Hogarth Press, 1961.

Glasser, W. *Reality Therapy: A New Approach to Psychiatry*. New York: Harper & Row, 1965.

Hall, R. C. W., Gardner, E. R., Perl M., Stickney, S. K., and Pfefferbaum, B. The professional burnout syndrome. *Psychiatric Opinion*, 1979, *(4)*:12–17.

Hartman, E. Sleep. In A. M. Nicholi, Jr., ed., *The Harvard Guide to Modern Psychiatry*. Cambridge, Mass.: Harvard University Press, 1978.

Hawkins, D. M., and White, E. M. Indications for group psychotherapy. In J. P. Brady and H. K. H. Brodie, eds., *Controversy in Psychiatry*. Philadelphia: Saunders, 1978.

Hinsie, L. E., and Campbell, R. J. *Psychiatric Dictionary.* 4th ed. New York: Oxford University Press, 1978.

Holmes, T. H., and Rahe, R. H. The social readjustment rating scale. *Journal of Psychosomatic Research,* 1967, *11*:213–218.

Houpt, J. L., Orleans, C. S., George, L. K., and Brodie, H. K. H. *The Importance of Mental Health Services to General Health Care.* Cambridge: Ballinger, 1979.

Jones, Ernest. *The Life and Work of Sigmund Freud,* edited and abridged by Lionel Trilling and Steven Marcus. New York: Basic Books, 1961.

Kahn, R. L., Goldfarb, A. I., Pollack, M., and Peck, A. Brief objective measures for the determination of mental status in the aged. *American Journal of Psychiatry,* 1960, *117*:326–328.

Kaplan, H. S. *The New Sex Therapy.* New York: Brunner/Mazel, 1974.

Karacan, I., and others. Prevalence of sleep disturbance in the general population. *Sleep Research,* 1973, *2*:158.

Keith, L. J., Gunderson, J. G., Reifman, A., Buchsbaum, L., and Mosher, L. R. Special report: Schizophrenia, 1976. *Schizophrenia Bulletin,* 1976, *2*:509–565.

Klerman, G. L. Affective disorders. In A. M. Nicholi, Jr., ed., *The Harvard Guide to Modern Psychiatry.* Cambridge, Mass.: Harvard University Press, 1978.

Klerman, G. L., and Hirschfeld, R. M. A. The use of antidepressants in clinical practice. *JAMA,* 1978, *240*:1403–1406.

Kolb, L. C. *Modern Clinical Psychiatry.* Philadelphia: Saunders, 1970.

Kramer, M. Dream disturbances. In I. Karacan, ed., *Diagnosis and Treatment of Sleep Disorders.* Rochester, N.Y.: Penwalt Corporations 1979.

Kronenberger, Louis and Beck, Emily M. *Brief Lives: A Biographical Companion to the Arts.* Boston: Little, Brown Co., 1971.

Lidz, T. *The Person: His and Her Development Throughout the Life Cycle.* New York: Basic Books, 1976.

Luce, G.C. and Segal J. *Insomnia: The Guide for Troubled Sleepers.* Garden City, N.Y.: Doubleday & Co., 1969.

M., Anthony. Al-Anon. *Journal of the American Medical Association,* 1977, *238*(10):1062–1063.

Macdonald, Linda. Drug Terms. In *University Medical, 13*(1):12–13, 1981.

Mack, R. B. Toxic encounters of the dangerous kind: PCP. *North Carolina Medical Journal*, 1981, *42*:407.

Marmor, J. The physician as psychotherapist. In G. Usdin and J. M. Lewis, eds., *Psychiatry in General Medical Practice*. New York: McGraw-Hill, 1979.

Matthysse, S., and Lipinsky, J. Biochemical aspects of schizophrenia. *Annual Review of Medicine*, 1975, *26*:551–563.

Masters, W., and Johnson, V. *Human sexual response*. Boston: Little, Brown, 1966.

Masters, W., and Johnson, V. *Human sexual inadequacy*. Boston: Little, Brown, 1970.

Meeks, J. E. Child psychiatry: Behavior disorders of childhood and adolescence. In A. M. Freedman, H. I. Kaplan, and B. J. Sadock, eds., *Comprehensive Textbook of Psychiatry*, vol. 2. 2nd ed. Baltimore: Williams and Wilkins, 1975.

Meyer, Bernard C. *Houdini: A Mind in Chains*. New York: E.P. Dutton, 1976.

Miller Milton L. *Nostalgia: A Psychoanalytic Study of Marcel Proust*. Port Washington, N.Y.: Kennikat Press, 1956.

National Institute of Mental Health. *Hospital InPatient Treatment Units For Emotionally Disturbed Children: United States 1971–1972*. DHEW Publication No. ADM 742—82. Washington, D.C.: U.S. Department of Health, Education and Welfare, 1972.

National Institute of Mental Health. *Residential Psychiatric Facilities For Children And Adolescents, United States 1971–1972*. DHEW Publication No. ADM 74–78. Washington, D.C.: U.S. Department of Health, Education and Welfare, 1974.

Norris, J. L. Prevention of chronicity in alcoholism. *Psychiatric Annals*, 1978, *8*(11):48–53.

Oates, Stephen B. *With Malice Toward None—The Life of Abraham Lincoln*. New York: Harper & Row, 1977.

Park, C. C., and Shapiro, L. N. *You Are Not Alone*. Boston: Little, Brown, 1976.

Pauly, I. B., and Goldstein, S. Prevalence of significant sexual problems in medical practice. *Medical Aspects of Human Sexuality*, 1970, *4*(11):48.

Pfeiffer, E., and Busse, E. Affective disorders. In E. W. Busse and E. Pfeiffer, eds., *Mental Illness in Later Life*. Washington, D. C. American Psychiatric Association, 1973.

Rahe, R. H., and Lind, E. Psychosocial factors and sudden cardiac death. *Journal of Psychosomatic Research*, 1971, *15*(1):19–24.

Rhoads, J. M. Overwork. *JAMA*, 1977, *237*(24):2615–2618.

Rhoads, J. M. When is overwork not overwork? Paper presented to annual meeting of the Academy of Psychosomatic Medicine, Atlanta, Georgia, November 17, 1978.

Rosenthal, D., Wender, P. H., Kety, S. S., Welner, J., and Schulsinger, F. The adopted away offspring of schizophrenics. *American Journal of Psychiatry*, 1971, *128*:307–311.

Selye, H. *Stress Without distress.* Philadelphia: Lippincott, 1974.

Selye, H. *The Stress of Life*, rev. ed. New York: McGraw-Hill, 1976.

Shader, R. I., ed., *Manual of Psychiatric Therapeutics.* Boston: Little, Brown, 1975.

Shipley, R. H., and Boudewyns, P. A. How to overcome phobias: Self-control techniques. *Behavioral Medicine*, 1979, 6:14–19.

Simpson, Eileen *Reversals* Boston: Houghton Mifflin, 1979.

Stone, Alan A. and Stone, Sue S. *The Abnormal Personality Through Literature.* Englewood Cliffs, N.J.: Prentice-Hall, 1966.

Strain, J. J., and Grossman, S. *Psychological Care of the Medically Ill: A Primer in Liaison Psychiatry.* Englewood Cliffs, N.J.: Prentice-Hall, 1975.

Tanner, Ogden. *Stress.* New York: Time-Life Books, 1976.

Truax, C. B., and Carkhuff, R. R. *Toward Effective Counseling and Psychotherapy.* Chicago: Aldine, 1962.

Vaillant, G. Alcoholism and drug dependence. In A. M. Nicholi, Jr., ed., *The Harvard Guide to Modern Psychiatry.* Cambridge, Mass.: Harvard University Press, 1978.

Walker, J, I., *Clinical Psychiatry in Primary Care.* Menlo Park: Addison-Wesley, 1981.

Walker, J., and Brodie, H. K. H. Current concepts of lithium treatment and prophylaxis. *Journal of Contnuing Education in Psychiatry*, 1978, *39*:19–30.

Wallace, Irving; Wallechinsky, David; Wallace, Amy; and Wallace, Sylvia: *The Book of Lists #2.* New York: Bantam Books, 1980.

Wallechinsky, David and Wallace, Irving: *The People's Almanac.* Garden City, New York: Doubleday and Company, 1975.

Wallechinsky, David and Wallace, Irving: *The People's Almanac #2.* New York: Bantam Books, 1978.

Wallechinsky, D., Wallace, I., and Wallace, A. *The Book of Lists.* New York: Morrow, 1977.

Weeks, E., and Mack, J. The child. In A. M. Nicholi, Jr., ed, *The Harvard Guide to Modern Psychiatry.* Cambridge, Mass.: Harvard University Press, 1978.

Weiner, R. J. Electrically induced seizures. *American Journal of Psychiatry,* 1979, *136*:12.

Wender, P. *The Hyperactive Child: A Handbook for Parents.* New York: Crown, 1973.